For my wife Amy, a beautiful and intelligent woman.

Without her support and patience, I would not be the person I am today.

ACKNOWLEDGMENTS

Many people worked hard to make this book possible. Steve Taylor helped immensely with the content; he provided technical information and even some early editing. I thank my editor, Estelle Manticas, for the many hours she spent helping me through the writing process. Thanks to Les Pardew, my technical editor and an all around good guy. Also, thanks go to Emi Smith and the entire team at Premier Press, who not only provided the opportunity to write this book, but also shared their expertise with me.

I also want to give a special thanks to my family for their patience while I spent many hours away from them working on this book.

Game Interface Design

Brent Fox

THOMSON

™

COURSE TECHNOLOGY

Professional ■ Trade ■ Reference

ISBN: 1-59200-593-4

Library of Congress Catalog Card Number: 2004111222

Printed in the United States of America

04 05 06 07 08 BU 10 9 8 7 6 5 4 3 2 1

THOMSON

COURSE TECHNOLOGY ™

Professional ■ Trade ■ Reference

Thomson Course Technology PTR, a division of Thomson Course Technology
25 Thomson Place ■ Boston, MA 02210 ■ http://www.courseptr.com

SVP, Thomson Course Technology PTR:
Andy Shafran

Publisher:
Stacy L. Hiquet

Senior Marketing Manager:
Sarah O'Donnell

Marketing Manager:
Heather Hurley

Manager of Editorial Services:
Heather Talbot

Senior Acquisitions Editor:
Emi Smith

Senior Editor:
Mark Garvey

Associate Marketing Manager:
Kristin Eisenzopf

Marketing Coordinator:
Jordan Casey

Project Editor/Copy Editor:
Estelle Manticas

Technical Reviewer:
Les Pardew

PTR Editorial Services Coordinator:
Elizabeth Furbish

Interior Layout Tech:
William Hartman

Cover Designer:
Mike Tanamachi

CD-ROM Producer:
Brandon Penticuff

Indexer:
Kelly Talbot

Proofreader:
Gene Redding

About the Author

Brent Fox worked his way through college as an art director for a package design company. While in college, he took a class in 3D animation and was hooked. Brent received his degree in Graphic Design from Brigham Young University, and shortly after graduation he began creating video games. He has worked in the video game industry for more than eight years, and he has worked on games for a wide variety of platforms. His title list includes games on the PC, Game Boy Color, PlayStation, Nintendo 64, Dreamcast, PlayStation 2, and GameCube.

Brent has not only created art for the games he has worked on, but he has also served as project manager and art director on many other games as well. He has managed development teams with up to 28 team members. He has created artwork for games published by Blizzard, EA, Midway, 3DO, and Konami, just to name a few. His published title list includes games such as *Brood War* (a *Starcraft* expansion set), *Army Men: Sarge's Heroes*, and many more.

Contents at a Glance

CONTENTS

x   Contents

Chapter 15
Creating an Interactive Mock-Up 179

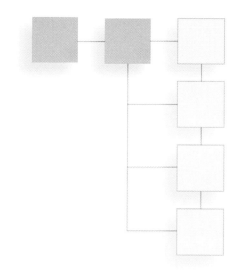

INTRODUCTION

An interface, as you no doubt already know, is the part of the game that allows the user to interact with the game. Interaction is what makes a video game different from a movie. When playing a video game, the user can make choices and respond to events. An interface is the connection between the user and the game, and a well-designed interface makes the video game experience more fun.

Interface design is a creative, exciting, and challenging subject. The purpose of this book is to introduce you to the game interface design principles and concepts used in the game industry. There is a huge amount of information to learn about interface design,

and I couldn't hope to cover it all. This book will, however, cover all of the basics you need to know in order to design your own game interface.

An interface has many pieces. This book will cover the interface from the first image that appears on the screen to the information displayed on screen during game-play. The player of your game interacts with buttons, sliders, menus, and many other components of an interface, and this book will show you how and when to use each of these input methods.

I hope that this book inspires you to create better and more effective game interfaces. You are capable of making a great, unique interface. Don't limit your vision by what has been done in the past.

Who Should Read This Book?

If you are just getting started in the game industry, this book will serve as a great introduction to interface design. It will also provide a little insight into the video game industry itself.

Game development is a unique and interesting field. It is fun, rewarding, and a lot of hard work. In this book you will get a glimpse at the developer and publisher relationship, as well as at the schedules, budget constraints, and politics that are found in the video game development industry.

Even if you are an experienced interface designer, this book will provide hints and tricks that can help you in your daily tasks. After reading this book, you will be able to better evaluate the effectiveness of an interface, and you will be aware of the areas in which you can improve.

The application of the principles I will show you in this book will help improve your design skills. It will also provide inspiration to go beyond the norm and create interfaces that captivate and entertain the user.

What's in This Book?

Great interfaces never happen by accident. They require a lot of planning. This book will outline the steps to good planning. You will be encouraged to define goals that will guide you through the design process and be shown how to plan and chart your menus before you begin to create art. You will learn how to be innovative and creative in the planning stages of the design process.

I will also walk you through the early planning stages for a game interface and present methods for crafting a unique look and feel for your interface. Creating icons, animation, and buttons will be covered.

Basic design and art principles are essential for any interface designer to understand. As you read through these pages, you will learn about these basic concepts and how they can guide you through the design process. You can use these design principles to effectively evaluate your own design and identify areas for improvement. You will begin to understand how much skill and talent is needed to produce a great interface. It's hard work, but it's worth it.

In this book, you will also explore the world of interface buttons. This simple-sounding topic is actually very complex. I will explain the concept of button states and teach you how to make a functioning button for a game interface. You'll learn how to create buttons that are easy to use and that look cool.

I will also show you how to avoid using too much text in your interface and how to replace as much text as possible with images and icons. This is not always an easy task, but a good use of icons can separate an extraordinary interface from a mediocre one. A screen full of text will turn users away; learn about methods you can use to communicate with the user without text.

Make it move! Animations can be a game interface designer's greatest asset. I'm not just talking about a spinning logo, but about serious animation. Understanding and applying solid animation techniques can bring a static interface to life. Learn these animation principles and how you can use them in an interface.

Chapter 14 will walk you through the step-by-step process of creating an interface. You will see how an interface is created using Photoshop. This process will help you understand how complex serious interface design can be.

In Chapter 15, you'll learn how to use Flash to create an interface with real interactivity. This software provides an effective method to mock-up and test a game interface design. Don't wait for a programmer to write code to see your design in action. You can do it yourself. Learn how to use Flash to make buttons function and objects move.

What's on the CD?

This book also comes with a CD containing images and examples. You will have access to many of the images in this book. You will also be able to open the Flash file created in the last chapter of the book and see it move. The CD also includes a free game demo and trial version of Macromedia Flash.

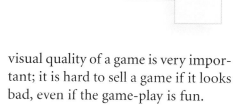

CHAPTER 1

INTRODUCTION TO VIDEO GAMES

Welcome to the world of interface design for video games. Of course, the best instruction you can receive is real life experience. No matter how good a game artist is before he begins developing video games, he learns a lot during the development process. Gaining this experience will take time. In the meantime, I hope to share a little of my experience with you and give you a head start.

The Importance of the Interface

Too often, video game interfaces are an afterthought. Sufficient time is not scheduled for interface design because too many project managers assume anyone can whip up an interface. They feel that interface design does not require any particular talent or very much time, so they assign the new guy to work on the interface. This is a big mistake, and when it happens, it's apparent to anyone who plays the game. It isn't hard for the user to immediately see poor quality. The visual quality of a game is very important; it is hard to sell a game if it looks bad, even if the game-play is fun.

Great art can do amazing things to boost game sales. Many game publishers claim that their number-one priority is game-play, but I've seen these same publishers look at a game and respond with "that looks great," even though they never picked up a controller or mouse. If a game doesn't look good, no one may ever play it and find out if the game-play is good. Consumers are used to seeing great art, and they demand high quality in any game they play. Great visuals can actually make a game more fun to play.

Even more important than the visual aspect of interface design is the functionality. A poor interface can ruin the entire video game experience. The game experience will be negative if the user is confused and can't figure out how to navigate the front-end menu or if he can't understand where to find information while playing the game. The more the user has to search for information and think about how to play, the less enjoyable the game becomes. The interface is a vital component of a game and should not be treated as a component that is unrelated to the game or as an unimportant task.

On the other hand, a great interface can significantly enhance the experience. A simple-to-use and visually appealing menu can set the tone for the game. The first thing that the user sees when he starts a game is the front-end menu. A good-looking interface with a lot of well-designed features can actually be fun to use and even seem like a game itself. Have you ever played around with a quality

"player editor"? Changing character outfits, hair, skin color, and tattoos can be a lot of fun. All of this takes place in the menu. Without ever starting the core game, the user feels like he is already playing.

Real-Life Game Development

In this book, I will discuss interface design for video games under perfect conditions—if there is no limit on time or budget. I will assume that you have been given total creative freedom and, as the interface designer, you can make decisions. In an ideal situation, a producer or designer won't mandate that the interface should look like a previous version of the game (most likely designed by a less-competent artist and designer than you) or direct that the interface must be in his favorite color. Too often, someone at your company notes that a competing game has a hair-color option in the player editor and demands that your game must have the same feature. It then becomes a requirement that this feature must be implemented exactly how it was done in the other game. Another one of my least-favorite

restrictions goes something like, "The Marketing Department says the game will sell better if the colors are brighter." Who can argue with that?

Artists who are new to video game development often believe that the perfect conditions I mentioned might actually exist. When these conditions don't exist at their current company, they assume that other developers at other companies have this freedom. These inexperienced interface designers don't understand all of the factors that contribute to final decisions when developing games. Unfortunately, total creative freedom is not usually given to most interface designers. Because of the restrictions that exist while making a game, I have rarely finished a game and felt like I had created the very best interface I was capable of creating. I feel satisfied if it was the best I could do under the circumstances and restrictions I was given.

Many factors apply to real-life interface design. Time and budget can greatly affect the amount of effort that can be applied. The bottom line is that budgets and schedules may have been set that may not allow for full 3D models to be used in the interface or for trips to a junkyard to collect photo references. Although the extra effort may result in a better interface, not working under the restrictions of the game can have disastrous results.

I have worked on many games that were canceled before they were finished. These games were cancelled for many reasons—most of them out of my control. If the game publisher thinks that they can't complete the game within the budget, they have a decision to make: They can try to come up with the extra money to complete the game or they can cut their losses and cancel the game. A surprising number of publishers decided to cancel the game.

Choose your battles and work well with others. Feedback and direction can actually make the completed game better. Sometimes the guys in charge actually know what they are talking about! If you are closed to ideas and suggestions, you may pass up some really good advice. Your skills and abilities will be trusted more as you demonstrate your skills and you learn more about the game development process. This will take

time. Telling everyone that you always know better than they do won't inspire others to join your cause (even if after reading this book you really do know better).

Don't be afraid to explain that you don't agree with feedback, but make sure you can explain why. "It will look better" is not as convincing as offering the explanation that serif fonts are hard to read at low resolutions. Don't be shy—offer constructive options, and tactfully point out potential problems. After a focus group has found a flaw in the design, you won't be very convincing when you try to explain that you knew it should have been done differently but didn't want to say anything.

Don't ever let these real-world limitations keep you from designing amazing interfaces, though. Let them serve as a challenge. Learn to work your best under these conditions. They aren't an excuse for poor design—if you really are good, you can still create great interfaces.

I have worked on games with very small budgets. One such game is on the CD that comes with this book. On

this game, we had to make some careful decisions about what to leave out and what to add. If we had had a bigger budget and more time, I would have done many things differently. I am proud of this game, not because it is the best game in the world, but because it was made really quickly by a few artists and programmers. It still is very fun, and it got some great reviews.

Working with a Team

Video game development requires a team effort. This is especially true with the really cool, big-budget games. While there may be few examples of a group of three or four people who make an entire game, these are rare exceptions, and it is often evident in the final product if a full team did not work on the game. The triple-A blockbuster games often involve amazingly large teams. The members of these big teams must learn to work well with one another.

Often, problems occur during game development because team members just can't get along. Fighting and arguing can cause just as many problems as incompetence. Because of this, putting 20 people who do not work well together on the same team may not be twice as effective as putting 10 people together who do. On the other hand, putting 20 people who work really well together on the same team can produce more than twice the results of a 10-person team. Cooperation is key.

Listen to Others

You may actually be right. You might even know more than the decision-makers. Your ideas may be better. But this doesn't mean that you should argue. Express your opinion politely when it is appropriate to do so. If you have an "I'm right, you're wrong" attitude, you won't get far.

Whether you have the authority over your co-workers or they have the ability to enforce their ideas, the best thing you can do is listen. Take the time to listen to their ideas and seriously consider what they are telling you. The best game and interface designers are not afraid to change things if they come across a better idea. They are able to recognize good ideas, even if the ideas are not their own.

Ask Questions

If someone has an idea that you think is wrong, the best thing to do is ask questions. Good questions require a lot of thought and effort on your part. These questions can demonstrate that you understand their point of view. Try to get all of the information you can. Make sure you completely understand the opposing point of view before you offer your suggestion. If you feel that an idea has flaws, politely ask if the person you are talking to has considered these problems. They may have a solution to the problems that they just have not described well. Or they may see the flaws and change their mind without an argument.

I once worked with a great game designer who was really good at this. Everyone liked him, and no one was afraid to approach him with a suggestion. The great thing was that when he made a decision, he was usually right. If anyone disagreed, he would talk things through with them and ask a lot of questions, like: "Have you thought about . . ." or "Why do you think that it would be better to do it that way?" Because of his great communication skills, everyone came out of the conversation understanding why he made his decision, even if they did not agree with it.

The bottom line is that working in a team is essential for game development. Don't be a problem in the game development process. Even if you are talented, you need to work well in a team.

A Career in Video Games

Reading about the potential obstacles may make video game development sound like a terrible experience. In reality, making video games is great! It is not easy, but that's one of the reasons it's so rewarding. If it were easy, anyone could do it.

The game industry is not easy to break into. The best way to get into the industry is to be really good. You will also need to be able to demonstrate how good you are. This is why a good portfolio is key. Having a great portfolio is essential to getting your first job in the game industry.

Interface design is important when developing games, but only big studios can afford to have an interface expert who spends all of his time creating interfaces. It may be harder to land a job at these bigger developers because they have more experienced artists who are applying for the same job. The way to combat this problem is to diversify. Make sure you have other skills that can be used when developing video games. Smaller development studios may have the same guy designing the interface and building 3D models. If you are trying to break into the industry as an interface designer, you might want to choose another area of game development and develop these skills along with your interface design skills.

I was lucky that a discerning art director saw my potential. When I think back to my portfolio when I first graduated from college and started looking for a job, I am not sure that I would have hired myself! I worked my way through college at a company that did packaging. I was hired just as the company was creating a Design department. By the time I graduated, I had been promoted to the Art Director position. This management experience is what helped me get my

first job in the game development industry. I found a company that was looking for someone to fill the role of art lead. I had more than just art skills, and that is why I got the job.

You should do something you love for a living. The best artists are the ones who have a passion for making great art and great games. The game industry is too demanding if you don't love it. It is very rewarding to see your game on the shelf in a store, but it is not easy to get it there. Many late nights must be spent and tedious tasks must be completed during the game-development process. If the process is not fun and rewarding for you, it will be hard to push through the tough spots.

I always get a good reaction when I tell teenagers what I do for a living, but I don't always get the same enthusiastic response from their parents. Many people assume that because some video games contain offensive material, all games are bad. This is tantamount to declaring that all movies are bad because some movies are violent. If you plan on working in the game industry, it is a good idea to decide early on what you are and

aren't willing to work on. A wide variety of games exist, from those that involve pornography and gambling to religious and educational games. If you want to work on a particular type of game, it is a good idea to develop a portfolio that fits with the kind of game you want to make.

After you have broken into the industry, you should continue to build your portfolio. Improve your skills and find a way to prove you can do the job. The most important thing for your next job is your title list. The most important game on your title list is the last one you worked on. Because games take so long to make, it is not easy to build this list. The experience you gain in making a game in invaluable.

The Publisher / Developer Relationship

Most of my experience has been developing video games for consoles. The most common model for console development is that a game publisher provides all (or part) of the funding to develop a game. The publisher also funds marketing, packaging, and distribution. Because the publisher is paying for the game, they have the final say. The power is in the money. Publishers often give a developer a great deal of creative freedom, but they always have the final say. They are taking the financial risk and, therefore, they have the right to get what they want.

The publisher typically pays for development by giving the developer payments along the development process. A milestone schedule is created at the beginning of development that outlines what will need to be completed for each milestone. The developer then presents these items to the publisher on the date they are due. If the publisher approves these milestones, then they make a payment to the developer. Because money is tied to each payment, getting these approvals from a publisher becomes very important to the developer.

In this book, I will refer to the publisher/developer relationship often. I will assume that a publisher is providing funding and that the publisher makes any final decisions. This is not always the case. Many independent game developers fund their own games and are, in essence, their own publisher. Many publishers do their own internal development. Even in these instances, there is often a person or group in charge of giving direction and making final decisions. This person or group fills the role of publisher. Every developer would like to make these decisions himself, but it is very expensive to develop a game. The reality is that most developers do not have the money to produce the big budget games on their own dime.

CHAPTER 2

PLANNING MENU FLOW

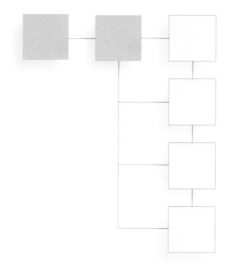

Planning is vital to a successful interface. If budget or time requirements are tight and corners must be cut, then cut something else. If you cut out the planning stage, your project will probably end up taking longer and costing more than it would have with careful planning. If you really want to complete an interface design quickly, spend more time planning. A large-budget project may afford the luxury of more experimentation and trials, but with a lean project, you need to get it right the first time.

Why Is Planning So Valuable?

The best way to speed up the design process is to only do things once, and careful planning gives you a shot at getting things right the first time. It may seem impossible to get a perfect interface on the first attempt, but if you don't plan your process, then you almost guarantee that things will need to be redone. You know that you will make changes, but that doesn't mean you should avoid planning. If you don't plan, you will end up having to make even more changes.

Without good planning, it is hard to know what needs to be done. It is easy for artists to waste time creating art for things that will never appear in the game. How many screens are needed? What pieces of art can be re-used in different areas? What information must be displayed in game? All of these questions should be answered in the planning stage. Good planning will generate a list of assets that are needed and there will never be a question of what art needs to be created.

Just like with everything else in the game development process, you should strive for the best but plan for the worst. In the ideal scenario, all of the details can be planned in advance and never changed. But in reality, some changes will always be necessary. Plan time for revisions but do all you can to avoid them. A trap many interface designers fall into is, when they see that time is planned for making changes, they use this "extra" time to justify incomplete work. "I can always fix it later," is a bad attitude. What usually happens in these cases is that the final polish is never added, and the game ships with an inferior interface.

Solid planning can also help determine schedules. If the design requires 100 screens, each with unique art, it may just take too long to create a fully animated 3D scene for each of these screens. If the design can be simplified and the resulting design only requires a handful of screens, then more time and attention can be given to each screen. More time will be required if the game design is so complicated that a large number of options and a lot of information must be displayed. You can make more reliable time estimates if the quantity of art needed for the game can be determined.

If I know how many screens will be needed for the front-end menu, then I can simply do a little math and know how much time I have for each individual screen. This will make it easy to determine if I am on schedule or if I am falling behind. You will need to ramp up and expect that the first tasks will take longer than the tasks at the end. If you have designed five other screens, it will be easy to make a sixth screen that fits into the design of the first five. Of course, make sure not to cut it too tight—add some time for revisions and adjustments. Without a good plan, it is difficult to know how much time you can spend on a task and if you are ahead or behind.

Accurate scheduling can reduce the panic level at the end of the project. There will always be a push at the end of the project, but you will be able to better manage things if you have a plan early on—you can attack problems early. A common result of poor planning is a string of "all-nighters" at the end of a project. This is one of the situations that cause your significant other to insist you find a job outside the video game industry. While crunch time is part of the industry it

can be greatly reduced by smart planning early in a project. This will only be beneficial if you are willing and able to react and adjust to the risks you identify early in the project.

Creativity in Planning

At first glance, the planning process may not seem very creative. It might even seem boring. Charts and graphs that are kept intentionally visually plain are often used in the planning stage. Little or no art is being created, and it can seem very tedious to someone who is bursting with creative energy.

If you have a complete understanding of the entire interface design process, this attitude will vanish. There are some very important and potentially creative decisions that are made in the planning process. Truly creative and innovative ideas can be conceived at this point. You can ask questions like, "What if we tried it this way?" Arguably, these ideas can be more important to the ultimate game than pretty art. It may be more important that you decide to have a 3D animated character guiding the user through the interface than it will be if you take the same approach as in every other game and just make a cool logo. In the planning stage, you can make these types of decisions. You are choosing the most important places in which to put your time and effort. If a 3D guide is not going to significantly add to the user's experience, you may find it better to spend your time creating cool, animated transitions between screens.

An interface designer who truly understands interface design can plan for creative and elegant concepts in the planning stage. It is much harder to find a designer who understands this concept and can come up with creative ideas that are also possible under the budget. These designers are more valuable than those who can create only cool-looking art. Creative planning is an area wherein an interface designer can become truly great. If you can come up with great ideas and you can skillfully execute these ideas, you will be in demand.

Getting Approval

Another reason for good planning is to get proper approval before starting to create art. A well-planned interface offers the game designer, project manger, or other team members the opportunity to give the go-ahead or voice concerns. Time can be wasted if the decision-makers decide halfway through the project that everything should be done differently. A producer could decide that the user should be able to choose a weapon before starting a level. If the producer has a chance to review the plan early, he could point this out.

You won't be able to avoid changes from the person in charge, but you can reduce the amount of changes you get. You can make it much easier for the producer to give you direction early if you present him with a good plan. He may not even know what he wants himself, and planning can help him to figure it out.

As you are presenting your plan to your boss or publisher, make sure that he understands that you are seeking approval and that this is the best stage to provide feedback. If the person in charge glosses over the plan, it can cause problems later. If you can make adjustments now, everything will go much more smoothly.

Getting approval can avoid your being blamed later because you can always refer back to the approved plan. Once you have received approval, it should never be used as a threat. This will make everyone hesitant to give you approval. You don't want to give the impression that you will fight against any reasonable changes after your plan has received approval, but the person giving approval needs to understand that there is a certain level of commitment in the approval.

Get as much information as you can before you even start to plan. This will help you get approval faster. If you understand the expectations, it is much easier to get approval. The more difficult problem comes when the publisher or producer doesn't know or can't articulate what he wants. This is where good communication skills come in. It is your job to understand what the producers or publishers are looking for and give it to them, even if they don't know what they want.

After a plan has been laid out, sufficient time must be spent evaluating the details of this plan. This should be done by anyone who has veto power. You can help make this clear by asking something like, "I need to get your approval on this layout to make sure that everything is the way you want it. This will help avoid changes." A polite request like this one conveys the idea that you expect this to be final approval. Just because flow charts don't look pretty doesn't mean they don't deserve serious consideration.

Interface Planning Helps Game Design

A detailed plan for a video game interface can really help drive game design. Fleshing out all of the details in the menus and the HUD will force many game-play decisions to be made early. It may also bring up important issues that may not have been considered until later in the game-creation process. The game designer may change actual game-play based on serious consideration of the interface design.

You can ask a lot of good questions in the planning stage. These questions can stimulate the imagination of the game designer. For example, a seemingly simple screen wherein the user chooses an environment can prompt questions that will help determine the game's ultimate design. Will the user be able to choose between different environments? How many choices will he have? Will some environments be locked and not available to the user until he completes certain tasks? Can the user choose an environment in every mode of the game or are there some modes that will dictate environment choice? Will environment choices, in the menu, be affected by other choices made during game-play? The questions could go on and on. They are questions that affect the flow of the menu. It is easy to see how game-play can be affected when serious thought is given the interface. It is difficult to have a solid plan if the game design is underdeveloped.

Don't forget to show your plan to a programmer. The planning stage is a great time to get feedback and suggestions from the programmer who will be working on the interface code. The features planned in an interface greatly affect the programming schedule. Something that may seem easy to an artist can provide a big headache for a programmer. If you plan on playing full-motion video in your menu while animating buttons on top of the movie, you will need to see if the engine has this capability. If you plan on using real-time 3D in the front-end menu, the programmer will need to make this possible. Do your best to work well with the programmer. Both of you will have to work as a team to get a functional interface—No one can go it alone.

Game Design Goals

A good way to for a game designer to make decisions about the features of a game is to have goals. If the interface designer also understands these goals, it will be much easier for him to make decisions about the interface. It's not always easy to define the overall game goals, but if the game designer takes the time to create concise goals for the entire game and the interface designer clearly understands these, many decisions will be easy to make. Goal-oriented design produces great results.

You may be wondering, "What kind of goals do I need to set when designing an interface?" *Make the coolest inter-*

face ever may be the first thing that comes to mind. This goal sounds great, but it probably shouldn't be the first priority. As much as everyone wants a cool interface, there may be other things that are more important. If you are making a kids' game, for example, it might be more important that the menu is easy for a six-year-old to use than that it looks cool. Prioritization is key to using these goals to guide your design.

The game designer, publisher, and project manager may need to work out the game goals. Everyone will need to agree on the goals. Each of these people has a different role and may have a different prospective. If they can agree on a prioritized list of goals, it can help everyone work together.

Some goals may not be what you would expect. For example, the first goal of the game may be to reach a broad market. If you are creating an online game that will be used to promote soap, the client's goal may be to reach a broad audience. This goal may not lend itself to the type of design that hard-core gamers might consider the coolest interface ever. You might choose a completely different art style because of this goal. You might use a little less rust and grunge than you would use in a game aimed at hard-core gamers, for example.

Possible Game Goals

Below is a list of possible goals that a developer or publisher may have. These goals may not match perfectly with your personal goals, but it is important to understand the goals of the guy in charge. This list is by no means a complete list of goals that could ever be used for game design. In fact, it is a very brief list. This list is just meant to stimulate thought about the real goals of your next game.

- Promote an existing license or famous personality.
- Capitalize on an existing license or famous personality.
- Meet a particular schedule.
- Reach a particular audience.
- Create something completely unique.
- Outdo a competing game.
- Capitalize on the success of a competing game.
- Continue a successful series.
- Sell another product (other than the game itself).
- Promote a moral issue.
- Create a buzz using controversy.
- Create an educational experience.
- Pass the approval process of the console manufacturer.
- Please the Marketing department.
- Tell a story.

Don't treat goals lightly. As an interface designer, if you are not given goals for the game, you might want to present the goals that you think everyone would agree on. This will give you a chance to see if you understand what everyone else is expecting. Ask questions about the target market, subject matter of the game, budget, schedule requirements, what the most important feature of the game is, what makes the game unique, what other games might be similar, and so on. A clear understanding of all aspects of the game will make it much easier to understand the overall goals of the game.

If you have input on creating the game goals, be honest with yourself. Get honest information from the game publisher. It may take a little coaxing to get a publisher to give you the direction you need. It is, however, very important to understand the publisher's vision. He is paying for the project, and therefore his goals and opinions are always the most important. It won't do any good to pretend that the number-one goal of the game is to be innovative when the number one goal of the publisher really is to reach a sales goal.

If you are working on a game that has a movie tie-in, the number-one goal may be to get the game on the shelf at the same time as the movie is released. This may be more important than adding cool new features. In such a case, the schedule should rule. Any feature that has the potential to delay the project may need to be scrapped, even if it would make the game "super cool." When making decisions, it will be easy to throw out anything that would jeopardize the schedule and choose the features wisely.

Breaking Down Your Goal into Specifics

Avoid the temptation to set one large goal that is actually several goals in one. This is often the easy way out—it is more difficult to articulate specific goals than it is to generalize. But a goal like "Make a cool game" is not nearly as clear as "Add three new and creative features that are not found in competing racing games." You could even break down this goal into several more detailed goals: Create one new feature that appeals to avid racing game fans and add two new features that appeal to the more casual gamer. All of these goals could be a subheading of "Create a game that will sell more copies than the last version." The point is to define useful goals that will provide direction during development. Understanding the motive behind the goal is very important.

How Priorities Affect Decision-Making

Now think about how priorities can affect decisions. Let's say that the first priority of a game is to be educational and teach kids about animals. A secondary goal is to make the interface intuitive and easy to use. This secondary goal is important, but it is lower on the priority list. If you are armed with this information about the game's priorities, decisions will be easier to make. For example, a lot of text describing the difference between amphibians and reptiles may be used in the interface. Using all of this text may not support the goal of a simple interface, but as the first goal of education is more important, the text must be kept. This does not mean that the lesser goal of a simple interface can be dumped. There may be ways to work around the text and create the best possible solutions that includes the text.

In the case described above, you may need to be a little creative and include the necessary text but not clutter an interface. One solution could be to create an information button with a recognizable icon. This button could be placed next to animals. When the information button is selected, a pop-up window appears with all of the text. This window can be closed and other information buttons can be selected. This way, the user can easily access all of the information, but the screens with the images of the animals can be kept simple.

Charting Methods

The menu system that appears before the game begins is often referred to as the *front-end*. This term helps distinguish this menu from all of the in-game and pause menus that can appear in a game. The best way to plan and organize a front-end menu is to create a flow chart. This will give you the chance to organize your ideas. Once you have a chart, it is also easy to give this information to others for approval or feedback. A great flow chart can even allow the programmer to begin programming the interface with temporary art, before the final art is completed. A flow chart makes it easy to see what tasks need to be done.

The important thing to remember when charting a menu is to be consistent and clear. The purpose of creating a flow chart is to be organized. Clear communication of the flow of the interface is the number one goal

of a flow chart. Don't worry about what the chart looks like so much as what information and options will be displayed on each screen. Just get the flow on paper and make it easy to understand. You can waste time making pretty borders and cool-looking backgrounds. Simplicity and clarity should be the governing factors.

There are many software programs that can help you create charts. I prefer to use Adobe Illustrator because I know it well and use it for other parts of game development. There are programs, like Visio, that are specifically made for creating flow charts. These programs can be much more efficient than a standard art program. Making changes should be easy. If you don't plan on using a program that was made for creating flow charts, I would strongly suggest at least using a vector program, like Illustrator, and not a raster program such as Photoshop. Vector files will be much more flexible when it comes to editing; they create smaller files and print clearly. I have seen some cool-looking flow charts created in Photoshop, but they were big files that were hard to send in an

e-mail, and it was much harder to make changes to them.

I have come up with a charting method that works well for me. There are many other methods that would work equally well, but I'll share my method as an example. Feel free to develop your own methods and symbols. The important thing is that your chart includes all of the information discussed here and is easy for others to understand.

Start by creating a box that represents the first screen that is seen when the user starts the game. Make a box that is large enough to fit several lines of text. All of the options for that screen should be listed in this box. Place a title at the top. As you choose the size of the document and the size of all of the elements that appear in this flow-chart, you should take several things into account. Most likely, this chart will be printed at some point. The text and images will need to be large enough to be easily read on paper. Think about the total number of screens that will appear in the flow chart, and make sure that the spacing and size will allow for all of these items to fit (See Figure 2.1).

```
┌─────────────────────┐
│    Title Screen     │
├─────────────────────┤
│                     │
│      New Game       │
│                     │
│      Load Game      │
│                     │
│      Options        │
│                     │
│      Credits        │
│                     │
│                     │
└─────────────────────┘
```

Figure 2.1
Create a box that represents the title screen. Carefully plan the size and spacing of your chart.

Tip

Your menu may become too complicated to fit on one page. Most software programs provide the option to print one document on multiple pages—when the chart is printed, these pages can be pasted together to make one big chart.

Charting may not be easy. It is very likely that you'll have questions that aren't easily answered during this charting process, and you'll need to make changes to your chart once these decisions have been made. Don't let this intimidate you. The best way to root out problems is just to get started. Take your best guess at the options that should appear in this first menu and type them into your chart. As you move onto other screens, you may discover something that will cause you to come back to the first screen and make changes. This is a natural part of the charting process.

Once you've listed the options, you need to decide where each of these buttons will take the user. Create new boxes, just like the first box, for each of these new screens. Type in all the options that should appear on these screens and decide where each of the buttons in these menus will send the user. Use this method to chart out the entire front-end menu. If important information or images (such as a tournament bracket in a sports game) will need to be displayed, make sure to list these items. Make sure that they are visually distinct from the items that will be interactive. I have created a sample of a chart that could be used for a sports game interface. All of the items that are not interactive have been italicized in this example. (See Figure 2.2.)

The next thing you need to do is create arrows that show the flow of the interface. Use these arrows to connect all of the various screens. Don't forget the Back buttons. Use a different colored arrow to represent the transition when the user presses a Back button. This will help keep things clear.

Video games often have items that are locked and are only accessible after certain tasks have been performed in the game. Levels may need to be unlocked by completing a previous level. The user may only have access to certain cars until he has won enough races. Most games have some items that are not available, or locked, at the beginning of the game. This is a good time to identify these items. Once an item is identified as one that is initially locked, it will be easier to visually design this screen later. (See Figure 2.3.) If you know that in the end 20 different soccer fields will be available, but in the beginning the user can only play in one of the three available fields, this will affect your design.

You may want to let the user know how many options are possible to unlock. In the example above, you might want to display all 20 fields and just mark some as locked. This is important to know before you start to design these screens.

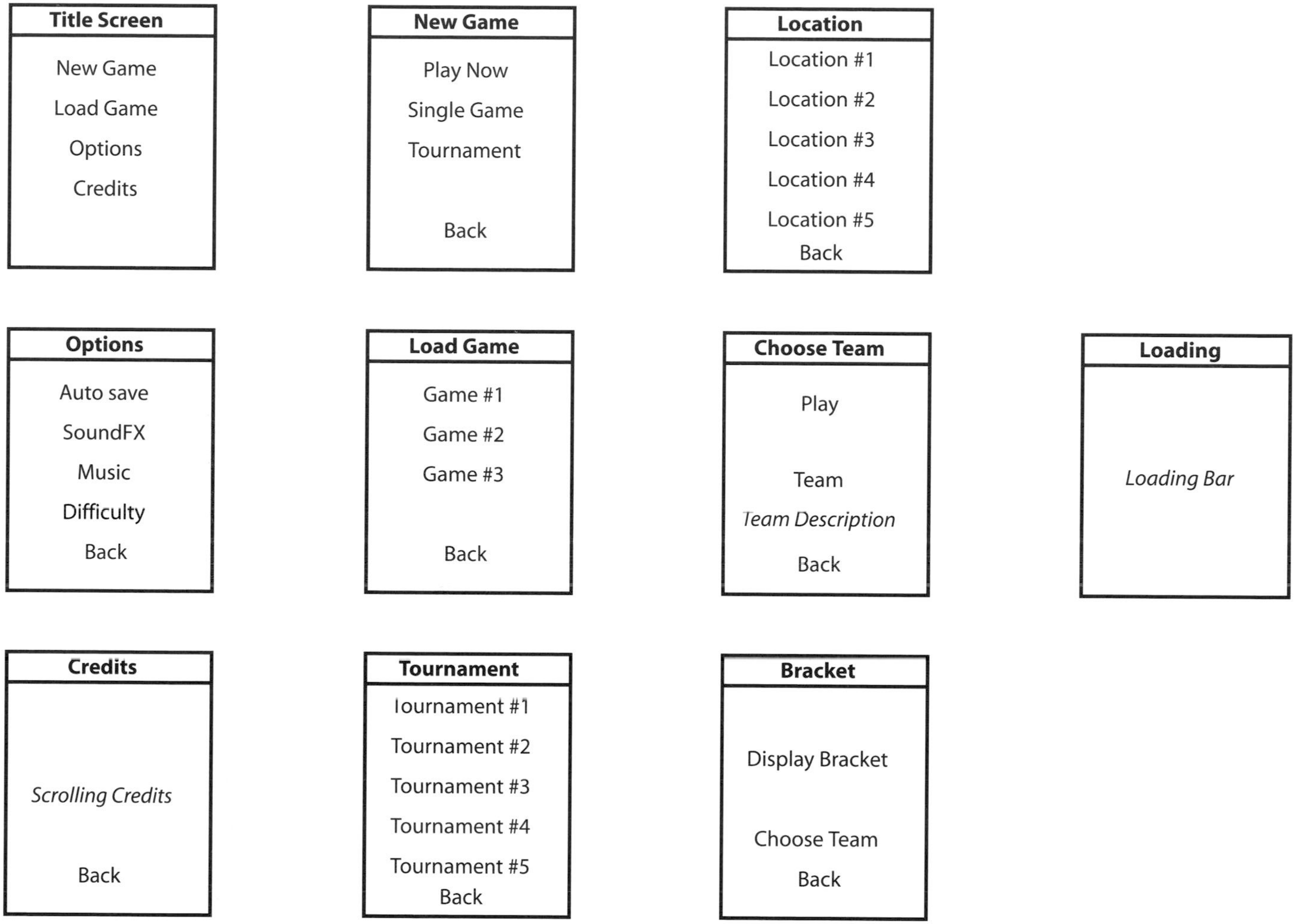

Title Screen
New Game
Load Game
Options
Credits

New Game
Play Now
Single Game
Tournament
Back

Location
Location #1
Location #2
Location #3
Location #4
Location #5
Back

Options
Auto save
SoundFX
Music
Difficulty
Back

Load Game
Game #1
Game #2
Game #3
Back

Choose Team
Play
Team
Team Description
Back

Loading
Loading Bar

Credits
Scrolling Credits
Back

Tournament
Tournament #1
Tournament #2
Tournament #3
Tournament #4
Tournament #5
Back

Bracket
Display Bracket
Choose Team
Back

Figure 2.2 Create boxes for every screen in the menu and list all of the options on each of the screens.

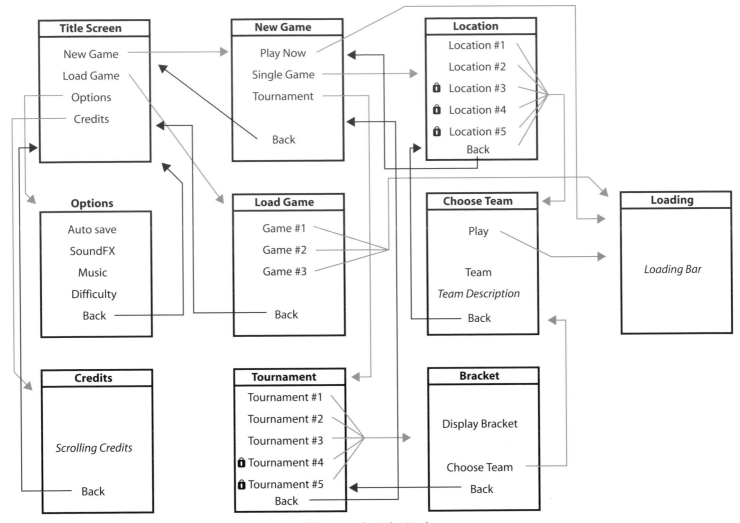

Figure 2.3 Notice the transitions and the locked items. This is a relatively simple menu.

The charting process may seem simple, but it can take a lot of thought to get it right. This first example is relatively simple and straightforward. It doesn't take long for a menu to become very complex, however. Take a look at Figure 2.4 and see how this same game, but with a bigger budget and more features, is more complex and will take more time to plan.

Notice another type of screen in Figure 2.4. These are pop-up menus. The traditional pop-up menu is different from a regular screen in two important ways. These menus are not stand-alone screens; they appear on top of the current screen. When they are activated, they "pop up" over the current screen. The screen that was visible before the pop-up appeared can often be seen in the background. The pop-up menu only covers part of the screen. Pop-up menus often appear when there is a small amount of information that needs to be displayed and this information does not justify a full-screen menu.

A common technique, used to avoid confusion, is to darken the previous menu, which is in the background. This way, the user does not think that the buttons on that part of the menu are active. Occasionally, a pop-up menu can advance a user onto a brand-new screen, but it is much more common to have these pop-up menus close and return the user to the screen he just came from—they are sort of "dead ends" in the menu flow. Because they are often small, they typically do not contain as many options and information as a full screen does.

Button Types

This is a good stage at which to examine the interactive aspects of the menu. How does the user make adjustments or choices? Most menus have several different ways of accepting user input. Buttons, sliders, and toggles are very common and are all used in many menus. The trick is to choose the appropriate input method for each item. What information does the user need to input, and what is the simplest method to get this information?

I will assume that the user will be using a mouse or a controller as an input device. There are, however, many other options. Voice recognition technology has improved and there are some games that use a microphone as an input device. Some systems use other input devices such as guns or drums. Not as many interfaces have taken advantage of these interesting input devices. This does not mean that there are not any great solutions that use this non-standard hardware.

The way to get input from the user is to detect which buttons have been chosen by the user. The user makes choices that advance him through the menu. Every time the user makes a selection, the game engine detects these choices and the appropriate changes are made when the game starts. Simply put, the user chooses features such as Single Player mode and Easy difficulty level by pressing the buttons or pressing Select on the controller. When the game starts, these settings take effect.

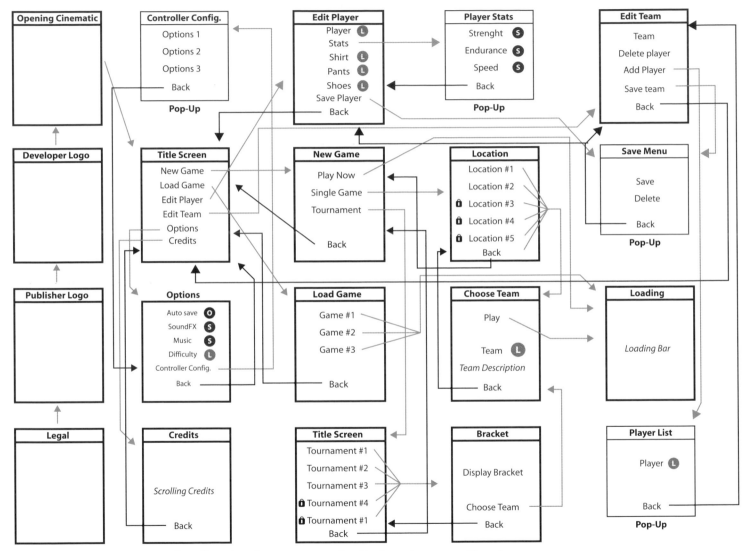

Figure 2.4 It is easy to see why a flow chart is necessary to visualize how the menu will work.

Sliders

Sliders are a great way to adjust values that have a wide range of possibilities. If the value that is being adjusted only has a small number of distinct choices, such as Easy, Moderate, and Difficult, then other methods work better. Numeric values like a range from 1 to 10 or 0 to 100 percent work great for sliders. Music volume is another good example of an input that could use a slider—the user can move the slider left and right and get a wide range of volumes. When using sliders, the settings are typically remembered by the game engine. If the user sets the volume at 3, and leaves the menu, the volume should remain at 3. If the game system has a method to save information on the hard drive or on a memory card, this setting should also remain the next time the user plays.

Just because you're using the standard input method for a slider doesn't mean there isn't any creativity involved. All sliders don't need to look the same. This is another area where you are only limited by your creative ability—the only thing that is important is that the user recognizes the control as a slider and

instinctively knows what to do with it. (See Figure 2.5.)

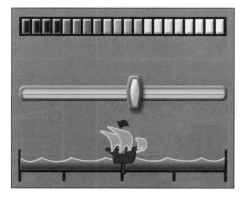

Figure 2.5 Be creative when designing the look of sliders. Just be sure not to confuse the user!

Toggle Switches

You can use a toggle input method when there are two possible states, such as On and Off. Methods for displaying these two states and getting the user input can vary. As the word *toggle* implies, the user can change from one state to the other by *toggling* or changing the switch.

A radio button is a commonly used toggle switch that is placed next to text or an icon. The text or icon represents one of the two states. When the

box is checked or the button filled, this means that the state represented is on. If it is empty, the state is off. For example, a radio button may be placed next to a line of text that reads "High Level of Detail." If the circle is empty, then High Level is off. If a dot appears in the circle, then this option is turned on. A radio button does not always have be a circle with a dot. For example, the same functionality could be accomplished with a check box. It is important that the empty version looks empty and the filled version looks filled. The user should be able to recognize it as a radio button.

Changing a toggle switch can be accomplished using several different methods. When playing a console game, the user can make a change by moving the control stick left and right when the option is highlighted. The toggle can also change as the user presses the Select button when the

Figure 2.6 These are some standard looks for a radio button.

option is highlighted. Look at the methods used by other games and see what will work best for your game. The goals are to use what you think will come naturally to the user, and to be consistent throughout the entire menu.

Lists

Lists are used in many different ways. If all of the screen options can be seen on the screen at once, then the user can move the selection indicator to the option he wants and the options remain in place. (See Figure 2.7.)

If there are too many options to display all at once, you can handle the situation in a couple of different ways. One method is to keep the selection indicator stationary and the options scroll on and off screen and move into place. (See Figure 2.8.)

You can use a combination method, but this can become confusing if it's not executed well. In the combination method, the cursor moves from option to option if it is visible on screen. Once the selection reaches the last visible option on the screen, and the user continues to move it in the

same direction, then the selection indicator remains still while the options move onscreen. (See Figure 2.9.)

Input Text

In some cases, the user may need to input text. For example, the user may be given the option to enter a name for his character. This can be a simple process when playing a game on a PC, but it can become very complicated

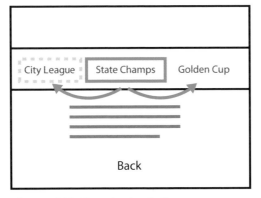

Figure 2.7 The selection indicator moves, and the options stay stationary.

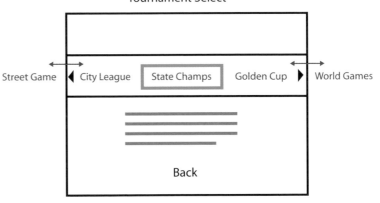

Figure 2.8 The selection indicator remains still and the options move.

without a keyboard, as when playing a game on a console.

This challenge has been addressed in basically the same way ever since the old arcade games asked the user to enter initials after receiving a high score. The most common method is to make three or four rows of text. This list should include every letter of the alphabet and any characters that can be used for input. There are also two additional options: Delete and Done (the Done button is only needed if the number of characters is not pre-determined). One of the letters is always highlighted, and the user can move this highlight left, right, up, and down. When the correct letter is highlighted, the user presses the Select button on the controller and this letter is added. If the user makes a mistake, he can select the Delete button and delete one letter. Each time the Delete button is selected, another letter is deleted. This method is effective and it can work with a very simple controller, such as a joystick and one button. The problem with this method is that it can take a long time to enter a name—it is much slower than typing. Figure 2.10 shows an example of this method for entering text.

Another approach is to start with one letter blinking. If the user moves the joystick up, the list cycles backward through the alphabet. If the user moves the joystick down, it moves forward through the alphabet. In both cases, the letter cycling wraps around and continues when at the end or beginning of the alphabet. When the

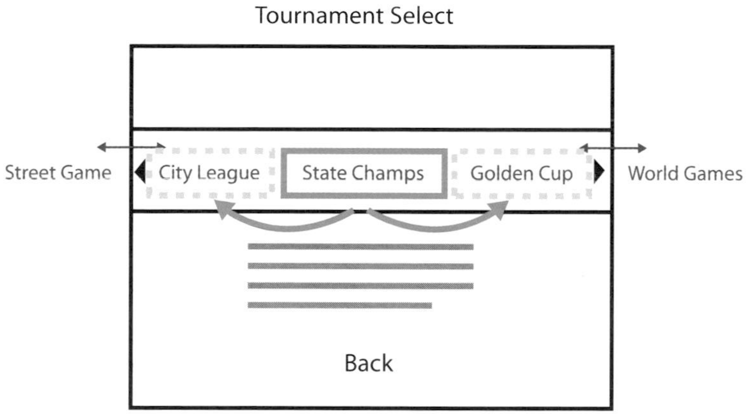

Figure 2.9 The selection indicator moves until it reaches the edge, and then the options move onto the screen

Figure 2.10 This is the traditional solution for entering text on a console or arcade machine.

Figure 2.11 This solution is also common. The advantage to this solution is that it uses much less space than the one shown in Figure 2.10.

user moves the joystick right, another letter is added. When the user moves the joystick left, a letter is deleted. Pressing the Select button on the controller finalizes the input and advances the menu.

These are just some of the most common solutions for allowing users to input text. There are many more that have been used, and I have heard some solutions described that would make the entry process much faster. I challenge interface designers to come up with a better text-entry solution for a console game, but I do so with caution. A new method can cause confusion and frustration in users. It must be very intuitive or explained really well. Neither of the methods described here is simple. The first time someone uses these methods to enter text, he is usually a bit confused. These methods do, however, have a huge advantage: Almost everyone who's played a game has used one of these methods and is familiar with them—in fact, users have come to expect them.

Drop-Down Menus

Drop-down menus are commonly used as an input method in PC games, but they are seldom used on a console game. Technically, a drop-down menu is just another way to use a list of items as input. It is just hidden until the user selects the correct option. Drop-down menus are a common solution in most PC operating systems and are very standard with application software. There aren't many software applications that don't use drop-down menus extensively.

While drop-down menus can be useful, remember that you are making a game. A lot of the Windows conventions may be very familiar to the user, but they aren't much fun. In general, it is better to get away from the feel of the operating system and make your game *feel* like a game. Drop-down menus typically don't make you feel like you're playing.

If you determine that a drop-down menu is still best for your game, you can at least do some variations. These menus can drop to the side or "drop" up. Interesting animations used for the transitions can also help give these menus a fun look. Just remember that you are making a game.

Other Variations

Not all of the methods for accepting input are listed in this book. In fact, there are many still waiting to be conceived. This is an area where vision and creativity can have a great impact on game design. Just be very careful when implementing new methods— if a new method makes the interface confusing, then it is not a better solution, even if it looks really cool. The user should know what to do without having to think very much. Stick with generally accepted methods most of the time; the user is familiar with these methods and will expect them. Use new and innovative methods sparingly and only when they will have a positive impact on the design.

Common Menu Screens

Some of the sample menus that were charted previously were simple. A big-budget game with a lot of options can get very complicated. Take a look at Figure 2.4. You can see that creating a flow chart for a menu like this can be complicated. I've worked on games that had interfaces that are even more complicated than this sample.

Below is a list of some commonly used menu screens. Again, this is by no means an exhaustive list. There are many other screens that appear in many games. Looking at this list may help you to begin to make a flow chart for your next game. Think about which of these menus could be used in your game and what your game might need that is not listed here.

- **Legal screen**. This can be a short sentence or a screen full of text. It will include legal issues like copyright notices.
- **Publisher logo screen**. It can be a requirement to show this screen before the developer logo. There may also be a requirement for how long it needs to be displayed before the user can move on.
- **Developer logo screen**. This is where your company logo is seen.
- **Console logo screen**. Some consoles require or encourage developers to display the system logo.

- **Title screen**. The name of the game appears here. It can also include interactive options.
- **Options**. An option screen allows the user to change many game settings.
- **Credits**. This is where everyone who worked on the game is listed.
- **Environment or level select**. This is used in games where the user can choose a level of location to play.
- **Player editor**. A player editor will allow the user to change the look and attributes of characters in the game.
- **Information**. This screen can have extra information, such as story, maps, and so on.
- **Save / Load game**. This screen lists how many games are saved and allows the user to load and save games.

Simplicity versus Depth

After you have created a flow chart, it's time to evaluate the flow of your menu. Before you move on to creating art is a good time to make changes to the flow. It is much easier to change your chart than to change elements after art is created and is working in the game. The goal is always to make the menu simple and easy to use. Ask yourself the following questions:

- How many options appear on each screen?
- Are they logically grouped?
- How fast can a new player get into a game?
- How fast can an experienced player get into the game?
- Which options will the player want to adjust often?
- Which options will be changed rarely?
- How does this menu compare with similar games?
- How many dead-ends are there? (When the user must back up to start the game.)

When designing interfaces, you should try to limit the number of screens you present. You should also try to limit the number of options on any one screen. These two goals sometimes conflict, and you must balance your solution. The user does not want to be forced to go through a lot of screens to accomplish what he wants to do. At the same time, if too many options are listed on a single screen, the menu can be more difficult to negotiate. It is much easier to quickly understand small amounts of information. This applies to both console and PC games, but too many options on a console can be even more problematic than on a PC. If there are too many options, screen resolution limitations can make them hard to read; it can also be tedious to scroll through a long list of items with a controller. A mouse allows the user to go directly to the option he is looking for. (The user will still need to read and comprehend all of the options on a PC game.)

A good test to see if your interface is designed well is this: When a user begins your game and just hits the Enter button repeatedly, can he get into the game? How many presses will it take to get into a game? Which options will be chosen with this default method? If your game has an option such as Multiplayer that will be used often but does not fall in this default path, how easy is it to choose this option and get into the game?

Make sure that the user is only forced to back up (go back to a previous screen) when he is adjusting options that most likely will not be accessed often. For example, music volume may only be set once and then left at the same level every time the user plays the game. Another option is to allow the user to start a game from what would be a dead end without a Start Game option. This doesn't always make sense, and it will only work if there aren't any other options that need to be selected before beginning a game.

Planning for HUD

What is HUD? It is not a replacement for a swear word. HUD is short for Heads Up Display, which refers to the interface that is displayed during game play—stuff like the radar, health meters, and score.

Because of the nature of the HUD, a flow chart is not typically necessary, but organization is important. You will need to know all of the information that will need to be displayed during game play and you will need to know any options that might need to be accessed in a Pause menu. You may need to get the information from a game designer. Get it as soon as possible. Many other screens may be needed for a game. Pop-up menus may occur at various stages and the player may need access to other information that is not visible in the HUD while playing the game. The user may need to check inventory or look at a map, for example. Do your best to get all of the information and list all of the possibilities that could occur during the entire game.

Because of the nature of the HUD, no matter how well you plan in the beginning, the game will change at least a little before you're done. It changes because of the close tie with game-play. You will discover that the user needs information that you did not anticipate displaying. You may also learn that when playing the game, some information is not necessary and should be removed. Many of these problems won't be discovered until the game is at a stage where it can be played. You will need to be flexible and even look for ways to improve the HUD.

I have changed the HUD partway through the development process on most of the games I have worked on. A great example is a change we made to the game demo on the CD of this book. We began by displaying a number as a percentage for the rating of the station. We later discovered that this number was confusing—the test users were not sure what the number meant. We changed to a five star system. I created five empty stars and the stars filled in as the rating increased. The disadvantage is that the user did not know if he was at 3.2 or 3.3 stars, but this information could be checked in the Goals pop-up menu. We found that this was a much better solution. All of the users seem to intuitively understand what three stars meant.

Get our your pencil and begin to sketch your HUD early. What you need to design will vary greatly from game to game. It also can be a little harder to design than the front-end interface, because there are fewer ways to chart the flow HUD. Just because the HUD is a little harder to plan does not mean it should be left until later. Get all of the information you can. List everything that could be possibly displayed! Prioritize all of the display items and determine how the user will access information that is not typically displayed on-screen. Determine what will be automatically displayed and what will require a separate menu. Identify any game events that will change the HUD. Organize all of the information to be displayed into logical categories, and plan as much as possible!

Creativity versus Conventional Methods

Most interface designers are bursting with creativity. They want to do things better than has been done in the past. They want to discover and implement original ideas—this is what makes the video game industry fun! The passion and desire to continually improve are essential.

When designing an interface (or working on any aspect of a game), remember that thousands of creative people have been doing the same thing for a long time. Most likely, someone else has already thought up what seems like a new idea to you. If it has never been implemented, then there might be a good reason. Be cautious when trying out new ideas—use your creativity wisely.

Video-game players have also come to expect the thing they have already experienced. Take advantage of this often by using these conventional methods. Don't give up on creativity, but don't think that something is better just because it is different. Make sure it really *is* better.

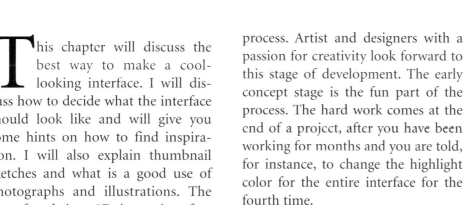

CHAPTER 3

THE LOOK AND FEEL OF YOUR INTERFACE

This chapter will discuss the best way to make a cool-looking interface. I will discuss how to decide what the interface should look like and will give you some hints on how to find inspiration. I will also explain thumbnail sketches and what is a good use of photographs and illustrations. The use of real-time 3D in an interface will also be covered.

Define a Look

Defining the look and feel of an interface is the fun part of the design process. Artist and designers with a passion for creativity look forward to this stage of development. The early concept stage is the fun part of the process. The hard work comes at the end of a project, after you have been working for months and you are told, for instance, to change the highlight color for the entire interface for the fourth time.

When working on the look and feel of a game, have fun and take the opportunity to be creative. This is a great place to experiment and to come up with something totally unique. The look of the design is what the end users will remember. If the functionality of an interface is good, the user won't even notice it. If you don't enjoy designing the look of a game, you may not be cut out for interface design.

Create a Mock-Up

The best way to define a distinctive look for your game is to create sample art, or a mock-up of the interface. The goal of creating this sample art is not to have a final product but to define and visualize the look and feel of the entire interface. Don't worry about having the right options listed. It is more important to show what your buttons will look like than it is to get the right button. By creating art that looks like a real interface, you make it easy for anyone who needs to review and approve your design. It does not require a lot of imagination or guesswork on the part of the producer or art director to get the idea if they can simply see it.

A mock-up can guide your design throughout the process. Once your mock-up has been created, reviewed, and approved, a standard has been set. The rest of the interface can be designed to fit in with the look and feel of the sample art. The entire interface should look and feel just like this sample art. It will be much faster to design the rest of the interface once you have set the look and feel. Much less experimentation is needed once you've found the style for your interface. Figure 3.1 shows an example of a mock-up.

A mock-up of a single screen of the interface and just a few more pieces of art, such as some important buttons from other screens, is all you need to define a look. Figure 3.2 shows a couple of these extra elements that you might want to include in the mock-up phase. You don't need every detail to establish your interface style. Often, the best screen to mock-up is the title screen. Legal screens, company logo screens, and even the opening cinematic sequence may appear before this title screen in the final game, but typically the title screen is the first in which options appear for the user. There are some games that have a separate title screen from the main menu, but it is usually the first screen with active buttons, and it will often contain the game logo, as well. Because it

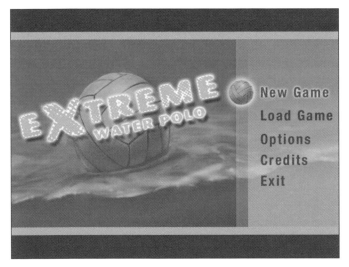

Figure 3.1 The mock-up of the title screen defines the colors and style of the entire interface.

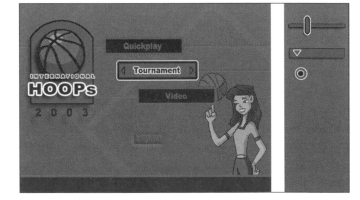

Figure 3.2 Creating a few more interface elements helps to better establish the look of the interface.

contains so many important elements, the title screen is ideal to use as a mock-up screen.

Working with Logos

Working with publishers and their game logos can be tricky business. The game publisher often provides the logo, and it is important to get this logo as early as you can. Too often, the publisher waits until near the end of the project to even decide on the name of the game, much less the design logo.

If the publisher is dragging its feet on coming up with a logo, create a temporary logo that captures the feel that will be used in the final logo. This may not be easy to guess, but it is better to have some reference, however flawed, than to have no reference.

Try to establish the look of the logo early, even if the name must change later. Communicate with the publisher and make sure they agree with the direction you're taking. It is always a pain when, say, the game has a black-and-orange interface and the publisher brings you a green and purple logo at the end of the project and asks you to change the entire interface to

match the cool, new logo. Even if the new logo *is* cool looking, if it doesn't mach the rest of the interface, it can mean you'll have to spend weeks reworking the art. Figure 3.3 shows how a logo can be out of place if the interface was not designed around the look of the logo.

Figure 3.3 The colors in this logo don't go well with the rest of the interface.

Define a Color Scheme

Color is a very important part of an interface. What color is your game? This is a good question to answer early. Anyone who looks at your interface should be able to see at a glance the color scheme of the entire game. Keeping the colors consistent throughout the game creates a unified look. Everything from the box cover to the in-game interface should reflect this color scheme and help define your game. Too many dramatic changes in color from screen to screen will make the game feel inconsistent.

When creating a color chart, make sure it feels like you want your game to feel. If you are working on a game for young children, for example, then bright, saturated colors may be appropriate. The colors would probably be very different for a game based on a horror story. In such a game, the colors should look like they belong in a horror movie—a lot of black with orange or green accents may be a good choice for such a scary game. Take a look at Figure 3.4 and compare the two color charts to see how a feel can be created using only color.

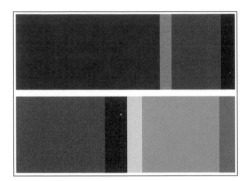

Figure 3.4 Just by looking at these two different color schemes, you can tell what kind of games they might be used for.

The subject matter of the game can often direct the color choice. If you are working on a game that takes place in a jungle, green is probably the wise color choice. If you are working on a game with demons and gargoyles, then red and black may be a logical choice. Your colors should feel like they fit with the subject matter.

Images sometimes actually get in the way of making a color choice. If you have an illustration or photo of a cool-looking red car, you may be influenced to choose red as one of the colors for your interface, even if red isn't the best color choice. It is better to make the color choice first and

then adjust the image to match your color scheme. This way, you have made the color choice independent of the colors in an image.

A good way to separate the color choice from all of the other decisions is to make a color chart. Create a file that is made up of the colors you will use in the interface. This color chart should not only contain the colors you will use in the design, but it should also have the correct proportions of each of the colors. It should roughly represent the amount of each color you will use in the actual interface. If an accent color is used in the design, it should only take up a small amount of space on the color chart. This way, the colors in your chart will feel like the final interface. Make sure to refer to this chart when working on the interface, so that you don't lose the color balance you've established.

Take a look at the color chart in Figure 3.5 and see how the yellow color is much smaller than the green tones. Now look at the final interface screen in Figure 3.6 and see how the color is balanced similarly to the color chart.

Figure 3.5 This color chart establishes the colors of an interface.

Figure 3.6 Compare the color chart with this final interface.

Express Yourself in the Design

Go for it! Make your design unique. This is your chance to really express your creativity. The best interface designs push the feel of the game. If you decide to design an interface with a retro, 1950s-America feel, then make sure that all of the elements fit together. Don't just design a standard interface that has a few elements that fit the 1950s theme—make it really feel like the 1950s. Look at clothing styles, colors, cars, and kitchen appliances that were used in the 1950s. Choose some of the elements that capture the feeling you are looking for. A button on a radio or the grill of a car may inspire the shape, color, and design of your interface. If the game takes place in ancient Japan and you decide to design the interface with a classic Japanese feel, then go all the way. Look at ancient Japanese art and calligraphy. Choose a font that looks Asian or like calligraphy. Use colors, plants, cloth patterns, or anything that imparts the feel you're striving for.

Take a look at Figure 3.7 to see how a design is less effective if a theme is only partially implemented. Then take a look at Figure 3.8 and see how this same theme produces a much more interesting design when it is pushed further. Choose an art direction and go with it—don't get caught with just an average design.

Figure 3.7 There may be nothing wrong with this interface, but it could be more interesting.

Figure 3.8 This menu takes advantage of the interesting images offered by the subject matter of the game.

Research and Inspiration

Coming up with ideas for your design is not always easy. It's not uncommon to hit a creative roadblock when designing an interface. When you feel like you can't come up with any good ideas, there are a couple of techniques that you can use to help inspire yourself. Don't let a slump hold you back for long!

Make Lists

A common and very effective brainstorming method is to create lists. Sit down and just start writing. Write down good ideas and even ideas that may not seem so good at the moment—just let them flow. Create several lists. List objects associated with the game. List emotions associated with the game. List actions associated with the game. Create as many categories as you can. Combine different words and phrases from different lists and see what you can come up with. You may come up with some unexpected solutions using this technique. Figure 3.9 shows an example of

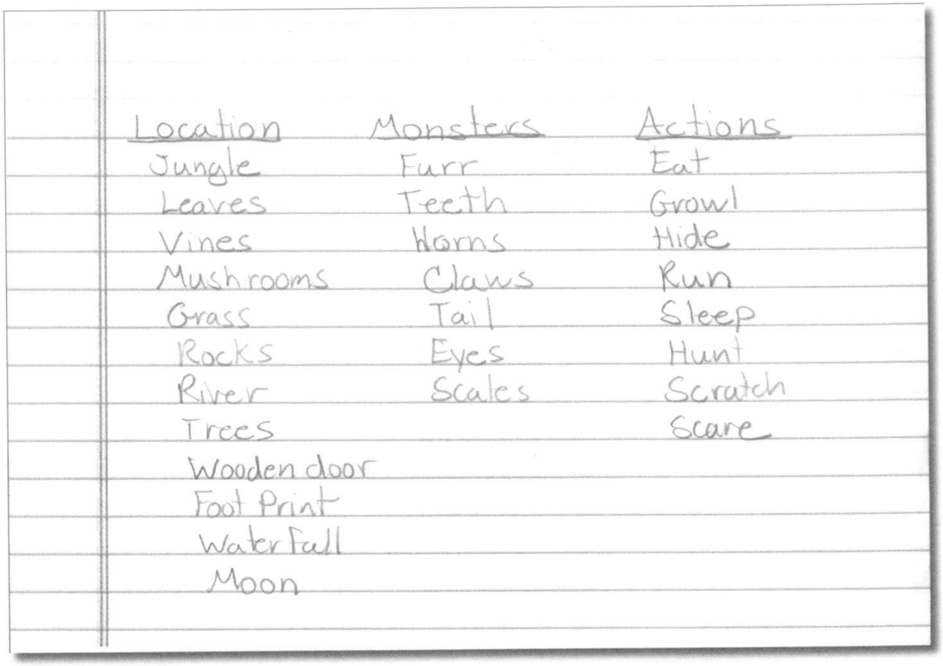

Figure 3.9 These are lists that were created for a children's game about a family of monsters that live in the jungle.

the beginnings of a brainstorming list.

Tip

Some of the most creative ideas come from mixing words from two very different lists that, at first, may not seem to work together. Don't be afraid to experiment. See if you can come up with something really interesting.

Search for Images

Another great creativity-inspiring technique is searching the Internet for cool, interesting, or thought-provoking images. You can go on a virtual field trip anywhere in world and see what things—buildings, clothing, flora, fauna, and so on—look like. If you are unfamiliar with the subject, you can quickly find visuals to help you approximate the look you're going for in your design. When creating an interface for a Formula One racing game, for example, you could search the Internet for photographs of the cars, the crowds, the tracks, and the drivers. You may find images of elements you wouldn't have thought of without looking at photos. Skid marks on the track, dented railing along the track, and helmets worn by the drivers may all provide inspiration and direction—and you may not have thought of them if you hadn't searched for images online.

Tip

The Web site http://www.google.com offers a great way to search for images. Click on the Images heading and enter any subject to find images on the Internet. You may want to have some sort of filtering turned on—you never know what you may see!

An amazingly large amount of information and photos can be found on the Internet. Be very careful not to violate any copyright laws, though. Use the photos and images you find for inspiration, but don't actually use any photos if you don't have the copyright on them. If you really need a specific photo, you may be able to purchase the rights to use it. Stock photography vendors will be happy to help you out.

You can find inspiration in other places, as well. Art galleries, libraries, and the theater can all be places where you can find inspiration. Constantly keep your eyes open. On my drive into the office, I pass several old factories with rusted metal walls, steel, and rivets. I think of how many great images and textures that can be found in these old, beat-up buildings. I often carry a digital camera so that I can stop and take a picture of anything visually arresting I come across during the day.

Another place I find a lot of inspiration is at the movies. There are so many visually stunning movies. For example, if I am working on a game that takes place in ancient Egypt, I will rent (or go see, if there is anything out) a great movie that shows architecture and art from Egypt. Animated movies are also great for inspiration. I have watched many movies with a sketchbook in my hand, ready to capture any inspiring image I see.

Check out your competition. Find out what they came up with when confronted with a similar design challenge. See what you're competing against and learn if any unique and interesting design solutions have appeared in other games. Understand what users have come to expect of games in the genre you're working in.

Avoid any urge to copy the design of other games, though. It's easy to make a game that looks only slightly different to a competing game. Playing a game like this won't be very enjoyable or impressive for users. Make your design original. Don't sell your own abilities short—even if a competitor has a great interface design, their design doesn't represent the only great solution available.

Thumbnails

Thumbnails are very small sketches. They are often only an inch or two wide. They are used to quickly run through a bunch of concepts. These little sketches can be very useful when designing an interface. When I skip thumbnails and go straight to working on a full size image, most of the time I end up getting stuck and having to go back and create the thumbnails after all.

It is easy to get too excited about an interface and either skip or spend too little time on the thumbnail sketch stage. Be patient, and make a lot of thumbnails. Thumbnails are easy and fast to make, and they can allow you to try out literally hundreds of ideas quickly. If you dig right in and start creating full-size color layouts before you make thumbnails, you'll only be able to try a limited number of approaches. Take advantage of the ease of creating thumbnails and create a lot of them.

Work Quickly

Keep your thumbnail designs small and simple. As the name implies, thumbnails are typically small, and they do not contain much detail; they are simply meant to help you arrange the basic layout. If they are drawn too large, you may be tempted to add too much unnecessary detail. Such

unnecessary detail will slow you down and can distract you from finishing the basic layout.

Make your thumbnails quickly and keep them rough. They should be used for internal direction and should not be shown to a publisher until they have been cleaned up. Spending extra time creating tight thumbnails can be a waste. Even without the details, it is amazing how much information you can convey in a small thumbnail. The best way to make thumbnails is the old fashioned way—with a pencil and paper. It is hard to match the speed of using a pencil for thumbnail sketches. Speed is the key with thumbnail sketches. You want to try a lot of ideas quickly.

Some artists struggle to maintain a small scale and to get the screen proportions correct. The best way to solve this problem is to print out a page of small, blank boxes that are the correct size and proportions. These boxes can then be used as borders for hand-drawn thumbnails. I have included a digital file on the CD included with this book that you can

use to print borders for thumbnail sketches. Figure 13.10 shows a page full of thumbnails sketches.

Push for Variation

It is a good idea to push yourself to create more thumbnails than you're initially inclined to make. You will often be more creative the further you go into the thumbnail process. At first, you may tend to create thumbnails that look similar to other interfaces you have created. Once you have run through your standard set of ideas, you will be forced to come up with more creative ideas. Don't stop when it starts to become difficult to come up with another idea. This is often the point when new ideas appear. When you get stuck, you can create variations on each design. It is also a good idea to create many completely new layouts.

Although it's good practice to create a lot of thumbnails, it's often a mistake to present hundreds of ideas to the publisher for approval. The publisher may legally own all of the art created in association with the game, but they seldom require that you show them

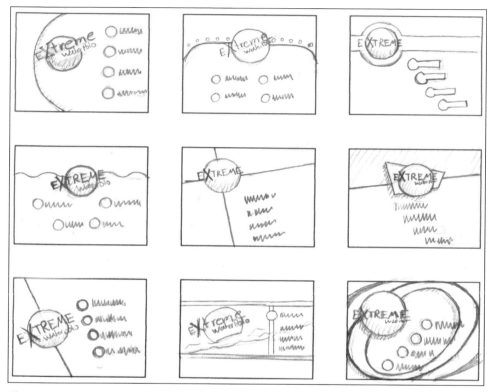

Figure 3.10 Keep thumbnail sketches small and simple.

Creativity versus Standards

Creativity is essential, but make sure that you use it in the right place. You must balance new and original ideas with standard approaches. Gamers have come to expect certain standards, and in many cases, it is better if they don't have to think too much about a new approach. Just because you think it will be cool to, say, have the "highlighted" button grow dark instead of light up does not mean it is necessarily a good idea; it may confuse the user and take him longer to understand which button is selected. This does not mean that darkening the selected button will *never* work. You just need to consider what the user is expecting to see and understand that if your menu does something different, then it may make it harder for the user to navigate.

Using Photographs

Photographs can be very useful and cool-looking in your interface, but they must be used correctly or they will hurt your design. In some cases, using photos may be the very best solution or even a requirement. If you

every scribble and sketch. Not only does it take longer for the publisher to sort through a large number of thumbnails, but inevitably the publisher will choose the one you like the least. Not everyone has the ability to envision a finished product from a thumbnail. Don't run the risk that a publisher can't see past your pencil

scribbling to the magic beneath. As I said before, most thumbnails should only be used internally; if a publisher requests to see thumbnails, it is a good idea to clean up and present one or two sketches. Choose the thumbnails that you have already determined to be the best solutions.

are making a game that uses the name of the latest sports star, you may need to include a photo of the athlete on the box and in the interface. A game with a movie license may also require a photo of the star. In many other instances, photos can be a crutch and can make a very bad or uninteresting interface. Photos should only be used when they are the logical solution, and not just because it's easier to use a photo than an illustration or to create your own background. It is very obvious when an interface designer uses a bunch of stock photographs that have not been properly touched up just to save time. It just looks bad.

I have a personal preference for using illustrations over photos. I usually avoid photos in an interface. Other than when you need to show a likeness of a famous person, I suggest always using an illustration. It will take more time and require more skill, but I think that a quality illustration has the potential to look much better than a photo. You will find that only a small percentage of the big, triple-A games use photos in the interface. Photos rarely fit well with the art in the game.

If your budget is tight, of course, you may need to use photos instead of illustrations. You need to be aware that this may be a weak point in your interface if you don't take the extra time to use the photos well. Making your own collage of several photos, using filters and effects, and making other adjustments to these photos can really help. Do your best to choose your photos wisely. I have seen some instances wherein an interface designer used photos and it resulted in a quality interface, but these instances are rare.

If you use photographs in your design, make sure they are of good quality. A digital camera can be incredibly useful when making games. The problem that comes along with using digital cameras, however, is that they are so easy to use that everyone thinks that he or she is a great photographer and that there is

no need to spend money on a professional photographer or purchase stock photography. Many designers think, "I can take a picture of my own football and get it just the way I want it." But in reality, the shot they end up with is not nearly as good as a professional photographer could do. Photos you have taken yourself are great for reference, but they must be high quality if you want to use them in your interface. Figure 3.11 is a photo that I took that is a little washed out. It is not a high-quality photo.

Figure 3.11 Digital photos that are not taken by a professional can hurt an interface design.

Don't be afraid to take digital photos, just understand your limits. There are many, many uses for photos. For example, they can serve as great references, as they capture details that you might not be able to remember without them. They can also provide a great start for textures. They can be used the same way the Internet can be used for research.

Photos that are to be used in your game can be touched up and edited. It's hard to fix a bad photo, but it's easy to improve a good photo. Whether you took the photos or they were taken by a professional photographer, there are many techniques that can be used to make the photo more interesting. Simple adjustments include changing the image levels and saturation. You can also try techniques like colorizing the photos or adding other filters. If you plan on using photos often, learn as many techniques as you can to get the most out of your photos. Figure 3.12 shows a photo that has been touched up using several different methods.

Figure 3.12 An average photo has been adjusted in several different way to help enhance the photo and make it more suitable for use in an interface.

Illustrations

In place of a photograph, you might want to consider using an illustration. This approach can really improve the look of an interface. The subject matter of your game can determine which to use. For example, while a sports game may be a great place to use a photograph of all the players, an illustration may be much better solution for a fantasy game. The style of illustrations used in an interface can help define the look and feel of a game. Are the illustrations stylized or realistic, detailed or simple, colorful or de-saturated? As with photographs, poor illustrations will hurt a design, but great illustrations can improve an interface significantly.

If you are confident in your skills as an illustrator, then you should do your own illustrations. If you can't produce top-notch illustrations in the style that would best fit your interface, get an illustrator with the style you need for your game. Just because your illustration style does not fit the game does not make you a bad illustrator. Don't force your illustration or illustration style into a design if it doesn't work just because you want the design to be "all yours." Figure 3.13 shows a sample of an illustration that would be hard to beat with a photograph.

3D Solutions

3D interfaces can be very compelling, and the idea of creating a 3D interface seems really cool. 3D interfaces can also be very expensive and time-consuming, though. Make sure to schedule plenty of time and prepare for the extra work that a 3D interface will demand. It will always take longer than you think, and you will run into more unanticipated problems than you would in creating a 2D interface.

Figure 3.13 Using an illustration instead of a photo here allowed for brighter colors. This image would have been difficult to photograph.

Pre-Rendered 2D Art

One way to get the look of a 3D interface without all of the hassle is to use pre-rendered 3D instead of real-time 3D. This option does not offer all of the advantages of a real-time 3D interface, but it certainly simplifies things. A pre-rendered 3D interface actually is just a 2D interface in which the 2D artwork is created using a 3D program. This approach doesn't allow for camera movement, but small objects can be animated and rendered in a 3D package and these frames can be played back. These animations typically need to be small because of memory limitations, but they can also look really cool.

I used this technique when making a Tiger Woods golf game for the N64. This game had an arcade feel, and we wanted to have a cool effect when the ball was hit perfectly. We wanted the 3D ball to morph and warp while in flight. The game engine would not have been able to handle the polygons needed to make this kind of animation in 3D. We instead rendered really cool animations and placed these 2D rendered animations over the ball when the effect happened.

This same effect can be used in the interface. You can use a 3D model to render a spinning animation of a button. These rendered frames can then be played back in the menu. It appears to be 3D even thought it is pre-rendered.

Involve the Programmers

Programmers should be involved from the beginning when you're considering an interface that involves real-time 3D. Real-time 3D involves a lot of technology, and the game engine must support all of the features that you plan to put in the interface. Good communication, tools, and patience are even more important when creating a real-time 3D interface than when creating a 2D interface.

Combining 3D and 2D

A common approach nowadays is to use real-time 3D in just a small part of the interface. 3D models are used in important areas where they are most effective. The trick is to determine where 3D models can provide the biggest benefit. For example, many games offer a player editor wherein the user can make changes to the character in the game. Many options, including clothes, hair, skin color, and even tattoos can be adjusted in these editors. Player editors often use the same models and textures that are used in the game. This way, the user can make adjustments and see the results instantly. In this combined approach, the 3D model is drawn on top of a 2D interface.

Cars in a racing game are an example of a common use of a 3D model on top of a 2D background. The user can often see the 3D model of the car he is choosing, right in the interface. One way to take advantage of 3D models that are used in an interface is to animate them or spin them around. This kind of movement would be very difficult with a 2D-only menu but it is simple when using a 3D model.

This can be a challenge when creating the 2D section of these menus. You will often need to guess at what the menu will look like after the 3D model has been incorporated. You will not be able to see the 3D model until everything works in the game engine.

3D Challenges

Making big changes to a 3D interface can be more difficult than making changes to a 2D interface. It can take a long time to build geometry and create textures for a 3D interface, and if you make too many changes you can waste a lot of precious time. Because each piece of art takes longer to create, changing or replacing this art is also more time-consuming. Spend a fair amount of time planning and designing before building a 3D model for an interface—and make sure you have solid concept designs.

This book covers many design principles. Principles like color balance, and eye movement should not be discarded because your interface is done in 3D. All of the same principles apply to 3D menus, just as they do to a 2D menu. Don't ignore any design principles just because you are using 3D.

Even though the source of the image on the screen may be a real-time 3D model, the end result is a 2D image on a computer or TV screen. This final image should be designed to take into account all the design principles for 2D art.

One of the big advantages of a completely real-time 3D interface is the ability to move the camera. Take advantage of this ability but do not abuse it. Too much movement can disorient the user. If the camera movement is too slow and takes too long, it can cause annoying delays in the game-play. Camera movement can be a benefit, but it can also be a challenge. As soon as you begin moving the camera, you will need to spend a lot of time trying to get it just right. Making these camera changes can take a lot of time.

Creating 3D interfaces can be a complex task. Experience is the best teacher. A good understanding of how 3D works in other aspects of the game is a must when using 3D in an interface. I have seen some incredible-looking interfaces that use 3D. If you have the time and the budget, these 3D interfaces can be very cool.

Don't Get Too Attached to Your Ideas

A big mistake that many designers often make is to get too attached to an idea early in the design process—they latch on to an idea that sounds appealing and then try to create the rest of the design around this element. It can be hard to do, but if an idea doesn't work well, you may need to scrap it.

For example, while working on a racing game, a designer may decide that using tires for buttons sounds really cool. But the black tires may stick out and not look good with the blue and yellow colors (which must be used because they are the colors of the sponsors) in the interface. The round shape of the button may not fit in well with the rest of the design, either. Rather than use a different image for the buttons, though, the designer wastes a lot of time changing everything else to match the tires.

If any element of the design is causing problems, just grit your teeth and throw it out. When something is broken, don't be afraid to fix it. You will be surprised how much better a design will turn out if you're not afraid to make dramatic changes.

In a game I worked on, we created an interface splash screen early in the process. It had a look and feel that we felt was appropriate for the game—a bright color scheme and a little bit of a retro feel to it. Our goal was to re-create the look of an old science-fiction movie. The game was goofy and fun. Both the game and the interface were created with the intention of appealing to a wide audience and not just to hard-core gamers.

The problem came when we showed the game to publishers and friends. They immediately thought that it was a game aimed at really young children. The game was a little too complex for really young players, and we did not want to scare off teenagers or adults, so we decided to scrap this interface and make adjustments that made it feel a little more sophisticated. The new interface still has the goofy cartoon characters, but because of the desaturated colors, it has a slightly more grown-up feel. Figure 3.14 shows the old design that was drastically changed before release.

Figure 3.14 This interface design appeared to be a little too young for the target audience.

Figure 3.15 A slightly more mature interface replaced the previous design.

Summary

The best interfaces have a very distinctive style. They capture the appropriate feel for the game. Great interfaces have a unique look and feel. These interfaces do not happen by accident. They are often a result of a lot of hard work. Good research and a lot of thumbnail sketches can really help you in this creative process. If you get stuck, do some brainstorming. Armed with the techniques discussed in this chapter and your personal creativity, you can create the best interface ever conceived by man.

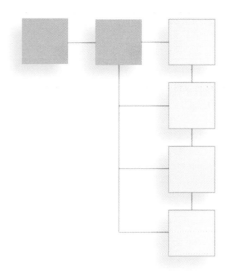

CHAPTER 4

BASIC DESIGN PRINCIPLES

Nothing will improve your design skills better than an understanding of basic design principles. Many interface designers learn these principles in college or a specialized art school but they forget them later—it is easy to go out and find a job in the industry, start working on real games, and just get sort of rusty on design basics. Ignoring or forgetting basic design principles will adversely affect your design ability. Once you have learned basic design principles, keep using them to evaluate and improve your interfaces. The best interface designers apply these principles every day.

Getting Back to Basics

I graduated from the design department of a large university. In my first year of college, I didn't get to design anything "real." All of my early assignments focused on abstract shapes and color because understanding how to design with abstract images will help you design anything better. Images of real objects can actually get in the way of seeing the real design. If you are looking at a racecar, it is harder to see the shapes and colors created by the car in the composition. It is easy to get lost in the illustration or photo of the car and not see how it works as a design element.

As you create your design game interface, try to look past any images of concrete objects, such as a ball, gun, or zombie, and look at the pure design. What shapes and colors are in your design, and how pleasing—or not—are they? If the images and text in your design were changed to abstract shapes and colors, would the design still have the right feel? Treat images and text in your interface as design elements. Be aware of their shape and color, and place them thoughtfully. Figure 4.1 demonstrates how you can look at all of the text and images in a design as shapes. This will help you better see the design and not be distracted by the basketball.

Really See Your Design

Looking past the images and focusing on the pure design may sound simple enough, but it is often difficult to do. It is especially difficult for the designer who has spent hours composing a design. Because of this, it is always easier to evaluate a design done by someone else. I have had the experience of not being able to evaluate my own design until it was being reviewed by the art director. As soon as I saw my design on his computer screen, I could see flaws that I didn't see on my computer monitor.

Try to get a fresh look on a design that you have been working on for a long time by squinting your eyes and making everything blurry, or by turning an image upside down. Flip it hori-

Figure 4.1 This design is easier to evaluate when you look at text and images as shapes.

zontally. Shrink it down so it is really small or look at the image from across the room. This will help you to ignore the details and look at the overall design—these details can be hard to ignore if you have spent a lot of time adjusting them. You want to make your viewing experience closer to that of a first-time viewer. It is surprising how problem areas will jump out at you when you use one of these methods to get a fresh look at your design.

Using Color

Color can be a very powerful design tool. Never underestimate the ability of color to set a mood. Color can express emotion and set an atmosphere. Colors are often linked to emotions—you've heard the phrases "feeling blue" or "green with envy." You can probably picture what these colors look like. The blue color is not very bright and saturated. It would most likely be a very gray-blue color. Gray, cloudy skies have a sad feeling associated with them. A design that uses a lot of neutral gray and very desaturated colors can also have the same sad feeling. On the other hand, bright yellows and blues feel very cheerful. What colors do you associate with a birthday party?

In order to harness the power of color, you need to have an understanding of how color works. Color is a complex subject and there is much more to learn about it than I can possibly cover in this book. I will briefly discuss a few of the important concepts in the next sections, though.

Johannes Itten published a book about color theory in Germany in 1961; check it out if you want to learn more about color. It is a very comprehensive and scientific approach to color and has been translated into many languages. The English version of the original book, *The Art of Color*, is not light reading, but there is a condensed version, called *Itten, The Elements of Color – A Treatise On The Color System Of Johannes Itten Based On His Book* The Art Of Color. This book contains just about everything you would want to know about color theory. Of course, every good library or book store carries other books on color and color theory. Pick up a few of these to become an expert at wielding color effectively in any situation.

Creating Color Harmony

One of the major challenges when working with color is finding a set of colors that work well together. When colors look good together, the effect is often referred to as *color harmony*. This subject has been studied for a long time and there are many interesting facts that have been discovered. If you understand the basic concepts of color harmony, it is easy to find colors that go well together.

Color harmony can be defined in a way that is very scientific and much less subjective than you may expect. There are scientific reasons that certain colors work well together. Color theory has been studies in depth by many people. Johannes Itten, whom I mentioned in the last section, is a great example of someone who has devoted his life to the study of color. He is considered by many people to be the greatest authority on color in modern times. He and many others have discovered that color harmony can be explained scientifically—color harmony is not just based on personal color preference.

Finding Complementary Colors

It is easy for someone without a strong art background to confuse color terms. Harmonious colors are colors that look good together. This can include colors that are similar to one another. For example, a range of blue colors can look good together. The term *harmonious colors* also includes a set of colors referred to as *complementary colors*. These are a special sub-set of harmonious colors.

If you need to use two colors that work well together, complementary colors are always a good choice. Complementary colors are the two colors opposite each other on the color wheel. Pick any color and draw a line to the exact opposite side on the color wheel to find the complementary color. (See Figure 4.2.) It is helpful to know the complementary color of all of the primary and secondary colors, as you may not always have a color wheel handy.

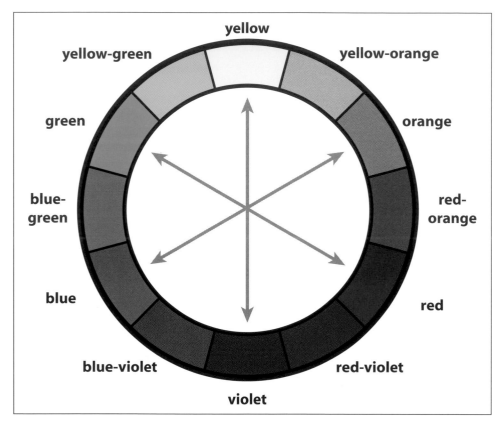

Figure 4.2 Complementary colors are found directly opposite each other on the color wheel.

When you use very saturated complementary colors together, they not only go well together but they impart a lively feel to your design. If you are looking for a less lively color scheme, you can use less saturated versions of these complementary colors.

There is a reason that complementary colors are pleasing to the eye when they are used together: If you mix two complementary colors together, the result is a neutral gray color. This neutral gray color is easy on the eye. The further away from neutral gray, the tougher time the human eye has seeing the color clearly. Think of how you would feel in a room with every wall painted a bright yellow. If the color is too strong, it can be hard to look at. Your eye (actually your brain, of course) reacts to colors by trying to adjust what it sees. Your eyes always try to shift colors as close as possible to this neutral gray.

In the room full of bright yellow walls, you could help out confused eyes by adding the complementary color. Adding a lot of purple can help counterbalance the bright yellow. A strong purple color would help your eyes better adjust to the yellow color. This counterbalancing effect is one of the reasons that complementary colors work well together. Yellow and purple may not be the best set of colors for interior decorating, but they might look good on a box of laundry detergent. Very saturated complementary colors are very lively and may be too powerful for every situation. However a soft yellow and a very calm purple might work well as an interior color scheme.

Afterimages

Stare at the box of color in Figure 4.3 for about 15 seconds, and then close your eyes tightly. For a couple of seconds after you close your eyes, you should see a box in the complementary color; this image is referred to as an *afterimage*. Your eyes have not had a chance to adjust to the fact that you

Figure 4.3 Stare at this color, close your eyes, and see what color the afterimage is.

are no longer looking at a block of color. The afterimage reveals a little about what your eyes are doing while you are looking the block of color—attempting to counteract the color in the square.

What you will see in the afterimage of a red square is a green square. The afterimage of a blue square is orange. Your eyes are trying to counterbalance the color you're staring at, and so when you close your eyes, you'll always "see" the complementary color. If you are looking at a black square, then the afterimage will be white, and if you are looking at a white square, the afterimage will be black.

Complementary colors look good together because they are naturally counterbalancing one another. If these complementary colors

were mixed, they would create the gray color that your eye is striving for—your eyes don't have to work as hard to do the counterbalancing. It is probably no surprise that a neutral gray square does not produce any afterimage.

Using More Than Two Colors

The same concept of finding colors that are pleasing to the eye can be applied to a color scheme with more than two colors. If you need three colors that work well together, you can use a color wheel and either an isosceles or equilateral triangle to find them. (See Figure 4.4.) By drawing a triangle inside the color wheel, you can find a set of colors that work well together by using the colors at each of the three angles in the triangle. You can also find four colors that go well together by drawing a square or rectangle in the middle of the color wheel. The principle is that when you mix all of the colors in any one of these color sets together they create a neutral gray color. (See Figure 4.5.)

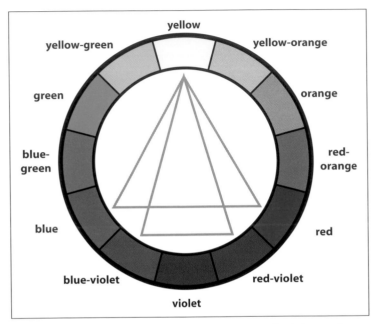

Figure 4.4 Using either type of triangle, you can find three colors that will mix to a neutral gray. Spin the triangles to see all of the possible color combinations.

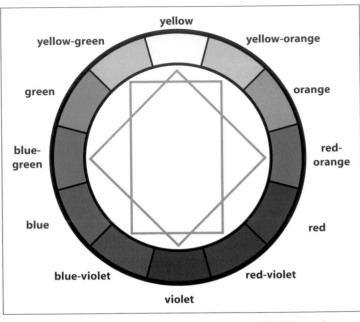

Figure 4.5 Using a rectangle or square, you can find four colors that will mix to a neutral gray. Spin the square or rectangle to see all of the possible color combination

Subjective Color

Each person has his or her own personal color preference. This can have a big effect on the colors that you find pleasing. You may assume that color preferences are a manifestation of one's individuality, but this may not be entirely true. Past experiences and personality do play a role in color preference, but it is interesting to learn the results of research done in this area. Some studies indicate that color preferences have a slight tendency to correlate with eye and hair color—blondes with blue eyes have a slight tendency to prefer very pure colors and brunettes with dark eyes tend to prefer color combinations that include black. (Obviously, this is not universal, and undoubtedly other factors apply to color preference.) These results would suggest that color preference is, at least partially, tied to the function of the eye. Blue-eyed blonds have different pigmentation in the eye and possibly see color differently than brunettes with dark-colored eyes.

Balancing Color Strength

Some colors have more visual strength than others. For instance, colors like yellow, red, and orange have more visual strength than the colors on the opposite side of the color wheel. When two colors of unequal visual strength are used in physically equal amounts—that is, half and half—the stronger color will appear to take over and will attract more attention than the other color. The saturation level of a color has a big effect on the visual strength of a color. A pure blue, for example, is much stronger than a gray-blue.

You should consider the balance and strength of each of the colors in your design. An exact balance between colors is seldom the goal, but you must be aware that even small amounts of a very strong color can have a big impact on your design. Figures 4.6 and 4.7 demonstrate how colors can differ in visual strength.

Warm and Cold Colors

Color "temperature" can be used to create a mood in your design. Certain colors seem to have visual temperature, and they are often referred to as being *warm* or *cold*. Yellow, red and orange are said to be warm colors. Colors like purple, blue, and green are said to be cool colors. Images that use these colors effectively can actually make the viewer perceive different temperatures in an illustration. Along with temperatures, emotions tend to be associated with these colors. Warm colors are perceived as happy, cheerful, and loud, while cool colors are more calm and quiet.

If your game takes place at night, or in the middle of Winter, blues and purples may be appropriate for the interface. These colors will help the users feel more like they are in the game world. Not only are these colors good for the interface, but also blue lighting can make a scene look cold. If your game takes place at midday on a tropical island, on the other hand, yellow and oranges can help set the mood. The lighting in a hot scene should also be bright and warm. Figures 4.8 and 4.9 demonstrate color temperature.

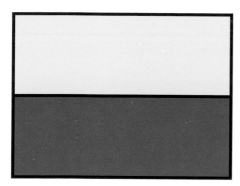

Figure 4.6 The yellow and purple cover an equal amount of space, but the yellow overpowers the purple.

Figure 4.7 The yellow and purple don't cover an equal amount of space. There is now less yellow, but the design is much closer to balancing visually.

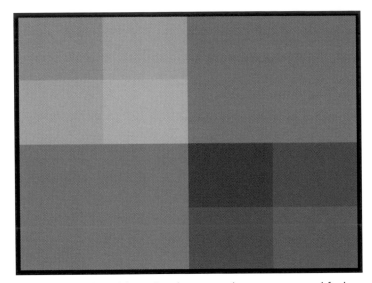

Figure 4.8 These blue colors have a cool temperature and feel very calm.

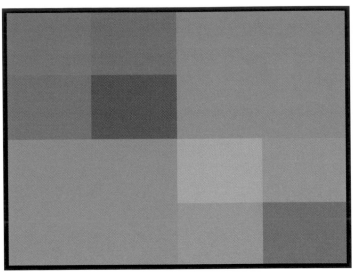

Figure 4.9 These orange colors are much warmer and feel cheerful.

Color on a Monitor or TV

Color on a computer monitor or a TV is created by three colors of light. Red, green, and blue lights are projected onto your screen and combinations of these three colors produce all of the colors you see on your monitor. All three colors at their full intensity produce a pure white. The absence of all three colors produces black.

Working with colors that are produced with light is very different from working with paint. When working with light, the more light you add, the closer the color is to white; the less light you add, the closer to black. A pure white color occurs when all colors of light are present, and black is the result of the absence of light. This is why RGB values work the way they do. I'll discuss RGB colors in more detail next.

Technically speaking, when you're working with paint, light still creates color. The difference is that you are not adjusting the light; you're adjusting the *material* that reflects the light. When a white light hits colored paint, some of the light rays are absorbed by the paint and others are reflected back to the eye. The color you see is the color of the light rays that are reflected back to your eye.

Creating Digital Colors

When creating colors digitally, there are several color systems you can use. Various software packages allow you to make these color adjustments in different ways. The most common color systems include RGB, CMYK, and HSB, but several other color systems, such as PANTONE, do exist. These other systems are used mainly in printing, and there is little need to use them in designing game interfaces. Figure 4.10 is Adobe Photoshop's Color Picker. You can choose any of these methods to choose a color.

RGB

RGB stands for *red, green* and *blue.* The RGB system allows you to adjust the values for each color from 0 to 255. Televisions and computer monitors use the red, green, and blue lights, just like the RGB system. Because televisions and monitors are using light, they can produce a much broader range of color than can be produced in the printing process. Because inks are not capable of reflecting every color back to the eye, they are limited as to the amount of colors they can produce. This is great for game developers—they can take advantage of the broader range of values that can be produced with light.

This wide range of colors you get with RGB is not found in the CMYK system, and it is the advantage of using the RGB color system to define digital colors. The RGB color system will offer the broadest range of colors. The difficulty with the RGB

system comes in understanding how to adjust the values to get the color you want. It is often counter-intuitive to adjust the RGB values because they function like light. Unlike with paint and ink, adding more color makes the color brighter and less color makes the color darker. Figure 4.11 shows how RGB values can be adjusted in Adobe Photoshop.

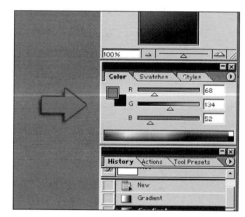

Figure 4.11 Adobe Photoshop users can adjust colors using RGB sliders.

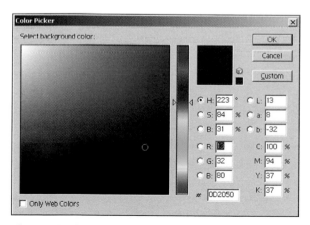

Figure 4.10 Adobe Photoshop's Color Picker allows you to choose between several different methods for mixing color.

Tip

Using the RGB color system can result in an unprintable color. Adobe Photoshop warns you when a color falls outside the printable range. If you click on the exclamation point that appears when these out-of-range colors are created, the printable color closest to the non-printable color will be selected. (See Figure 4.12.) Not all software will warn you when you fall out of the printable range. If you are creating art that will be printed, you may need to account for this discrepancy.

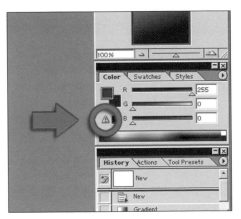

Figure 4.12 Adobe Photoshop alerts the user when a color has been created that is out of the printable range.

CMYK

Everyone mixed paint as a kid. If you are an artist (and even if you aren't), your finger painting mess may have been beneficial to your understanding of colors and color mixing. And artists who have worked with traditional media understand mixing paint and ink even better than your average kid. These experiences make the CMYK system a little easier to understand because CMYK works just like mixing paint.

Paint and ink actually absorb some light and reflect back the rest. The colors that are reflected are what the eye can see. This is why mixing ink or paint produces a darker color. When the colors mix, the colors absorbed by the two individual colors are now all absorbed by the new color. Less light is reflected back to the eye, and the resulting color is darker.

The CMYK color system is derived from the printing process. Printers use cyan, magenta, yellow, and black inks to print full-color images. Small dot patterns are printed in each of these colors. The dots are printed in a range of sizes across the image. The eye then mixes the colors, and it appears that the image contains a wide range of colors.

If you take any full-color, printed image and look at it through a powerful magnifying glass, you can see the dot pattern. It is much more visible in lighter areas because the dots are smaller and further apart. Many home printers also use CMYK ink. They also print using these small dots. Printers will often tout their printing capabilities by giving you a number for DPI. DPI stands for *Dots Per Iinch*. The more dots a printer can print in an inch, the smaller the dots must be. The smaller the dots, the harder they are to see and the better the image looks.

Understanding how the CMYK system works can make it much easier to mix colors. The problem with this color system is it can't produce a wide range of colors like the RGB system can. Figure 4.13 shows you what Photoshop's CMYK mixing system looks like.

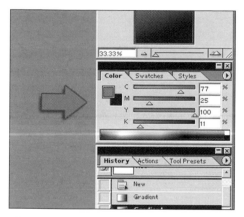

Figure 4.13 Adobe Photoshop also offers the option of mixing colors using the CMYK system.

HSB

The HSB system offers the same range of colors as the RGB system and is easier to understand. HSB stands for *hue, saturation, and brightness*. If you understand these terms, it can be easy to mix colors using the HSB system.

Hue is what most people think of when they use the word *color*. Changing the hue can change a color from red to blue. Saturation defines how powerful the color is. When saturation is low, the color is closer to gray. When saturation is high, the color is much closer to the full color. Brightness works like it sounds: The higher the brightness value, the closer to white the color is; the lower the brightness value, the closer to black. Figure 4.14 shows Photoshop's HSB mixing system.

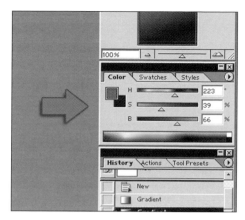

Figure 4.14 HSB may be the easiest color system to understand.

Visual Organization

A good rule when creating an interface is to space elements evenly and align them well. Paying attention to spacing and alignment results in visual organization. If the elements in your design are scattered and the spacing between them isn't consistent, your design will appear unorganized. This is displeasing to the user. Most people are attracted to organization.

If your design calls for objects that are not aligned, then make sure that these elements are not positioned only slightly off-alignment with other objects—in other word, move them far enough out of alignment that there is no doubt that it was intentional. It can be very disconcerting to the user if objects look like they should be aligned but they aren't. Many designs can be improved by simply fixing the spacing between objects.

Use your eyes and not your ruler when creating spacing between objects. Visual spacing may not always be exactly the same as the actual physical spacing. For example, elements with circular edges may need to be closer than objects with square edges. The important thing is that everything appears evenly spaced. Trust your eyes. It is often helpful to imagine that you will fill the space between two objects with sand. If the spacing is visually correct, the amount of sand between each object should be roughly equal.

In Figure 4.15, the upper set of shapes is evenly spaced and aligned along the bottom of all three shapes. The middle set of shapes is center aligned. This improves the alignment but even though they are technically spaced evenly, the circle seems a little too far away. The bottom set of shapes is visually spaced correctly.

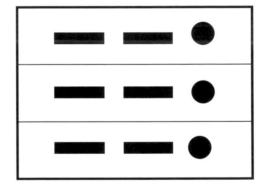

Figure 4.15 The bottom image is visually spaced correctly.

Unity and Variation

When you're creating an interface design, one of the biggest challenges is striking a balance between unity and variation. If your design is composed of a group of unrelated elements, then there is no unity. If all of the elements in your design are a different shape or color, then the composition will appear to be thrown together and it will lack the cohesiveness found in good design. On the other hand, if all of the colors and shapes in your design are exactly the same, then your design won't be very visually interesting. A little variation is required to make a design pleasing to the eye.

The best approach is to start with unity. Everything should feel like it fits together. Unity in your design is accomplished by repeating visual elements such as color, shape, and size. An obvious place to start is color. Use color consistently throughout the interface. Look at the rest of the elements in your design and make sure that shapes, sizes, and other elements repeat often. If you are using circular shapes in your design, then be sure to use these curved shapes throughout the design. A square shape with harsh edges may not fit with the rest of your design.

When you've achieved visual unity, then you can create some variations that will create visual interest. If your design consists of circular shapes, you can make them different sizes or colors. If you are using square shapes, you can set them at different angles. The difficult part is striking the balance between making the variation different enough to be interesting and not losing the unity of the design.

Negative Space

When placing an element in your design, you should be aware of the negative space that is created by the object. Negative space is the empty area around an object—not the shape of the object itself, but the shape of the background. Negative space is just as important a design element as the shape of the object. The negative shape will contribute to the overall feeling of your design just as the positive space does.

At first, it may be difficult to see the negative space. It may take practice before you are able to instinctively notice the shapes created in the negative space. Your natural reaction is to only see the positive space. Figure 4.16 illustrates negative space.

Movement

Even if an image is static—without any animation—it can still impart the feeling of movement. Certain shapes have an inherent movement, while others appear to be stationary. Angled lines give the feeling of motion, for

Figure 4.16 The fancy F creates a negative shape. Part of this shape can be seen in red in the smaller image.

example. The more visual space and power the angled object has, the stronger the feeling of motion. Figure 4.17 demonstrates how angled lines have an inherent motion. You can also line objects up in a way that together they produce an angle with motion.

If you are working on a racing game, you might want to consider a design with a strong angled line. If movement and speed are important elements of your game, then angles may be much better than vertical lines. If

you have a design that seems too static, you might improve the design by simply tilting the entire menu at an angle.

If you are working on a city simulation game, it may be more important to give a feeling of power and stability than a feeling of motion. A feeling of stability comes from lines that are vertical or horizontal. These lines do not have much movement, but they feel much more solid. If your interface needs to feel strong and stable, vertical or horizontal lines can really help.

Figure 4.18 demonstrates how these lines have a feeling of stability.

Eye Movement

In addition to the inherent motion of the shapes in an image, you should think about eye movement. *Eye movement* refers to the order in which a viewer looks at an image. What is the first thing the viewer sees? Is this the most important object in the scene? Where is his eye drawn next? At any point is the viewer drawn out of the

Figure 4.17 These angled lines create a feeling of motion.

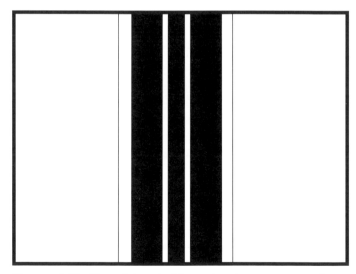

Figure 4.18 The solid vertical lines give the appearance of strength and stability.

design and off the screen, rather than on to the next item? As the designer, you can control the user's eye movement with the composition of elements.

Many attributes of the objects in your scene can contribute to eye movement. Size, color, and shape can all attract attention and control the movement of the user's eye. You can see how your eye moves across the image in Figure 4.19. Figure 4.19 docs a better job of keeping the viewer's eye

on the page than Figure 4.20 does. To test your own designs you will need to learn how to recognize your own eye movement.

Balance and Weight

Shapes and objects in any image have a visual *weight*. Dark areas appear heavier than thin, light-colored objects. When designing an interface, pay attention to the overall layout and control how the visual weight is dis-

tributed. Look to see where the heavy areas are located in relationship to the light areas. Visual weight can be affected by the color, size, and shape of an object.

If all of the elements in your design appear to have equal visual weight, your design may not have enough variation to be interesting. Not all designs require dramatic differences in visual wcight, but if your design lacks energy, you can try adjusting visual weight.

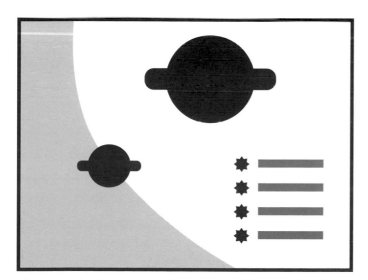

Figure 4.19 The eye movement starts at the large shape, moves to the medium shape, and then the curved line draws the eye to the shapes in the bottom-right.

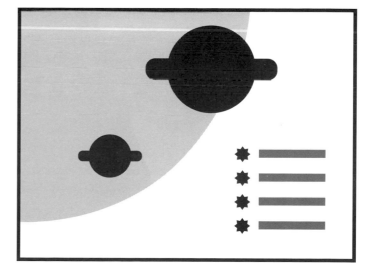

Figure 4.20 This design is similar to that in Figure 4.19, but the curved line now draws the viewer's eye off the screen before it reaches the shapes in the bottom-right.

In the real world, physical objects that are unbalanced don't stay that way very long. They fall over. We are used to seeing objects in a balanced state. It is the same with visual weight within a design. We expect to see visual weight distributed in a way that feels stable. When objects with more visual weight appear at the bottom of an image, it brings a feeling of stability. When these objects appear at the top of an image, the design can appear a little top-heavy. This effect can appear even more dramatic if the visual weight is off-center. Figure 4.21 is a design that is not balanced. It seems like it is just about to fall over.

There are two types of balance that can be used in a design. The first is formal, or symmetrical, balance. If you can draw a line down the center of the screen, all the objects on one side of the screen are mirrored on the other side. All of the objects do not need to be exact copies of the objects on the other side, but they may be similar in size, shape, and color.

The second type of balance is *informal,* or *asymmetrical,* balance. If you divide the screen, when using informal balance, a large item on one side balances several smaller items on the other side. Size is not the only attribute that can be used to informally balance your design. A darker item may be used to balance several lighter items. It is much harder to achieve balance using informal balance. When using formal balance, you can simply mirror the image. Informal balance requires more planning and skill, but it also can be much more visually interesting and appealing.

Unbalancing Your Design to Create Tension

If you understand how to use visual balance, you can use this knowledge to create a feeling of tension. If a design is very top-heavy, it can appear as though the objects in your scene are about to fall over. A feeling of stability is not always what you're shooting for. Many times, you can correct a design by making changes in the visual weight of objects that result in a stable and grounded-feeling design. Other times, you can make an interface that is a little boring much more dynamic by shifting the visual weight into a position that appears unbalanced.

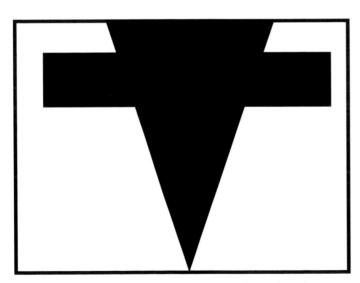

Figure 4.21 This design is top-heavy. It looks as though it would be easy to tip over.

Odd Numbers

When placing repeating objects into your design, you will find that having an odd numbers of objects is more visually pleasing than an even numbers of objects. One of the reasons that odd numbers are appealing is that they have a center object. This is more comfortable to look at. Even numbers of objects can work if they are well placed, but if you have a choice, it is good to remember the odd-even rule.

It is easiest to see the effect of odd numbers when working with a small number of items. Three or five objects is much more visually interesting than two, four, or six objects. Once the number of objects in your design gets much past seven, it is harder for your eye to even detect if there is an even or odd amount of objects. Figure 4.22 demonstrates how odd numbers look best.

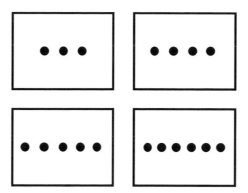

Figure 4.22 Notice how the odd numbers seem more interesting.

Dividing an Image

When introducing an element into your design that divides the image, make sure to carefully place the division. Any object that stretches the length or height of the screen could possibly divide your image. The division doesn't have to completely divide the screen. You should treat a division that covers a large portion of the screen in the same way you treat a complete division, though.

Dividing an image evenly can make it much more pleasing to the eye. If an image is divided near the center but the division is not centered, it may look like a mistake. Good places to divide an image are in the center, at the two-thirds point, and at the quarter point. A two-thirds division tends to be particularly visually pleasing. Figure 4.23 illustrates how even division is visually pleasing.

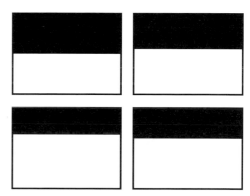

Figure 4.23 The images on the left are divided in half and in thirds. Notice how this is more visually pleasing then dividing an image at positions that are a little off.

Intersections

When objects intersect, it is particularly important to make sure that there is nothing that looks like a mistake. If two objects intersect in such a way that they do not line up perfectly but are close to lining up, make some adjustments—either make them line up perfectly with one another or move them so they are far enough off that no one thinks you tried to line them up and missed. Figure 4.24 demonstrates how alignment can be important to your design.

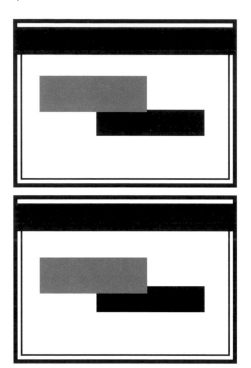

Figure 4.24 The top image looks as if the designer tried to align the boxes and just messed up. The bottom image looks better because the two boxes are clearly not intended to be aligned.

Summary

If your interface does not boast as good of a visual design as you would like, it might be helpful to go through a checklist of basic design principles. If you follow these basic design principles, you can create great interfaces. These principles apply to everyone—no one becomes a good designer and then can ignore these principles. Following the guidelines presented in this chapter makes an interface designer effective.

CHAPTER 5

CONSOLE OR PC?

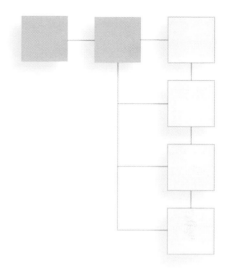

Big differences exist between video game development for consoles and development for PC games. Each platform has its benefits and drawbacks. One of the biggest and most apparent differences between the PC and a console is that they use different input devices. A mouse is very different from a controller. The entire game can change if it is on a console instead of a PC. Understanding these differences can help an interface designer create a better interface for either platform.

Bad Conversions

The differences between a console and a PC are most apparent when a PC game is converted to a console game. PC games are often converted to a console, but the conversion is not always successful. Most PC games have been created so that both the interface and game-play work well with a mouse. When these games are converted to console without all of the necessary adjustments, a great PC game can become difficult or impossibly hard to play.

An interface designed for a mouse may be very difficult to navigate with a controller. Buttons can be placed almost anywhere on the screen in a PC game. They don't need be placed the same way they are placed on a console. Often, this means that a PC interface needs to be redesigned for the console.

When converting a PC game to console, it is imperative that the entire game, including the interface, be modified to work well with a controller. It is not always easy to switch a game from mouse control to console-style control without changing the core game mechanics. In some conversions, an attempt has been made to turn the controller into a mouse. A cursor appears on the screen, and the user moves the cursor around with the joystick or d-pad as if it were a mouse. This is seldom a good solution. It can be very tedious to move the cursor completely across the screen using a joystick because the joystick can't move as fast—but if it moved fast, the cursor would be hard to control. It is much easier to move a mouse around your desk at varying speeds than it is to use a controller to move a cursor like a mouse. A controller can't easily vary the speed of movement. Moving a mouse is much faster than it is to fake mouse control with a controller.

Console Development

The more you know about the entire game-development process, the more effective you will be at creating great interfaces. I will give you a little background about how games are made and explain how this can have an effect on the interface. Some of the differences between PC games and console games are not only a result of the differences between a mouse and a controller, but are a result of the differences in the development process as well.

Console Hardware Manufacturers

The current major hardware manufacturers for console systems are Nintendo, Sony, and Microsoft. Because these companies manufacture the consoles and all of the games that can be played on their game systems, they make the rules. Even if another company has actually developed the game, the hardware manufacturers themselves actually make the game disks. The only way to get a game on the market for one of these console systems is to learn and follow the manufacturer's rules.

The console game developer is not the only one who must comply with all of the guidelines set by the hardware manufacturer—the game publisher must also work around the hardware manufacturer's schedule. This can get really tricky when everyone is trying to get games out for Christmas and they all need to get approval and have the disks created at one company. This can cause a bottleneck, and it can take a lot longer to get a game into the stores. Because of this potential delay, PC games often have a much quicker turnaround time from completion to the shelf. This means that delays in console development can be even more detrimental and harder to overcome than they might be for a PC game. Console games cannot be manufactured overnight.

Developer Approval

Before a developer can use development hardware and gain access to the technical information he needs to make a game for a console, the hardware manufacturer must approve the company. This approval is not simple to obtain. One of the only ways for a new developer to get such approval is to find an experienced publisher that is willing to pay a less-experienced developer to make a game. The publisher can then ask the hardware manufacturer to approve the developer. The problem is that publishers are looking for experienced developers who are already approved. Yes, this is as complicated as it sounds.

Concept Approval

Even after a developer has received approval, he can't just make any game he wants. Most of the console manufacturers require a concept approval for each game. Because of this concept approval requirement, most publishers hesitate to invest money into a concept that has not been approved. Even after the concept is approved and the game is complete, the game still needs to meet certain technical requirements.

If the game concept does not appear up to the standards of the hardware manufacturer, it will not be approved. This decision is completely up to the hardware manufacturer—they and they alone decide if your game is good enough. The game is judged on a number of factors, including depth, quality, target audience, competing products, release schedule, expected sales, and whether they believe that it will be good enough for their system.

Technical Approval

Each hardware manufacturer has stringent technical requirements that must be met before a completed game can be approved for final manufacturing. These requirements affect the programmers, and they also affect the interface design. For example, saving and loading games usually must be done in a specific way. Often there are also specific text requirements that need to be met in the interface. I've had a game rejected because I didn't use a capital letter when referring to a piece of hardware.

Each hardware manufacturer provides a lot of documentation and online help. All of these guidelines are listed in this documentation. Even with all of the documentation they provide, you may come across situation in which you are unsure what to do. When this happens, you can ask questions. But you must be an approved developer to have access to this information.

When developing a game for a console, make sure to follow the manufacturer's guidelines strictly. Even one tiny mistake can cause a game to be rejected and result in costly delays. The problems will need to be fixed and the game re-submitted. Even if the developer can make the changes and have the game ready the next day, it can take anywhere from a couple of days up to a couple of weeks for the game to be reviewed again.

You will save time if you read and follow these requirements from the beginning of a project. Rejection can come as a nasty surprise at the end of a project, especially for inexperienced developers who planned on getting approval quickly. You should do your best on your first game submission to a console manufacturer, but prepare to be rejected—a high percentage of games don't pass on the first attempt.

Console Game Cost

It typically costs a lot more to make a console game than it does to make most PC games. And because the cost is higher, the stakes are also higher. While console games average more sales, the higher costs of development can still make them a bigger risk. Because of this bigger risk, it is difficult to convince a publisher to make a new and original game. Publishers are looking for guaranteed successes.

One of the reasons for the higher cost of developing console games is that the development equipment is extremely expensive. A lot of equipment is needed to program and test a console game. Each programmer may need a special development system that allows him to actually program and run the game on the console system. These systems come directly from the hardware manufacturers and some of them cost more than your car—especially right after a new console has been released. Often, special hardware is used to burn the CDs that can only run on special versions of the consoles. All of this hardware is expensive and can only be obtained by approved developers. Even the disks needed for a final submission are costly.

Another reason for the high cost of console game development is that these games must meet the standards of the hardware manufacturers. This often means that console games need more features than a PC game. The hardware manufacturer may not approve your game if the feature set is not up their standards. If you have made a kids' dodge-ball game and you only have 10 characters to choose from, you may be obliged to bump the number of characters up to 30 or 40 before the game will be approved. No matter what your budget is, you will be compared with all of the other big games on the market. More features means a bigger team, and large teams can be expensive.

Not only is the actual development cost higher for console games, but also it is more expensive to actually produce the final game disks. The game publisher must pay the hardware manufacturer a fee for every disk that is produced. This is how the hardware manufacturers make money. Because of this extra cost, it is much more expensive for the publisher to get a console game on the shelf than to release a PC game.

Effect on the Interface

A publisher may ask you to design your interface exactly like that of another game that has already been approved. This may be frustrating, especially when what you really want is to try something new. Understanding the approval process can help you understand why the publisher wants you to design something tried-and-true—any small deviation may cause the game to be rejected. If you don't pass on your first submission because of this change, it will take time to correct the problem. This time-delay could cause the game to miss shipping in the correct quarter.

It would be great to be able to design your game interface without thinking about the business side of game development, but unfortunately, business decisions do often directly affect an interface designer.

The biggest business question is, of course: How many copies of the game will be sold? This may have an effect on your design. The Marketing department may have a different idea of what will sell than you do. You may need to follow their advice even if you think your idea is much cooler than what the Marketing department thinks will sell best. If they feel that the ability to scan your own face and put it on the player is the hottest new technology, you may have to build the interface to do this.

Handheld Development

Handheld development is much like console development. The control is often similar to a console, and the approval process is also similar. The difference is that traditionally, the game sizes and budgets have been smaller than for console games. The hardware and the price of the games have limited the amount of money that can be spent on development. This may change in the future.

Both Sony and Nintendo's latest handheld systems will add their own new twist. The PSP will be very powerful for a handheld game system, and the DS will introduce a new control system with both a touch screen and a second screen.

PC Development

Developing video games for the PC presents its own unique challenges. Many of the differences from console development are a result of the variation in PC hardware. When you're developing for a console, you can count on the hardware remaining the same on every system—every Playstation2 has the same video card, for example. There are no variations. You can't buy a Playstation2 with a better processor or video card than all of the other Playstation2 systems. They are all identical. If the game works on one GameCube, it will work on all GameCubes.

This is dramatically different for PC games. A huge variety of computers will be used to play your game—there are countless types of video cards alone. Compound this with sound cards, RAM, operating systems, and so on and you've got thousands of possible configurations for a personal PC. When creating PC games, the developer must be aware and design the game to run on large variety of these possible configurations.

Minimum Requirements for PC Games

PC games list the minimum hardware requirements needed to run the game right on the box. The lower the minimum requirement, the bigger the potential audience for the game—meaning more people may buy it. Because of this reality, many publishers want the minimum requirements to be kept low. These lower requirements limit the kinds of features you can have in the game.

The minimum requirements for a game can directly affect its interface design. The video card affects the amount, size, and shape of the textures that can be used in an interface. Once the minimum requirements are established, work with the programmers to see how they affect the interface.

Often, big-budget PC games support cool features that are only in the latest video cards, but they must still support much lower minimum requirements. In these cases, the game may require different art for high-end machines. The questions that must be answered early in development are: What percentage of end users will have good enough PCs to see the advanced effects, and are they worth the effort? The target market of the game can greatly the answers to these questions. If you are developing a first-person shooter game that is directly aimed at hard-core gamers, then you can safely assume that much better hardware will be used to play it. If you are creating a puzzle game that may be played mostly by middle-aged people, then you'll need to account for the fact that older people tend to own older computers.

Find out what the minimum requirements are early and learn the limitations of the low-end hardware. Create the best interface you can under the restrictions. Establish any special advanced features that your game will support, and determine whether these features will affect the interface. Early planning will prevent time-consuming changes to the interface later.

The Controller

One of the big challenges for developers who are familiar with PC games but have never designed an interface for a console game is to create menus that work well with a controller. Controllers have many buttons, but they do not give you the freedom of movement you get with a mouse. A mouse can be moved around a computer screen rapidly, so the location of the buttons onscreen is much less important than when using a controller.

The basic principle when designing interfaces for a controller is to place all of the onscreen buttons in a row. The user should be able to cycle

between all of the buttons by moving the onscreen cursor in a single direction by pressing buttons on the controller. All of the options should be accessible by moving the cursor either up and down or left and right, but not in both directions. If the buttons are stacked vertically, so that moving the onscreen cursor up and down moves the player from option to option, then moving the controller left and right should change the settings for the selected option. In this case, if you have difficulty levels selected, moving left or right should cycle through Difficult, Medium, and Easy.

In addition to moving the controller left and right, the user could also change some options by using the button on the controller that is designated as the Select button. The Select button can also be used to advance the user to the next screen. Figures 5.1 and 5.2 demonstrate how buttons should be aligned in a row. They don't need to be perfectly aligned, but the user should recognize that moving the button down will change options, it won't make changes to the currently selected option.

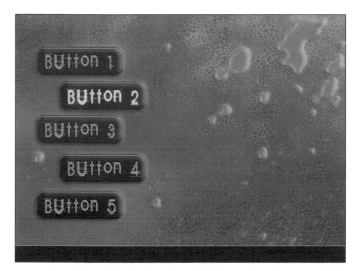

Figure 5.1 Moving up and down moves the selection from button to button. Moving left and right makes changes.

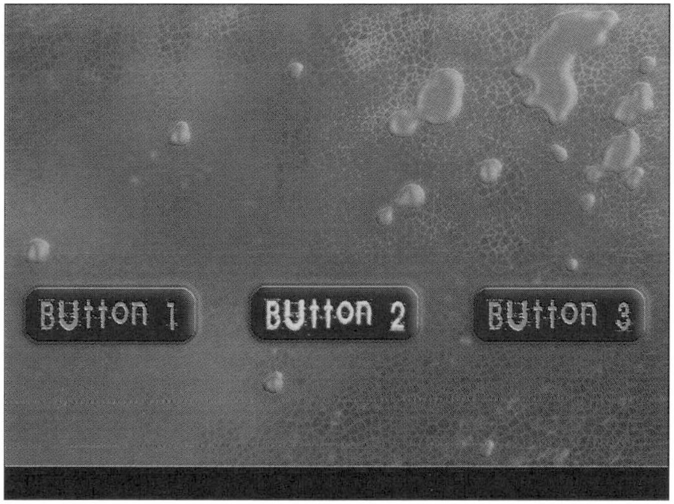

Figure 5.2 Moving left and right moves the selection from button to button. Moving up and down makes changes.

Getting the Timing Right

Changing options by moving the stick or direction pad can cause problems if the speed of this change is not implemented properly. Game programmers often address most of the problems that can occur with bad timing, but it is important to understand how changing highlighted options in your menu should function.

The challenge of getting the timing correct comes in adjusting how the stick or directional pad works. There are several viable options, but I suggest using the most common approach. If the user presses the controller in one direction and holds the d-pad or joystick down, the onscreen selection should change once. After the selection stays on this new option for just under a second, the selection should change again, and it should then continue to change fairly rapidly until the button on the controller is released.

It is sometimes tough to get the timing right. When the button on the controller is held down, the cursor changes the first time it pauses on the next selection for an instant. This pause should hold long enough so that the user does not accidentally move further than he wants to. If the pause is too brief, the user could accidentally hold the button on the controller too long and move two spaces instead of one. It should also not pause so long that if he wants to move

Power Controller Users

At the same time that you make the interface easier for new gamers to navigate, you can also make the interface easy for the expert gamer, too. Consider allowing the user to use the shoulder buttons (the buttons on the top-side of the controller) to pick minimum and maximum option settings, for instance, or provide shortcuts for jumping from screen to screen.

A well-designed console interface can actually be quicker for a power console user to navigate than for a user with a mouse. For instance, a few quick button presses can bring up a menu to which a mouse user would have to carefully navigate using movement and clicks. Don't just adapt to the limitations of the console controller—embrace the advantages of it, including the directness, simplicity, and feel.

In addition, take into account the uniqueness of a given console's controller compared to the controllers on other console systems. Play other games on the specific target hardware and decide what you like and don't like about how the designers implemented navigation and control using that specific hardware.

more than one space, he feels as if the controls are unresponsive. The option-changing speed should be rapid enough that the user can change options quickly but still be able to stop at his desired location. The options shouldn't change so fast that the player overshoots the one he wants.

Limiting Buttons

Another rule for console interfaces is to use only a limited number of buttons on each screen. Too many buttons on a single screen can make navigation tedious. Because the user must cycle through all of the buttons, it can take an unacceptable amount of time to get from an option at the top of the screen to an option at the bottom. With a mouse, a player can skip all of the intermediate buttons and go directly to the correct button, but with a controller he can't. If a screen begins to have too many options, you should probably create another screen and move several of these options to it.

You also don't want to have too many screens. You may have to work to reduce the total number of options so

they are manageable on a console. Striking the perfect balance is not easy.

Displaying Navigation Information

Because the controls for navigating an interface in a console game are not necessarily as intuitive as clicking on buttons with a mouse, it's often important to display more help information in a console interface than you would in a PC game interface. Some console games display a list of buttons and their associated actions. Some designate a Help button that, when pushed, shows a new window summarizing the functionality of the buttons on the current screen.

The Mouse

The mouse opens up a lot more opportunities for interface layout. The ability of a mouse to move the cursor quickly to any spot on the screen allows much more freedom of design and layout. Buttons do not necessarily need to be positioned in a row as they do when using a controller.

Keep the Design Simple

The design freedom a mouse affords is no excuse for a disorganized layout or having too many options on the screen. Simplicity and organization should still be your design goal. The user will enjoy being able to look at a screen and instantly know what to do. Keep your design simple.

If there is a chance that the game will be converted to a console game in the future, it is a good idea to design an interface that is simple to convert. Design the menu as though you were designing it for a console. Think about how the menu would work with a controller. This will prepare your menu to be converted and it will help keep your PC game menu simple and easy to understand.

Console interfaces tend to be much easier to convert to the PC. If the layout works well for a controller, it is easy to turn the console buttons into buttons that can be selected with a mouse. Converting the gameplay mechanics can be a little more difficult.

Image-Based Interfaces

A common approach to designing a PC interface is to use a detailed image as the interface. In such a design, the buttons are actually objects in the image. As the user moves the mouse over the image, areas light up for each option. For example, an image of a locker room might be used for a football game; as the user moves the mouse over the chalkboard, it lights up, and if he clicks on it he can create and modify plays. As the user moves the mouse over the team logo, it lights up, and if he clicks on it he can switch teams.

This approach can create a very interesting interface, but it also can be problematic—images can look really cool, but they can make it easy for a user to get lost. The user should never have to stop and figure out what (or where) all of the options are. A quick glance should reveal all of the options and tell the user where to click.

A game menu is not a good place to play hide and seek. The screen should include a clear visual identification of each clickable area. This can be done in many ways. For example, a brightly colored border around each clickable object will clearly indicate their locations onscreen. It is also helpful to make each clickable object relate logically to the option. It wouldn't make much sense if objects led to random options that had no real correlation to

Figure 5.3 An interface that uses images as buttons can be interesting, but you need to make sure that it is still easy to use.

the object. If your interface was an illustration of a rural village, and an image of a well was a button that led to game options and an image of a donkey led to the scenario select screen, the user could get really confused. It requires a lot of creativity to design an interface that has the correct combination of objects to fit all of the options.

Resolution

PC monitors and televisions are very different from one another. One of the big differences between a television and a computer monitor is resolution. *Resolution* refers to the number of colored dots that are used to make up the image on the screen. The more colored dots, the sharper the picture. The more of these dot or pixels that are displayed, the higher the resolution. A standard TV resolution is 640×480, and a computer monitor can display a resolution like 1280×1024 or even higher.

PC Game Resolution

The resolution capability of a PC depends on the video card in the computer. The more pixels that are displayed, the harder the computer needs

to work. Often, the game developers make the choice to support various resolutions in one game. In these cases, the user can change the game resolution in the options menu. If the user chooses an option that is too high for his computer, he may experience sluggish game play. Allowing the user to change the resolutions allows the game to be played on a larger variety of computers. Slower computers can simply run the game at a lower resolution.

Most PC games don't run any lower than 640×480 and some offer very large resolutions, such as 1024×768 or higher. The resolution of a game can affect game-play. For example, if you are playing a network first-person shooter against a buddy with a computer that can't handle the resolution that your computer can handle, you will have the advantage. You will be able to see more, as objects in the distance will be comprised of more pixels than on your buddy's computer. These resolution changes often only affect the in-game resolution.

Front-End Menu Resolution

In PC games that offer changes in resolution, typically, the front-end menu

remains at a fixed resolution no matter what game resolution the player chooses—only the in-game resolution changes. The HUD (or in-game interface) is much more affected by changes in resolution than the front-end menu. The simple way to handle resolution changes is to design the HUD for the lowest resolution; if the game runs at a higher resolution, then the HUD elements appear proportionately smaller. When you are creating mock-ups and making final art, create and design your interface at the smallest game resolution. If you work at larger resolutions and then reduce the size later, critical detail can be lost. You need to know if text can be read and that everything is clear at the lowest resolution. If you create art that is too small and it is scaled larger, it will become blurry. This applies to both the front-end interface and the HUD.

Standard TV Resolution

Traditionally, the resolution of a television has been really low. A standard TV in North America has a resolution of 640×480. This is smaller than the lowest resolution of most PC games. This low resolution can pose a challenge for console game developers, as there is not much room to work with. Fonts can't be too small, and icons may need to be displayed with a limited number of pixels. Every pixel is very important on a television and you can't hide anything. As HDTV becomes more popular, more console games will support higher resolutions. The need to also support standard TV resolutions will remain in place for a long time. Console games will need to look good at 640 × 480 even as HD resolutions become more common. It is important to determine whether your game will support a higher resolution even if it is a console game.

PAL versus NTSC Television

When designing your interface, you'll need to take into account the fact that there are several different television standards in the world, not counting HDTV. The two most common standards are NTSC, which is used mostly in North America and Japan, and PAL, which is used primarily in Europe. Among other differences, NTSC and PAL televisions have different refresh rates and resolutions.

The PAL television has a resolution of 640×512.

Overscan

The term *overscan* refers to the fact that not all of an image is displayed on a TV screen. Almost no television displays the entire available image. All four edges of the image that the console is sending to the TV are cut off. The amount that is cut off varies from TV to TV. When working with console games, it's essential that you account for overscan and do not put important information on the very edges of the screen. In fact, console hardware manufacturers require you to keep critical data away from the edges, and will usually not approve your title if a piece of text, for example, is too close to the edge. Review the specific approval requirements for the target platform to make sure your design and final work take overscan into account.

TV Color

Computer monitors have the capability to display a much broader color range than a television can. Many software packages provide filters that help keep your colors within a range that works well on a television. For example, Adobe Photoshop has an NTSC colors filter. This filter is found under the Filter/Video/NTSC color. It will take any of the colors in your image that are out of the color range for television and convert them to colors that work well on a TV. This filter is helpful in many cases, but it can also produce some unexpected results. When the colors are converted, they may not look good with the other colors in your image. It is always best to work within a safe color range rather than working in a broader range of color and running this filter. You can't rely on the NTSC filter to fix all of your images.

Figure 5.4 demonstrates how the bright colors in the image were darkened by the NTSC Color filter.

There are two color issues to remember when creating an interface for a console game. The first is that saturated colors in the range of yellow to red should be used sparingly. Even if your colors fall within the NTSC range, these colors can bleed, and the edges of these brightly colored objects can become very fuzzy on a television

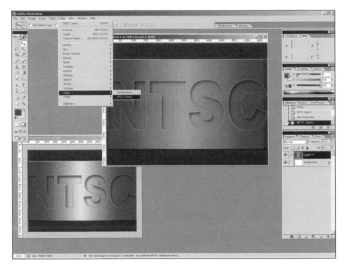

Figure 5.4 This filter can help but if you use too many colors that are out of the NTSC range, the filter may not be enough to fix the problem.

screen. The second thing to remember is that any high-contrast colors, such as pure black on pure white, may also bleed on a TV. Small white text on a black background can be much harder to read than light gray text on a dark gray background.

Interlace Flicker

Small, high-contrast lines and text can flicker on a television screen because most televisions actually display half the lines of an image in one 1/60th of a second update (1/50th of a second in the PAL standard) and the other half in the next update. This is called *interlacing.* Some console systems have hardware that reduce the effect. It's important to check your art *as displayed by the target hardware* on a television. Your development team should have test machines or development hardware that you can use to check your art before you commit to a specific look.

If your images flicker, you will need to make adjustments. The problem is most visible when the contrasting areas become a pixel or smaller. In such a case, you can make the contrasting areas larger and less contrasting. This will help the flicker.

Color Variation

Colors vary greatly from television to television. What you see on your monitor is different from what will be displayed on a television. Every television will also display colors slightly differently. It is essential that you review your work. Make sure to look at your menu on many different televisions and not depend on how it looks on a computer monitor. If slight color changes on various TVs cause problems, you may need to adjust your colors so they work well across a variety of televisions.

Summary

Learn the differences between console game development and PC game development. Understanding these differences can help you design for either system. Don't assume that because you have developed for one of these platforms you can automatically develop for the other. Consider the resolution of your game when designing the interface and be careful to use safe colors when working on a game that will be displayed on a TV. You must look at your art on the final platform before you know how it will really look.

CHAPTER 6

BUTTON STATES

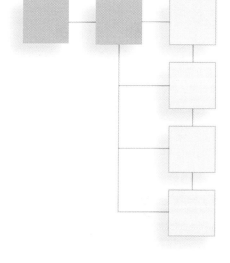

In this chapter, I will be discussing buttons. When I use the word *button*, I am referring to anything that can be used to make a selection in a game interface. I call these controls *buttons* because they often appear to be a button that can be pressed. They are shaped, colored, and appear to be raised like a button on a VCR or dishwasher. These buttons also often function like a button. When they are pressed, they give the illusion that they are moving down. Using art that looks like a button helps the player understand how to use the interface.

Everyone has used buttons. At an early age, we all learn that buttons should be pressed. If you hand a toddler a television remote or telephone that she has never seen before, she will instantly begin pressing the buttons. This does not mean that images that don't look like buttons can't be used in an interface. Images that look like a bullet or space ship can be used as buttons. The player will still need to know that they function like buttons. In the rest of this chapter, I will refer to any image that can be clicked or selected to navigate the interface as a *button*.

Buttons change appearance when they are selected or when they are pressed. Each of these changes is referred to as a button *state*. Although the three button states (standard, selected, and pressed) may seem to cover every possible situation, there are many more possibilities, some of which you will read about in this chapter. You should carefully consider what button states will be needed for your interface. The number of states needed for an interface can vary.

Controller Button States

When you are designing an interface that will rely on a controller to navigate it, you must include some basic button states. However, it isn't always necessary to support all button states for every game. Look at all of the screens that will appear in your menu and decide what will be necessary for your game. The only two states that are always necessary are standard and selected. It is possible to create a very simple interface using only these two button states.

Some button states make the interface look better, and some button states provide information that will help the player navigate the interface. The following is a list of the basic button states for a controller interface:

- Standard
- Selected
- Pressed
- Active
- Active-selected
- Disabled

The Standard Button State

A standard state of a button is just what it sounds like. This is the normal state of a button when nothing has happened—meaning the player has not pressed or selected it. A button in this state should appear to be a button (or something clickable) so that the player knows that it can be clicked. This state should be designed with the other states in mind. Think about what the button will look like in all of the other states. If you want the button to glow when it is selected, you will need to make sure that the button is designed in a way that the glow does not obscure anything important. If you want the button to appear to move down when it is pressed, you will want to design a button that has a component that looks like it can be pressed down.

Figure 6.1 shows a set of buttons in a standard state. Each of the three images has been placed on a box with rounded corners. This box has slightly beveled edges that provide a little visual depth and have the appearance

Figure 6.1 This is a button in a standard state. This is what it looks like when no action has been taken.

of a button. Each icon helps the player understand what each button does.

The Selected Button State

The selected state is the state of a button after it has been selected. This state is often referred to as "highlighted" because typically the button appears to glow or appears in a brighter color. The player's eye should be drawn to the selected button first. The selected button state should be the most visually powerful state of all of the buttons on the screen—there should be no doubt that this button is selected.

Because of the importance of this state, the selected effect is often animated. When the highlighted button is moving, it can really catch your eye.

It tells the player to look here and make a decision. A simple pulsing glow can be effective. Figure 6.2 shows the center button in a selected state.

Figure 6.2 The selected button state is used when the current button has been selected (or when the mouse curser moves over the button on a PC).

The Pressed Button State

The pressed button state occurs when the player presses the Select button on the controller. The highlighted button often appears to move down. Darkening this button is also a common effect used for a pressed button state. This change tells the player that the game recognized that a controller button was pressed.

The pressed button state is frequently included in games, often just because it looks good. This is a state that can usually be left out of a game. The pressed state is usually only necessary when there is a delayed reaction from the time of selection until the player sees the change. If the player presses the button on the controller and there is no visual change on the screen, he may think that something is wrong.

Some option selections may require the game to load something from a disk, and this can causes a delay. For example, if the player chooses to start a game and nothing moves on the screen, he won't know if the button press worked. That's where the pressed state comes in handy. The delay may not be long enough to justify a loading bar, but the wait may be long enough to cause confusion. Even a one-second delay can seem like a long time when you're expecting an instant reaction. Without the visual feedback indicated by the pressed button state, it may appear to the player that his selection did not register. He might even become confused and try to select the option again if he does not see any change.

Tip

Audio clues can really improve an interface. Adding a sound to a button selection event helps the player to recognize that a button has been selected.

Figure 6.3 The pressed button state is used right after the player presses the Select button on the controller (or clicks the mouse on a PC).

Figure 6.3 shows the middle button in the pressed state. It looks as though the button has been pressed down. The lighting has changed to create this illusion.

The Active Button State

Some menus are designed so that buttons can be active even when other buttons are selected (or highlighted). For example, a soccer game may include the option to choose between 15 different stadiums. The player needs to know which stadium is currently active, even when the Start Game button is selected. The Current Stadium button should appear as if it is active. Figure 6.4 shows a button in the active state.

Figure 6.4 When a button has been selected but the player has moved to another button, the active button state is used.

The active state should be second in visual power, after the selected state. It should be clear that that this button or option is active, but it shouldn't overpower the selected button. If you are using a glowing and brightening effect for the selected button state, then the effect on the active item shouldn't be as bright. Another common method is to place a marker object around or next to the active button. This extra image is helpful when other effects in the active button state are subtle because it can help the player recognize that this button is active. Figure 6.5 has a small arrow to the side of the button to make it clear that the button is active.

Figure 6.5 When a button has been selected but the player has moved to another button, the active button state is used.

The Active-Selected Button State

The active-selected button state occurs when the player selects the button that is also active. The active-selected state is optional. It provides more information, but it is only necessary when an item can be active. Even in this case, it is not completely necessary. The normal selected state can be used in place of active-selected if the active button is similar to the selected state.

The active-selected state can help the appearance of the interface and at the same time provide more information for the player. The problem with not using an active-selected button state is that it may not be clear to the player that the selected button is also active. The only way the player will know that the selected button is also active is if he remembers that the button was active before it was selected.

This may sound confusing in print, but everyone has seen the active-selected button state in action, and when it is executed well, it is not confusing at all—The active button state is very common in many software programs. For example, the latest version of Internet Explorer uses the active-selected button state. When the Search button is active (it has been pressed) and then the player moves the mouse over it and it becomes selected, the highlight effect is different from the highlighted state when the button is not active.

Figure 6.6 is a button in the active-selected state. The glow around the effect has a green tint that is similar to the active state, but it is brighter than the active state so that the player will know it is selected. Visually, it is a combination of the active and selected button states.

Figure 6.6 The active-selected button state is used when a button has been selected previously so it is active and it is the selected button (the mouse is hovering over this button on the PC).

The Disabled Button State

When certain options are not available but the player needs to be aware that they still exist, a disabled button state can be used. When the player must play through the game levels in order—say, he can't skip to a higher level but is allowed to go back and play a previous level—the levels that can't be played yet are disabled. You could simply not show the buttons for the levels that can't be played yet, but the advantage of using the disabled button state is that the player can see how many levels are left to play.

The disabled button state is not only for options that need to be unlocked; it can also be used when other choices limit the options that are available. For example, if the player chooses the single-player option, then multi-player levels become disabled.

Buttons in a disabled state should not appear to be click-able. A common solution for creating disabled buttons is to have the programmers cover the button with a gray color at 50 percent opacity or make the button itself semi-transparent. Because of the appearance of the buttons when using these techniques, these buttons are often referred to as being "grayed out."

Figure 6.7 When a button can't be selected, the disabled button state should be used.

PC Button States

Many of the button states for a PC game are the same as those for a game with a controller. There are some slight differences, though. It is less important to draw attention to the selected button state, for example. The selected button will always be under the mouse cursor. For this reason, the selected state in a PC game is often called the *mouseover* state.

Other States

You might need to design for unique button states in your game. There are many cases in which a button state that is not one of the standard states described in this book could be useful. For example, there may be a need to select a button that is disabled. If you display information about a level when it is selected and you want to display this information about levels that are locked, you will need to allow the player to select the disabled levels. In this case, a disabled-selected state might be appropriate. If you are making a multi-player sports game and you allow both players to move around the Team Select screen at the same time, you will need a Player One button select state and a Player Two button select state. You might even want to have a new button state if both players have one team selected at the same time.

There is no real limit to the number of button states that could be used in an interface. You may come up with many innovative ways to give the player more information by creating new button states. Don't be limited to the states listed above. Let your game dictate how many button states you will use.

Animated States

Animation can add a lot of impact to an interface. Movement is always more interesting than a static screen. Movement can also be very effective in attracting attention (see Figure 6.8). While animation can be a powerful tool, if it is used incorrectly, it can also cause problems. For example, if every button is animating in the standard button state, the interface can become confusing. Be sure that button animation does not conflict with any background animation.

Figure 6.8 The arrow next to the button pulsates.

The most logical place to use an animation is in the selected button state. This is where you want the player to look first, as it is the most important location on the screen. Movement on the selected button will let the player know that this is the location where a choice can be made.

One way to create animated buttons is for the artist to actually create all of the frames and give these frames to the programmer. The game engine then cycles through these frames to create the animation. A simple, cycling animation is usually the best. In cycling animation, when the engine reaches the last frame in the animation it starts over at the beginning. If the animation is created correctly, the transition is smooth. The number of frames you can use in the animation will usually be limited—talk to the

programmer and determine how many frames you can use. An animation created by the artists instead of by the programmer allows for 3D rotation and other impressive effects, even if everything in the interface is really just 2D.

The game programmers can also do some of the animations; this can save time and file space. They may be able to animate the opacity, position, rotation, or scale of any piece of 2D art you give them. For example, if you give the programmer a button and then give him a separate glowing highlight, he can place this highlight over the button. He then can animate the opacity of the highlight and make it appear to pulsate.

One advantage of having a programmer do the animation is that if it is done correctly, a programmer can make adjustments like changing the animation speed of all of the buttons at once. These types of adjustments can be made easily, and a large amount of time that it would take an artist to create animations can also be cut out. The problem with this solution is that the interface designer gives up a little control. You will need to rely on the programmer to set the speed and amount of movement in an animation. Unless the animation is done using good software, it will also limit the effects that can be animated.

If you are creating a game using a program like Macromedia Flash, you may have more control over animations. Even if you are working with a programmer who will be doing the scripting, this tool offers you the ability to animate interfaces right in the game environment. Many of the high-end 3D game engines also have tools for creating interfaces. In both of these instances, the artists may have more control over the final look of animations than they would if they are in a situation where the programmer is creating animations.

Another solution for creating animated buttons is to use real-time 3D geometry instead of 2D art. You could use an actual 3D model as a button, for example. It is a greater technical challenge to use 3D elements in an interface, but it can provide more options. For example, longer animations can be used because they do not require a lot of 2D frames. Also, a greater number of animations can be used because of the small file size of 3D animations. 3D interface elements can also rotate and move in 3D space. These effects are much more difficult to accomplish in a totally 2D interface.

Workload

When making the decision about how many button states you will support in your interface, make sure to consider the workload added for every button state. If your interface has 50 buttons and you add just two more states, this could mean you have 100 new buttons to create. Your schedule may limit the amount of button states you can support.

I recently worked on a game that was a modification of another game. One of the changes we made to the new game was to change the colors in the interface. The game had a lot of buttons and a lot of states for each button. It took me a lot of time to get them all switched to the correct color.

Saving Time

There are some techniques you can use to greatly reduce the workload when designing for button states. For example, if you design the buttons correctly, you create one piece of art for a new button state rather than a new piece of art for every button in the game. If you design the buttons in your interface so that the background of the button is always the same, and text or icons are placed on top of the background in the game, the programmer can combine art to create different button states. This way, you create one piece of art for each state and a different icon for each button. Everything is put together in the game. If you decide that the selection button state should be a little brighter, you only have to change one piece of art and all of the buttons change. The disadvantage to this technique is that the icons do not change for each button state. If you want the icon to light up or darken in any of the button states, the method of combining art will not work.

The programmers can use several techniques to limit the amount of art that needs to be created. They can take the standard state button and use transparency to create a disabled state so that the artist does not need to create a disabled button state, for example. Or the pressed buttons can be a darkened version of the standard button that is created in the game engine. While these techniques can save time, again they also limit the variety of visual effects that can be used. If you want the pressed button to actually *look* like a button that has been pressed down, you may need to create the art yourself.

Audio

Good audio can really add to an interface. Interface designers typically do not have complete control over the audio used in an interface, but they can make suggestions for creating the audio or making it better. When creating the art, it can be helpful to picture what the object you are creating might sound like. Do your buttons beep or honk when they are selected? When your screens transition, does the player hear a whoosh sound or a ding? You don't need to stick with a traditional click for your buttons. Pick a sound that helps set the mood of the game.

As always, the number one goal is to make the interface player-friendly. Don't confuse the player by adding too many sounds. The sounds need to seem right for the actions they are attached to. This may mean that sound effects for a button in a selected state may need to be subtle, so that the button-press sound will stand out more.

Summary

Examine the button states of your favorite game or software. If they have been designed correctly, you may not have noticed before how many are used but you still understood how to use the interface. Button states should provide information that will help the player. Evaluate your game and determine how many button states are necessary for your game. Some of the most common button states are standard, selected, pressed, active, active-selected, and disabled. You will use these states a lot, but you will also now and then need to come up with more useful button states that are specifically designed for your game.

CHAPTER 7

CREATING A FOCAL POINT

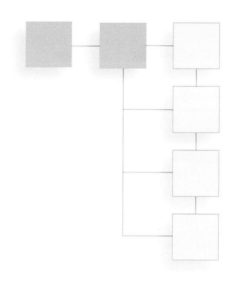

The concept of creating a focal point and creating a composition that leads the eye is a common art and design principle. Painters, illustrators, and designers pay close attention to the focal point in their art. The principles discussed in this chapter are even more important for video game interfaces. Because the player must interact with a game interface, it is critical that he knows where to look and what to do.

The Most Important Element

When designing an interface, you should figure out what is the most important object on screen, and then determine what is the second most important object, and so on. Your design should correlate with this hierarchy of importance. A well-designed interface will help the player quickly find the most important element on screen without having to search. Good design will lead the player's eye where you want it to go.

Put careful thought into determining the most important element on your screen. The most important element may not always be obvious, and the decision might be difficult to make. For example, should the game title be the most prominent or the Select button? A natural reaction might be to have the name of the game the biggest, brightest image on the screen, but is the name really the most important item on the screen? The player usually knows what game he is playing before he gets to the title screen. If the Start Game button is selected, it might be more important to let the player that know if he presses the Select button on the controller, the game will start.

Don't fall into the trap of making no one element stand out because you think several elements carry equal importance—this will seriously limit the visual power of your design. You should always have one element that is undoubtedly the most prominent element on the screen. If you included three elements that have equal visual weight because you can't decide which to make prominent, then the interface will be harder to navigate. You don't need to fear that everything other than the main element will be lost. Just because the visual impact of the second object is not as strong as the first does not mean that it will be overlooked. In fact, I would suggest it is more likely to be seen if there is a clear path for the player to follow.

This concept of creating a visual hierarchy can be applied to all kinds of design and layout, including text documents. If you are typing a proposal or design document, you can apply this design principle. For example, if you use bold text too often, nothing will stand out. I have seen many people make half of the text on the page bold because they believe that everything is important. If you use bold text on only one phrase on the entire page, this phrase will immediately catch the reader's eye. Figure 7.1 illustrates how much more effective a bold phrase is if it is the only bold text on the page.

It is easy to find examples of bad document design. I get them delivered to my house every week—my mailbox is filled with poorly designed coupons.

When designing an interface you need to figure out what is the **most important object on screen**, and then determine what is the **second most important object** and so on. Your design should correlate with this hierarchy of importance. A well-designed interface will help the user quickly find the **most important element on screen** without any searching. Good design will lead the users eye.

Careful thought should be given when determining the most important element on your screen. **It may not always be what you would expect** and it may be a hard decision, but it must be made. Should the game title be the most prominent or the selected button?

Make a decision. Don't fall into the trap of making nothing stand out because you think the second most important item is really important so you decide to make give it **almost as much visual strength as the most important item**. If you only make slight differences nothing will stand out. Just because the visual impact of the second object is dramatically different does not mean that it will be overlooked. In fact, I would suggest it is more likely to be seen if there is a clear **path for the user to follow**.

This principle can be applied to all kinds of design and layout. It can be also be applied when typing a document. **If you use bold text too often, nothing will stand out.** On the other hand, if you only use bold text on one phrase on the entire page, **it will immediately catch the user's eye.**

When designing an interface you need to figure out what is the most important object on screen, and then determine what is the second most important object and so on. Your design should correlate with this hierarchy of importance. A well-designed interface will help the user quickly find **the most important element on screen** without any searching. Good design will lead the users eye.

Careful thought should be given when determining the most important element on your screen. It may not always be what you would expect and it may be a hard decision, but it must be made. Should the game title be the most prominent or the selected button?

Make a decision. Don't fall into the trap of making nothing stand out because you think the second most important item is really important so you decide to make give it almost as much visual strength as the most important item. If you only make slight differences nothing will stand out. Just because the visual impact of the second object is dramatically different does not mean that it will be overlooked. In fact, I would suggest it is more likely to be seen if there is a clear path for the user to follow.

This principle can be applied to all kinds of design and layout. It can be also be applied when typing a document. If you use bold text too often, nothing will stand out. On the other hand, if you only use bold text on one phrase on the entire page, it will immediately catch the user's eye.

Figure 7.1 Notice how the bold phrase stands out on the second page.

The designers of these ads seem to think that everything is terribly important, and so they make all of the text the same size or surrounded by a different bright color. When everything is highlighted, nothing stands out. This visual confusion can cause people to stop reading because they don't know what to look at next and they can't be bothered to search for the main point. The average viewer's attention span (and patience) is short, and in a split-second of confusion the viewer can give up.

Figure 7.2 is a fictional advertisement that is similar to some of the junk mail I routinely receive. The sad thing is that I have even seen worse design than this! In Figure 7.3 you can see how much the same advertisement can be improved by creating focal point. The ad still includes basically the same colors and text; the only major change is that a visual hierarchy has been created. It still may not be great design, but it looks much better than in Figure 7.2.

Size Variation

One of the obvious ways to get the player to look where you want him to look is to adjust the size of the visual elements. Usually the largest object gets the most attention, so make the most important object the biggest (see Figure 7.4). Make the size differences dramatic to show the importance of one element over another.

Figure 7.2 This ad is poorly designed—everything has the same visual strength and nothing stands out.

Figure 7.3 This may not be great design, but look how much better the advertisement looks when there is more variation in the visual weight of the elements.

In cases where a group of objects need to be the same size, other properties can be changed to give more or less visual impact. If you have a row of icons across the bottom of the screen in the HUD, these icons may need to be small, and they are likely to all be the same size. Once an icon is selected, it should stand out so that the player knows where to look. You may not have enough room to make the highlighted button bigger when it is selected. Size is important, but it is not the only way to draw attention. For example, changing color may be a good option in a multiple-icon scenario.

Color

Color can be a great way to highlight important objects in your menu. Even small objects that are a vibrant color can really attract attention. Using complementary colors can really make an item stand out. Just as with the other techniques for establishing a focal point, color is most effective when it is used dramatically and should be reserved for only the most important items on the screen. In Figure 7.5, a white outline is used to attract attention. The title gets the attention first and the highlighted button next. The white color stands out on this screen because all of the other colors are darker and very saturated. The white outline is used sparingly.

Figure 7.4 The first thing that catches your eye in this design is the biggest object.

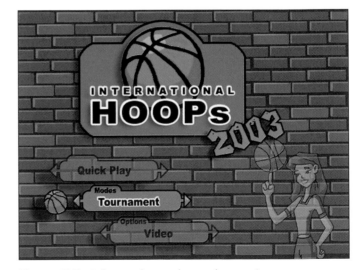

Figure 7.5 Color can be used to grab attention.

Value

Just like color, value can help you attract attention. The brightness or darkness of an image can help create a focal point. When using value to guide the player's eye, the key is to have a lot of contrast. Bright objects stand out much more on a dark background, and dark objects stand out better on a light background. Figure 7.6 doesn't have any color, but the selected button stands out because it is so much brighter than the rest of the screen.

Figure 7.6 Even without color, value can be used to create a focal point.

Movement

Use animation, or movement, on every screen. A static screen is much less interesting than a moving screen. Movement brings life to your interface. Animation will attract attention, so you need to use it wisely—choose important elements to animate and avoid animating unimportant background images. If possible, the player should never have to look at a static screen. Creating animation is not a trivial task. Creating good animation requires a lot more effort than a motionless screen, but it is worth it. Even simple animations can liven up your interface.

We are inundated by movement onscreen every day. Web pages and Internet advertisements often move. And of course, television images move. In an attempt to push more information and grab your atten-tion, TV commercials move even faster than they did in the past. Images flash rapidly in front of your eyes—it is amazing how much a view-er can comprehend in a split second. Video game players have also come to expect movement in their games. A static screen can be very boring; it is harder and harder to get attract atten-tion in a game without using move-ment.

Movement can easily add visual power to anything on screen. Animation is by far the best way to get attention. Even if you use some or all of the other techniques that can attract attention, the player will almost always see the movement first. A small and simple animation can be powerful, and a dramatic animation can overpower everything else on the screen.

Imagine a slow-moving fog in the background of your interface. This could be really cool as long as the movement is slow and does not detract from the rest of the interface. Highlighted buttons should attract attention so that you can really make them move. A simple, pulsating glow is a common approach, but you can get more creative than that. The button could bounce, spin, scale up, or ripple like water. Decide what kind of motion would fit your subject matter. In a basketball game, for instance, basketball-shaped icons could spin on a finger when they are highlighted. Figure 7.7 shows how a spinning animation could be used to emphasize the highlighted button.

Be careful to only use animations on important elements. Because of the power of movement, the player can be easily distracted from other important elements on the screen. The most important object on the screen can be a great place for an animation. If you use background animations, make them subtle so as not to distract the player from quickly using the interface.

Summary

Creating a focal point will help your design and also help the player know how to navigate the interface. You can use several techniques to attract attention. You can use size, color, value, and movement to designate the area on the screen where you want the player to look. The most important item will not stand out by accident. Carefully plan your interface with a focal point in mind.

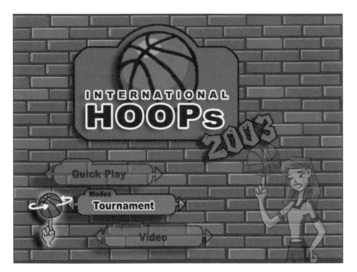

Figure 7.7 A spinning ball would really attract attention.

CHAPTER 8

USING TEXT IN YOUR INTERFACE

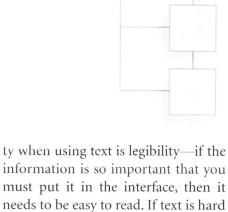

Text is a powerful tool that is often overlooked or at least underestimated by designers working on game interfaces. The style of text in an interface can set the mood of the game. Each font has a personality. A font that is handwritten and "scratched up-looking" might be a great choice for an extreme sports game. A smooth, flowing script font might be great for a horse riding game targeted at young girls.

It is possible to make a great interface design using only text. Font choice, size, placement, color, and type effects can greatly improve the design of an interface. Become a type expert and take the time to tweak your fonts until they are perfect. There is a lot more to learn on this subject than I can present in one chapter. Consider this a quick overview and learn more every chance you get.

Using Text Wisely

No one likes to read a lot of text when playing a video game; therefore, text should only be used when it absolutely necessary. Your number-one priori-ty when using text is legibility—if the information is so important that you must put it in the interface, then it needs to be easy to read. If text is hard to read because it is too small or blur-ry onscreen, the user is likely to just ignore it and move on.

In some instances, however, legibility may not be so important. Text can be used in the background merely as a design element. The purpose of this background text is to set a mood. Remember, you can't use text like this if you expect the user to read the text.

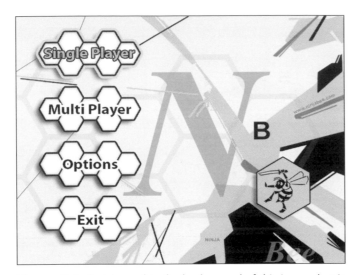

Figure 8.1 Text is used in the background of this image, but it is there just for looks.

Figure 8.1 shows a lot of text in the background. None of this text was intended to provide information; it is just decorative.

Type Anatomy

It is important to understand the elements that make up text style. You should know the terminology so that you can talk about fonts intelligently. It also makes using software to manipulate your font design much easier when you know what all of the adjustments do.

It is well worth your time to study typography. Understanding the structure of type will help you to make effective adjustments to fonts. Figure 8.2 shows many of the important pieces of a font labeled.

In the following sections, I'll discuss some of the most important components of type and how to use them in your interface design.

Serif versus Sans-Serif

Serifs are the little "feet" on the ends of letters, such as on the letter H. Printed fonts that have serifs are easier to read because the serifs guide the eye along the line. Serifs are found on the classic font, Times Roman. This book is printed in a serif font. Figure 8.3 shows a letter that has serifs.

Fonts without serifs are called *sans-serif* fonts. Arial and Helvetica are examples of popular sans-serif fonts. Sans-serif fonts are considered "modern," and are becoming more popular and widely used; people are getting better at, and more accustomed to, reading them.

The rules for using text in an interface are different than they are for printed text. The reason for the difference lies in the way text is drawn on a computer monitor or a TV. When choosing a font that will be displayed at a small size in your interface, it is best to choose a sans-serif font. Because there are so few pixels that can be used to display these small fonts, serifs just make it harder to read—the serifs can be less than one pixel and will make the text appear blurry and harder to read than would a sans-serif font.

Arial and Helvetica may seem like plain fonts with less personality than many other fonts, but they are easy to read in an interface. If you choose a font with serifs, you must make sure it is still very easy to read in the smallest version you will use.

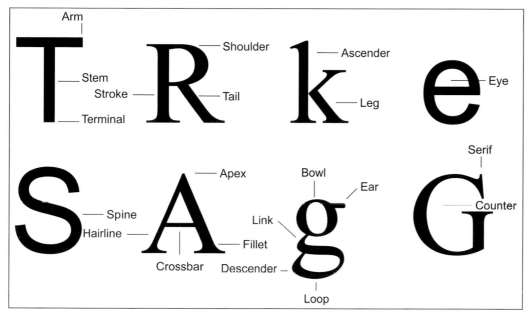

Figure 8.2 It will be very helpful to learn all of the terms used to describe text.

Figure 8.3 The little strokes on the end of letters are called *serifs*.

Ascenders and Descenders

Figure 8.4 diagrams several font terms. *Ascenders* are letters that extend above the *cap line*, the high point on most uppercase letters. Descenders are letters that extend below the *base line*, the bottom of most upper and lowercase letters. These letters are important because they affect the entire alphabet when creating a font for a game. If you only have 18 pixels for your font, this small space will need to include room for both ascenders and descenders. One of the best ways to get more out of these 18 pixels is to use a font

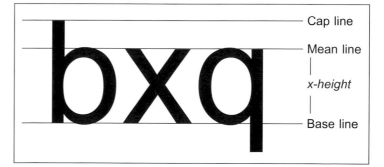

Figure 8.4 When working with fonts, you need to consider all of the different vertical heights in a single font.

wherein the descenders do not extend very far below the base line. This will give you more room for the space between the base line and the mean line (the x height). This is where a majority of the letters of the alphabet will fall. If you can't find a font that fits this description, you can always make your own. This is a very common solution for video game interfaces. There are some good fonts that can become great solutions for interfaces with some minor changes.

Uppercase and Lowercase

Another way to avoid taking up valuable pixel space for descenders is to use an all-uppercase font. Some fonts only have uppercase letters. (This is more common with free or inexpensive fonts.) You can also, of course, use only the uppercase letters in a font that has both uppercase and lowercase letters. The problem with all-uppercase fonts is that they are naturally harder to read than a font that uses a mix of uppercase and lowercase letters.

Many people think a bold font with all uppercase letters will stand out more, but the truth is that they may not. The faster and easier it is to distinguish between letters, the easier it is to read text. Capital letters are more similar to one another than lowercase letters are. It is easier for your eye to see the different shapes of letters when reading a mix of uppercase and lowercase letters. Uppercase letters used in conjunction with lowercase letters help to visually signify the beginning of sentences. An all-uppercase font does not give this same visual signal at the beginning of each sentence. An all-uppercase-letters font is particularly hard to read in block text. Figure 8.5 demonstrates the difference between a line of text that uses all uppercase letters and one that uses a mixture.

Points and Picas

The system for measuring fonts allows for very precise measurement. This system uses points and picas as the basic units of measurement. Most software packages use points to measure fonts, rarely picas. Picas are 12 points tall. A printer who is working with large text may use a pica as a measurement.

Points measure an actual physical distance, like centimeters or inches. This can become confusing when working with digital fonts. When working in a raster format (images that use pixels), there are two numbers that are often used to adjust the "size" of a file—points and pixels. These two numbers are very different, but they work together. Understanding both of these numbers can help you understand

> I think Steve is really cool!
>
> I THINK STEVE IS REALLY COOL!

Figure 8.5 It is harder to read a font that is all caps.

how point size of text works in your image.

Points are really only used in the software used to create the art for an interface, such as Photoshop. Game engines are only concerned with the number of pixels. If a font is 16 pixels tall, the physical size of the text onscreen will vary. The size of the television or the size and resolution of the monitor will dictate how large the text will appear. The size of a pixel will vary in every situation.

File Size and DPI

When trying to manage file sizes, the first thing you should look at is the pixel dimension of your image. This defines the number of pixels used in your images. A standard TV can display 640×480. Computer monitor resolutions vary. The more pixels in your file, the more space it will take up on your hard drive. More pixels result in a more detailed image but it also means that there is more information in the file and therefore bigger files.

A second number is commonly used in conjunction with file sizes. The second number is the DPI (Dots Per Inch). This term comes from the printing industry. During the printing process, small dots of ink are laid down on the paper. The more dots used in an inch, the smaller the dots must be and the crisper the image will appear to the eye. When adjusting this number, you are really adjusting the physical size of an image and not the amount of pixels used in the entire image. In many cases, you can just ignore the DPI when working with interfaces. However, if you are using physical sizes—like points and inches—in your software, you will need to understand how these sizes relate to DPI. If you ignore the DPI, you also have to ignore any measurements that refer to physical size.

If you have an image that is 640×480 at 64 DPI, and you printed it on a piece of paper, the image would be 10 inches wide. Only 10 pixels would be used for every inch, so the image will appear very *pixilated*—it would appear as if the image were created

out of large blocks of color. If you took this image and changed only the DPI to 320 and left the image at 640 × 480, then the image would only be two inches wide, but it would look really good because every inch would have 320 dots.

The relation of resolution, DPI, and size becomes even more confusing when printing. Each printer prints images at a particular DPI. This is actually referring to the quality of the printer and doesn't have anything to do with the DPI of the image. A printer who prints at 600 DPI is actually putting down 600 dots of ink in every inch. This does not mean a printer can improve on an image that only has 100 DPI. The printer can't add more color information than exists in the file. In this case, the printer will use six dots of ink to print each of the larger pixels of color in the 100 DPI image. The image will still only look like a 100 DPI image when it is printed. This concept can be hard to understand, but it will be important only if you must print your interface images. When using the image for a game interface, the only thing that is important is the image resolution. When these files are used in a game, the DPI of the file does not matter.

What does all of this have to do with type size? Understanding these relationships will help you understand how a 16-point font in Photoshop will turn out in your interface. Points (or other type measurements, such as inches) are a physical size, so the number of pixels a font uses changes when the DPI of an image changes. This means that point size does not always correlate with pixel size. If you have an image that is 640×480 at 72 DPI and you have a font that is 72 points tall (one inch) the font will be 72 pixels tall. If you change the DPI to 144, then a 72-point (one inch) font will be 144 pixels tall.

One of the best solutions to all of this confusion when working with Photoshop is to change the units for fonts in Photoshop's Preferences. If you never need to print, you will only need to worry about the number of pixels you are using and you won't have to deal with the DPI of an image.

Kerning

The space between individual letters is called *kerning*. If the amount of space between letters is exactly the same for every letter in a font, then the font is referred to as a *monospaced* font. Monospaced fonts are hard to read, and therefore they are seldom used. They are, however, much easier to implement in a game engine. If you notice that the engine is spacing using a monospaced font, you may want to recommend an improvement to the font system that adjusts the kerning. Most game engines actually adjust kerning so the fonts are more legible.

If you take a close look at text that is typed on a computer, you will notice that there are small differences in the spacing between each letter. If you measure between letters, the spaces are not actually equal. Even though the distance between the letters is not consistent, the letters do appear to be spaced correctly.

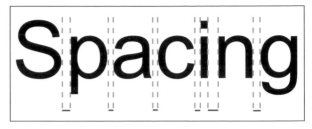

Figure 8.6 Letters should be spaced for maximum readability, even if that means the letters are not equally spaced.

Figure 8.6 shows how the spacing between letters varies, but the text still looks as if it is evenly spaced. Text generated by most software packages is typically spaced correctly; however, if you plan on using large text, you may need to do a little hand-adjusting to the kerning.

Thicks and Thins

Most fonts have variations in the thickness of the strokes that make up the letters. Times Roman is a great example of a popular font that has thick and thin parts in the letters. If you look closely, you can see that the font in this book has variations of thickness in each letter.

These *thicks* and *thins* are remnants of hand-written fonts. In the pre-computer, pre-typewriter "old days," text was often written with pens (and before that, with quills) with wide metal tips dipped in ink. The angle at which these metal tips were held as they touched the paper determined where the lines varied in thickness. The important thing is to keep this angle consistent even when creating your own digital fonts or making adjustments to existing fonts. If the way the thick and thin parts of the lines are drawn changes from letter to letter, the font won't be pleasing to the eye, and it will be harder to read. Figure 8.7 shows a script font that has very dramatic thicks and thins.

Scaling Fonts

Avoid scaling fonts in one direction and not the other. Many art programs, such as Photoshop, give you the ability to non-uniformly scale fonts. This usually makes a font harder to read. If you want a tall, skinny font, you should find a font that is designed tall and skinny rather than stretch another font. Disproportionate scaling changes the carefully

Figure 8.7 Keep the variations in thickness of the strokes consistent.

Figure 8.8 A font stretched in only one direction often doesn't look quite right. It's usually better to choose a font that has the look you're going for right from the beginning.

designed ratio of thick to thin. Fonts that have been scaled this way look like they have been stretched. Figure 8.8 demonstrates how bad a stretched font can look.

Font Choice

Choosing a font can be a big decision, and it can take a long time to find just the right font for your game. Great software, such as Macromedia Fontographer, has made it very easy for anyone to create a font, and as a result, there are thousands of bad fonts floating around on the Internet. There are several Web sites out there offering a huge number of free, or almost free, fonts. The problem with many of these sites is that there may only be a couple of good fonts on the entire site. You will probably need to sort through a thousand bad fonts before you find a good one. Looking at so many bad fonts can make an average-quality font look much better than it really is.

If you are willing to purchase a font package, you can get hold of some great fonts. For example, Adobe has a variety of great fonts that can be used to achieve many different effects. If you don't want to buy an entire font package, you can often just purchase a single font.

Theme Fonts

An inexperienced designer is easily enticed into choosing a bad, "theme" font. These fonts use letters that appear to be constructed from a material that fits a theme—for example, a font designed to look as if it

were made out of bamboo or water puddles. Just because you are making a Wild West game and you find a font that looks like it was made out of wood does not mean it is a good choice. In fact, a theme font is much more likely to be a bad font.

There are so many bad theme fonts out there for the simple reason that good theme fonts are hard to create. It is much harder to create an easily readable font made out of paper clips than it would be to just make an ordinary readable font. You can find good theme fonts but you need to be aware that a high percentage of these fonts are hard to read and very cheesy.

Figure 8.9 shows several fonts that are hard to read and would not look good in a game interface.

You must choose the font used to display body text in a game carefully. It is more important to use a legible font for text than it is for headlines because body text will be smaller, and there will usually be more of it. Fonts used in a logo or as a heading can be larger than body text and will therefore offer a little more freedom. For example, you might be able to get away with using a theme-style font in the game logo, but probably not in body text.

Figure 8.9 These fonts are hard to read.

When making a logo, I often adjust the letters from the standard font. I like to fine-tune the letters. Such adjustments can improve a logo, but can be dangerous—if you are not experienced with fonts, adjusting thickness, kerning and so on can actually make a font worse. If you adjust curves of a letter, they may no longer match and look out of place. Even subtle differences will be noticed.

Multiple Fonts

Using multiple fonts in one interface can make it more difficult to get the right look—not only do you need to choose good fonts, but you must also consider whether the fonts work together. If you need to use two fonts, it is usually best to use a standard font like Helvetica or Arial with a more stylistic font. Finding two distinctive fonts that work well together can be very difficult, and if you don't make a good choice, the results can be disastrous—the two fonts end up fighting each other. They just don't work well together, either because they are too different from one another or because they are so similar that they look as if they should match, and so their slight differences appear to be a mistake.

The mark of a bad designer is an interface filled with a ton of different fonts. I'm sure you have had a friend who gets a bunch of new fonts, and suddenly every document he produces has a different font on every line. Such documents are difficult and annoying to read. I use a pretty basic and standard font for body text in most of the menus I create. I like Helvetica or Arial and use them often. I often choose another font to use for larger captions and buttons, and I make sure to choose a font that won't be mistaken for Helvetica or Arial. If this second font is substantially different, then there is less chance of a conflict with my body text. This second font is often the font that shows the "personality" of the game.

Know Your Fonts

You don't need to know the name of every font in existence, but you should get to know a handful of fonts really well. Collect a small set of versatile fonts. When a publisher or art director asks for a "retro style" font, you should be able to quickly find one. It is also helpful to recall the font name from memory. You can save a lot of time if you are familiar with a handful of good fonts that can work for a variety of needs.

It will be helpful to have a favorite font for a variety of styles like a script font or serif font. This knowledge can save hours of time searching for fonts. You will find that a small set of quality fonts will work for 90 percent of the things you do.

Creating a Game Font

Most game engines require that an artist create all of the fonts. Some advanced engines have tools that can take a standard font and convert it to the game format. Even in these cases, it is good to understand how a font works because often it is helpful to edit the font directly. You might be able to make some adjustments that are better than those the tool can make automatically.

The most common format for a game font is white text placed in a grid. The files are usually square, and the dimensions of the entire file are a power of two (128, 256, or 512). The important thing to determine is how many pixels each letter will use. Will you create a 10-pixel tall font or an 18-pixel tall font? Find out how much space has been allotted for fonts and how big your files can be. When you choose the font size, make sure that there is enough room in the file for all of the letters and images that you will need. You will also need to think about how tall each letter will be on the screen. How much text will need to be displayed, and how much screen space will this text take up?

The first thing to do is set a grid to the proper size. You can then type the letters of the alphabet in all uppercase and then in lowercase. Make sure that every letter fits in the box—they can't extend past the edges of the grid even slightly. The game engine will most likely look at your file and find the first pixel, moving left to right, that is not 100 percent transparent. It will consider this the start of the letter. It will then move right until it reaches a vertical row of pixels in the grid square that is completely transparent. It will consider this the end of the let-

ter. The font system will then place space between this letter and the next letter. If the letter extends the entire width of the grid square, the font system will stop at the last pixel in the grid.

Transparency information must be saved with your font file. Only certain file formats contain transparency information. This transparency information will make the file slightly larger. If an option appears allowing you to choose the bit depth when you save your file, save your image at 32 bits, as 24-bit images usually don't contain transparency information. Work with your programmers to determine what type of files the game engine will support.

You will also need to make sure your letters line up vertically. If you have descenders in your font, you will need to leave space at the bottom of all of the letters. The space between letters will change, but the letters will be placed in the same vertical location that they are in within the grid.

Using a standard font in a program like Adobe Photoshop can really speed up the font-creation process.

You can hand-create each letter in Photoshop, but it would take much longer to do.

Even when starting with a good font, you may need to touch up many letters. Very small changes to individual pixels can make letters crisper and easier to read. Look at your final font and see if there is any adjustments you can make to improve readability. Get up close and make adjustments at the pixel level. The right touch-ups can really improve your font.

Figure 8.10 shows a close up on the letter S. Making slight changes to this

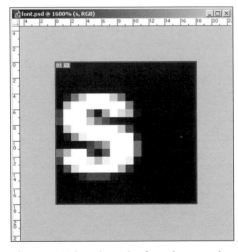

Figure 8.10 Adjust the font down to the pixel level.

letter can affect its appearance. If letter looks a little flat on top at regular size, you can make it appear slightly more round by adding a dark gray pixel or two above the letter. Notice how these gray pixels appear at the bottom of the S.

Icons in Fonts

Fonts can be a great place to put all kinds of images. Numbers, dashes, symbols, and icons can all be put into a font file. These icons and images can be used in the game just like a font. A common example of using icons in a font is when you're creating a console game and you place small images of the controller buttons in the font. You can use these images just like a font. Directions on how to play the game can be given by simply using the font. If you have ever see a line of text like "Press [image of a button] to select," there is a good chance the image was in the font.

Typically, a text file is used to tell the game engine where each letter is located in the font file. Numbers can be used in this file to identify a grid square. When this number is used in the game, the icon will appear in this spot. As always, the font system will vary from game engine to game engine. Talk with the programmers and figure out how it works in your game.

Figure 8.11 shows a font that includes several icons.

Font Effects

Typically, it is best to leave the font in your font file plain and white. Remember that the goal is legibility. The programmers can color this font in the game and use the same font to create a variety of colors. If you have enough pixels in your file, then you can add small effects, such as a drop shadow or an outline. Just make sure that these effects don't detract from the legibility of the font.

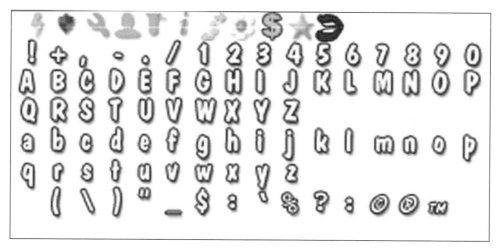

Figure 8.11 This font has both an outline and a drop shadow.

Summary

Creating good fonts is an art. Give the fonts in your interface the attention they deserve. Paying attention to the details can really help your font to be legible. Learn all you can about fonts, as you will use the information you learn often when working on video games.

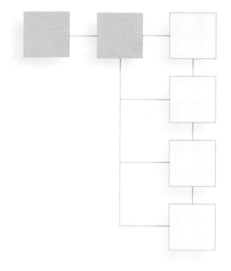

CHAPTER 9

TECHNICAL REQUIREMENTS AND TRICKS

Creating art for video games requires a lot of technical expertise. This may not be the fun part of making games, but it is very important. Just because you can create great art does not mean it will work in the game. If your art won't work, it doesn't matter how good it is.

You need to have both artistic skills and technical skills to create effective art for games. The ideal game artist has both artistic and technical skills. This may not come naturally to all artists. I have learned hundreds of tricks over the years—there is a lot to

learn about making video games, and practical experience is the best way to go about it. Many new artist and designers think that they know a lot because they have played a lot of games or even made one or two. All of these artists seem to look back after they have made a handful of games and realize how little they really knew.

Though creating interface art is a little less technical than modeling and creating animation, there is still a lot to learn and understand. I will cover a few important technical issues in this chapter.

File Sizes

Keeping file sizes small is key when you're creating video games. Small files are advantageous for many reasons. In some cases, file size may not be a critical issue, but it is always good to think about conserving space. If you can do anything to reduce the file size, you should. Large files can cause unexpected problems later, and small files can help you avoid these problems. This section will describe some of these problems and suggest ways to avoid them.

Limited RAM

A limited amount of memory is available for use in loading all of the elements in a game. The amount of memory available depends on the hardware. The RAM in your PC and in your video card limits the size of the files that can be loaded at one time. It is the same for a console or handheld system. No matter how much memory the hardware has, there is always a limit.

There are many ways for the game engine to use this memory. You will need to talk to a programmer who understands how your game engine works and how big your files can be in your game engine. Typically, a plan is made early on, and a particular size chunk of memory is allocated to each of the items that will need to be loaded. You will want to know how many files you can use in an interface and how big they can be.

Memory limitation on a PC is also an issue of minimum requirements. Your interface must fit into the allotted amount of memory for the minimum requirements for your game. Even if your game is really best played on powerful PCs, you may need to make your game run on older computers as well. Communicate with your programmers and see how big your interface files can be on the minimum specs.

In a console game, typically smaller amounts of memory are available for textures. Some systems have a block of memory that can be divided up however the programmer needs to divide it. You may need to share space in this memory with sound, animations, and other files. In other cases, the console has a set amount of texture memory that can only be used for textures, and files such as sounds, 3D models, and animations can't be stored in this memory. Find out how much texture memory is available for your game and keep your interface within these limits. Remember that other 2D files may need to be loaded in this same memory.

Tip

Just because you are allocated a certain size does not mean you must use it all. When you get toward the end of the project, it seems there is always one more thing to add that you didn't think of before. If you have used all the space available to you, you'll have to cut or reduce another element before you can add something new.

Being efficient with file sizes is not always easy. It can take a lot more time for both the artist and the programmer to make files smaller than it would to just be lazy and leave large files. Breaking files into smaller pieces and getting palettes just right can take weeks—or even longer—if you have a lot of files. Programmers can write programs to help speed up many of these processes, but these tools don't come free, as they require a lot of time for a programmer to create and modify.

It can also take the programmer a long time to write the code that will put together interfaces that have been dissected into small pieces. It is always faster for the programmer to take one big image and put it in the background, but it can really waste space.

When making decisions about how to create your interface and deal with file sizes, don't base your decision on laziness. Make sure that your approach will not limit you later or cause problems. Some game-development schedules may call for shortcuts, but be aware that using these shortcuts may mean that your demo level may result in a huge download size or not enough room on the CD for the cool *Making Of* video. If the game looks good, no one will complain because a file is too small.

A game interface can quickly become a big space hog. If you use a new, full-size background on every screen in your interface, your files can become big very quickly. Animations are another place where file sizes can shoot up and quickly become out-of-control. It takes some skill to produce an interface that looks great and is small. Such an interface is something to be extra proud of.

When I give a new artist a file size limit, he often responds as if I were asking too much of him, but I know it is possible to make a good game with a small file size—I have created full 3D games on consoles like the N64 and the PS1. These consoles had very tight limits, and yet some amazingly big games ran on them. Artists always want bigger files to create better art. The really skilled artists can create amazing art and still keep the file sizes down.

Disk Space

Disk space can become an issue with large-size games because, of course, the entire game must fit onto a CD or DVD. With a PC game, many files also need to be copied to the user's hard drive. While many users have large hard drives, you should still try to limit the amount of space that is used. I personally hate when games take up a large amount of space. Even with a big hard drive, I am often limited in the number of games I can have installed on my computer at once. If your game is taking up space on my hard drive, it better be for good reason—not just because it was faster to create big files.

Early in the project, you need to figure out how much room you have for the interface. How big can your files be? Find out if the game will be on a CD or on a DVD or how big the cartridge will be, if it is a handheld game. Discuss whether files other than the game files will be on the disk.

PC games are usually distributed on standard-sized disks, but they can also be put on a DVD. Console games are often distributed on special disks that are made specifically for that console. These disks may be different sizes than a standard CD or DVD. On a console, there is also often both a CD and a DVD. The user might not see the difference.

You might think that the best choice would be to use the larger disk, but more space can cost the publisher more money. Even a small amount of extra space can add up when a lot of copies of the game are produced. Your publisher will always be happy to hear that your game fits on a smaller disk.

It is always funny to me when new artists, upon learning their size restrictions, groan and complain. They seem to think that it is impossible to create anything good that is so small. I like to point out the history of video games to such artists: Old gaming systems had very little disk or cartridge space for large files, and yet some of these games were quite complicated. I have worked on several projects wherein the entire game had to fit on a 12M cartridge. Yes, the entire game!

Load Time

Even if you have room on a disk to use huge files in your interface, it may take a long time to load all of these images, and that's not good. Have you ever had to sit and watch a loading bar for a seemingly endless amount of time before a game began? This can be very annoying and frustrating. Keeping your load times fast can really improve the user's game experience. No matter how cool the game is, no one likes to wait a long time for it to load.

Loading time is not all about file size. There are some tricks that the programmers can use to load files faster, but the basic rule for you as an artist is to keep files as small as you can. It is also good to use fewer files, if possible.

It can take a long time for the game engine to look in a bunch of different locations on the disk for a file or files. The time the game engine spends looking for files is referred to as *seek time*, and it contributes to the overall load time of the game.

Online Content

If your game will be downloaded on the Internet, you need to consider download time and file size—this can be a huge issue. This is true for small shareware games and for big PC games that have a free, downloadable demo. Too many developers think their game is so cool that the user will be willing to wait forever for it to download. While it might be true that some games are worth the wait, think how much happier the player would be if he only had to wait half as long. Everyone will be happier with smaller download sizes.

File Compression

One way to reduce size is to use compression. There are many ways to do so. Some file types have built-in compression. For instance, using a JPG file

can result in really small files because of the compression used in this format. The problem is that the compression used in a JPG file can be *lossy*. This means that some information is lost, and the files may not look as good. When you save a JPG file, you can control the amount of compression and the quality of the image. After being compressed, the image is not exactly the same. Depending on the way the file is compressed, it can affect the image differently. Colors may slightly change or files may become blurry.

Be careful when using a compression format that loses data. Once it has been lost, you can't get it back. Figure 9.1 shows the difference in a file before and after compression.

Not all files use compression, and not all compression techniques lose data. A .PNG file uses compression that results in a much smaller file, but no data is ever lost. Because of this fact, .PNG is a popular format for games. In the future, new and improved file formats will no doubt be introduced that will be even more efficient.

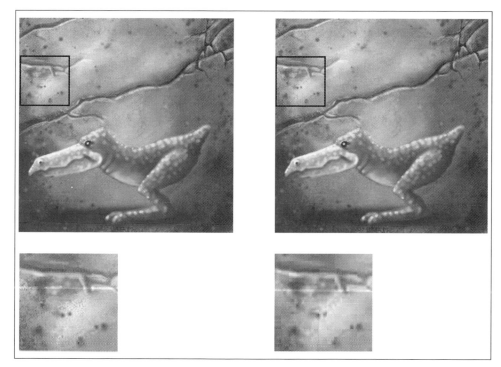

Figure 9.1 You can see that the quality has been lowered in the compressed file.

When making a game, compression is not only used on individual files. The programmers can also use compression to make files smaller before they are put on the disk. The game engine can often open files directly from this compressed format. Good compression may allow you to have bigger files, which is always good. It will have the biggest impact on disk space.

These files may need to be uncompressed when they are loaded and still take up the same amount of memory.

Even if you use a format that does not lose information, when game files are later compressed it can result in a loss of quality in your interface. If your interface looks good while you are designing, it but then, at the end of the

project, the colors are off slightly, banding appears, and you see other problems in your image, you might want to check and see if the files have been compressed. If they have, you might want to talk it over with the programmers and see how much compression is really needed and if there is a way to preserve more quality. While programmers are often efficient, they may not always care about the look of the game as much as you do.

Compression can allow you to use more and bigger files in your interface, but it also can be a trade-off. If the programmers plan on using compression, don't wait until the day before you ship the game to look at your interface after it has gone through the compression process. You don't want the interface to look bad, but you may have to sacrifice a tiny bit of quality to get more out of your art.

Using Palettes

In the past, game artists were required to use a *palette*, or small set of specific colors, for every piece of art in a game. It had to be done this way so that the whole game could fit on the cartridge or in memory. Cartridge sizes were small and the amount of memory was also very limited, so there wasn't much room for big files. The need for paletted images has been reduced greatly as hardware becomes better. Some video cards don't even support paletted images. There are still many cases where palettes can be used, and they can be very useful. Even if you don't use them often, it is good to understand how they work.

The color of every pixel must be stored in a saved image file. When you save a file and open it up again, the color of every pixel in the image must be displayed. An image that uses a wide variety of colors has a lot of information to store when the file is saved. When an image is changed from a full-color image to a paletted image, a specific number of colors is used in the image. Every pixel in the image must be one of the colors in the palette. Typically, there are 16, 32, 64, 128, or 256 colors in a palette. The fewer colors there are, the smaller the file.

One palette can also be used for many images. When files share a palette, the only information the image file needs to keep for each pixel is the palette entry (the color position in the palette) for every pixel. The palette can be attached to this file or even a separate file. The palette contains all of the color information. It might be hard to imagine creating an image with only 16 colors. 256 colors may even seem like a pretty big limitation.

The images that use palettes are typically created using many more colors, and then they are converted to an image that uses a palette. There are some tools that do this conversion. Adobe Photoshop does a great job and has several conversion method options. Photoshop also has the ability to batch-convert files (convert as many as you want in one action) for when you need to convert a bunch of files to images that use palettes so that file sizes can be reduced.

Although Photoshop does a good job of choosing colors for your palette, it is best, when you are creating an image that will later be converted to a palletized image, to not use a wide variety of colors. If most of the colors in the image are similar, it will look much better when it is converted. Figure 9.2 shows an image that uses a palette. You can see all of the colors that are used in the image.

Currently, a more common approach than using an image with a small palette is to choose a bit depth. The

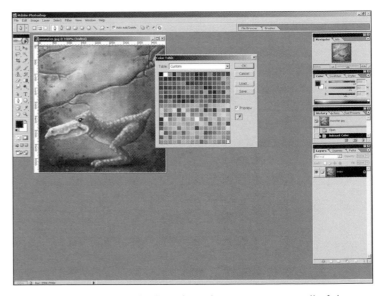

Figure 9.2 When you look at the palette, you can see all of the colors in the image.

number of colors used in your image can be affected by the choice of bit depth. The smaller the number, the fewer colors will be used in your image. However, when choosing a 16-, 24-, or 32-bit depth image, you do not need to worry about which colors to use, as this will be calculated for you. A 16-bit image uses a limited amount of colors. A 24-bit image gives you a full range of colors. A 32-bit image gives you the same range of colors as a 24-bit image, but it contains other information, such as alpha (transparency). Of course, the bigger bit depth images are also bigger files.

Using Programmer Art

You can save space if you use programmer art. Typically, when I use the phrase *programmer art*, I am referring to an image or set of images that looks as if it was created by someone without much artistic talent, but in this case I am referring to useful art generated by the game engine and not by artists.

Programmers are not known for creating great art. However, there are actually some good uses for programmer art. Simple pieces of art, such as

solid-color lines or solid-color boxes, can be created by a programmer. Art like this can be created in code and it may not actually require the artist to save a file. If you need a big, blue background with a small image in the center, you can have the programmer set the background color and you can provide just the small piece of art for the center of the screen. There is no reason to waste space in an image file on a solid color when it can be drawn by the game engine.

Working with the programmer to have the game engine generate images requires some effort. It is usually easier for the programmer to just use a piece of art from a file that was generated by an artist. It will take more time for the programmer to set a background color or draw a thin line across the screen than it would for him to use an image you have created. This may not sound like it would take much effort for the programmer, but imagine if you wanted to change the background from blue to green—you no longer have control of the background color and you have to wait for the programmer to take time to change it.

The space savings of using programmer art is often worth the effort. If you are creating art that could easily be replaced by art that is generated by the game engine, you might want to consider having the game engine do the work for you. Code used to create the visual on-screen is much smaller than is a file created by an artist.

Good tools can help avoid the problem of a programmer needing to make artistic changes. The rule I like to use is that if an artist must change something more than once, then the programmer should give the artist the ability to go ahead and make the change himself, without even telling a programmer. The programmer can create a tool that will allow the artist to make the change without writing any code.

In our background color example, the programmer could create a menu that shows up in the game when a button is pressed. (This only works in development, not in the final game.) Sliders appear that allow the artist to change the color and see the changes right in the game. Creating this tool can take the programmer even longer than changing the color once, but it will result in a better game because the artist can tweak things until they are perfect rather than stopping when he believes that all the changes are annoying the programmer. This is just a simple example. Tools written by the programmers can be very elaborate.

Texture Size

Texture sizes typically need to follow certain rules. One of the most common restrictions is the texture size. Some PC video cards and many consoles require that every texture dimension is a power of two. This means textures can be 2, 4, 8, 16, 32, 64, 128, 256, 512, or 1024 pixels large. Often there is a size limit, and a single texture can't be bigger than 512 pixels. You will also find that there are some consoles that require square textures. Many times, the engine and the hardware will support a texture that is 128 pixels wide and only 32 tall. Your textures do not always need to be square. Just remember that this could cause problems if you ever convert the game to a platform (or support a video card) that requires square textures.

If you are using only square textures and you have an image this is not square, you may need to leave extra space in a texture so that it fits these size requirements. You can avoid some of the problems that arise when you are meeting the texture requirements by planning ahead. If you design a button that is 33 pixels tall, it will require a 64-pixel tall texture. If you can design that same button one pixel smaller, you can save a lot of wasted space. This problem is compounded at larger sizes. A 129-pixel tall image adds another 128 pixels in height over a 128-pixel tall image.

Figure 9.3 shows how you can fit a non-square piece of art into a square file.

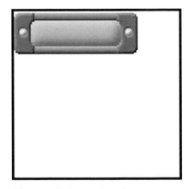

Figure 9.3 Notice the extra space that is needed for this piece of art.

One trick you can use to avoid this wasted space is to divide one texture into several smaller pieces. If you have an image that must be 70 pixels wide, then you can cut it into a 64-pixel wide image and then create an 8-pixel wide image that contains the extra six pixels (two pixels of extra space). The programmer will then need to put these two images in the right place in the game so that they seem like one full-size image. Again, this can take a little more programmer effort, but it can save a lot of wasted space.

Scalable Objects

An even more advanced approach to meeting texture requirements than simply cutting up an image and putting it back together is to re-use a section of art many times. A simple example of this technique would be to create a button with a right and left end piece and a very small middle that is repeated. If you design your button in a way that there is no variation in the middle section of the button, this can be a very effective method to reduce file sizes. If you have a lot of variation in the middle of your button, this approach may not be useful.

Figure 9.4 shows a simple example of pieces of art that can be put back together.

Figure 9.4 Look at the small pieces that are used to create this button.

I call this type of image *scalable* because they offer another advantage besides than small file size. The engine can use these scalable files to create images of varying sizes. The middle section can be repeated many times to make the button longer or fewer times to make it shorter. In essence, the objects become saleable in the engine.

The programmer can manually place these images where they belong, but there is an even more effective method. The programmer can give the artist a set of parameters for several types of objects that will be placed using method described above. You then can create artwork that fits these guidelines. The programmer can write code that supports several of these types of images. In the exam-ple of a scalable but-ton, when the length of the button is spec-ified, the engine puts the pieces together in a way so that it end up with a button that is the correct size. You can pick any length and the button will be created out of the single piece of art. Your artwork becomes scalable.

Figure 9.5 This button is made up of three pieces. These pieces can be put together to make any size button.

In the ideal situation, the program-mer will have time to write a custom tool and the interface designer can open this tool and adjust the size of these buttons by dragging a handle. This can all be done right in the game engine using a small piece of art.

There are two basic types of scalable objects. The first is bar- or rectangle-shaped, with a right, middle, and left piece. The file that is created by the artist is divided into four equal pieces and only the first three are used. The quarter on the far left is the left side, the next quarter is the middle of the button, and the third section is the right end of the image. The far right quarter is left blank. The game then grabs all of these pieces and can make an image any width using this art. Figure 9.5 shows a scalable button.

The second type of scalable object is more like a box. It can be scaled both in width and height. It is very useful for pop-up menus. It is composed of nine pieces, and. like the button, it can restrict the type of box that you can design. The sides, top, bottom, left, and right function like the bar object described above. They can't have any variation within the sides. The middle also needs to be pretty plain. This type of art also requires good planning. It works best if the corners and sides fit into a convenient size, like 32×32. Figure 9.6 show all the pieces that can be used to create a dialog box of any size.

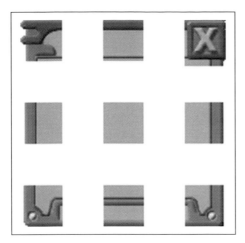

Figure 9.6 This button is made up of nine sections that can be put together to make many different-sized boxes.

You can add more variations to both of these types of scalable art if you are willing to limit the scaling size to increments of your grid. In a scalable button scenario, the programmer could scale the image just a couple of pixels larger by using only a couple of pixels from the middle piece. This requires all of the horizontal pixels in this middle section to be the same. In this same scenario, if the middle section was 32 pixels wide and the button scale was restricted to 64, 96, 128, or 160 pixels wide, using this restriction would allow a little more freedom to make variations in the middle section. The same principle can be applied to the box type of scalable art to allow the middle section to have more variation. The center piece would have to be a perfectly tiling texture that tiled on all four sides.

Tiling Textures

The edges of a tiling texture match up in a way such that if you place multiple copies of this same texture side by side, they will appear to be one continuous image. No visual seams will appear.

There are many techniques for creating tiling textures. I prefer the approach used by Painter. This program makes it incredibly easy to create tiling textures. If you turn on the Define Pattern option under the Pattern roll out, everything you paint will tile perfectly. As you paint off the side of the image, the brush will wrap around and begin painting on the other side of the image. You can't mess up now.

If you already have an image and you want to make it tile, turn on this same option. If you then hold down Shift and the Spacebar and click and drag with the left mouse button, you can move the image. It will wrap around to create a tiling image. If you move the edges to the middle of the image you will see the seam. Simply paint over this seam and you will have a seamless, tiling image. Figure 9.7 shows you where to find the Define Pattern option in Painter.

Creating good tiling textures requires a lot of skill and practice. If you make a distinctive pattern and repeat it many times, the texture will look tiled, even if you can't see the seams. Good textures will not appear to tile. Figure 9.8 shows a texture that will not tile well. Figure 9.9 will look much better when tiled.

Alpha Channels

Images that include transparent pixels use an *alpha channel*. This is the part of the file that contains the information on which pixels are transparent and which are opaque.

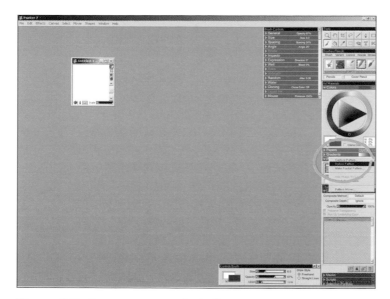

Figure 9.7 Once you turn on the Define Pattern option, everything you paint will create a tiling texture.

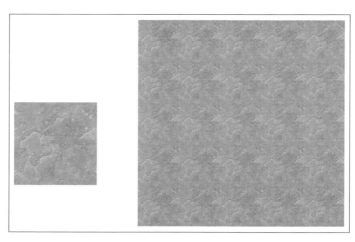

Figure 9.8 This texture does not tile well. You can easily see the repeating pattern.

Figure 9.9 This texture will tile much better.

Different software handles alpha channel information in different ways. Some actually show you the transparency in the image; the advantage of this approach is that you can see what the transparency will look like—you can see through the image. The problem with this approach is that the part of the image that is transparent is usually missing from the file. You can't go back and make a transparent section opaque. The image is lost in the transparent area, and you can't get it back.

Another way to work with alphas is to display another black and white image. Black represents the transparent sections and white represents the opaque. There are some file formats that only store completely black and white images. The pixel is either 100 percent transparent or 100 percent white. Other formats store a range of transparency, so a mid-range gray color can be 50 percent transparent. The advantage to such a format is that you can retain the entire image, even the stuff in the transparent area, but you can't see what it looks like with the transparency added.

If you need transparency in your image, you will need to save your file in a format that has the transparency information. Check with the programmers to see which file formats the game supports that contain this information. If you save into a file that doesn't have this information, the transparency will be lost and the entire image will become opaque. If you convert a file without transparency to a file that saves this information, the transparency will not magically reappear.

Some engines save space by using a color key instead of saving the transparency information. Instead of saving this extra information—which makes the file bigger—the engine recognizes a certain color as transparent. Solid black is sometimes used, but it can cause problems because you can never use solid black in your image, as it will become transparent. Another solution is to use a color you will never find in your game, such as hot pink, and use this color as a color key. A limitation with this format is that the transparency has a harsh edge. Every pixel is either 100 percent transparent or 100 percent opaque.

Localization

Localization is a term used when a game is changed to adapt to a different area of the world. The biggest part of this change is usually a change in language. When a game is localized, it usually must be translated into several different languages. This can be a simple or a very complex process. It is best to plan from the very beginning to make translation easy by setting up the game correctly. If it takes a lot of effort to change a language, it will be much more expensive to create the new version. This may discourage the publisher from putting money into creating multiple versions of the game, resulting in fewer sales. If there is even a remote chance that your game will need to be translated, it is best to work in a way that will make translation easy.

The best way for an interface designer to prepare for localization is to never put any text in the art. Make sure all text is in the font and the text is generated by the game engine. This may limit some of your text effects, but it is well worth it. If you put anything that needs to be translated in the art, a new piece of art will need to be created for every new language. If the programmer has set things up correctly, and all text uses the font system, all of the current text can easily be replaced.

Often, when a word or phrase is translated, the results are longer than the English version. This can cause a lot of problems if there is no extra room in your interface design. The best way to avoid running out of space is to leave a lot of extra room wherever text appears in our interface even in the English version. If the text is tight, be aware that this might be problematic in other languages.

Source Files

Source files are art files used to create the final assets that go into the game. *Final assets* are the files actually used by the game engine. You may typically work in Photoshop using many layers and effects; then, when you are finished with your design, you will need to save it to a file that will be used in the game. For example, the game may actually use a PNG file. This final file does not contain all of the layer and other information that may be contained in the Photoshop file. This source Photoshop file should never be placed with the final assets that get shipped with the final game because it would take up unnecessary space, but it should always be saved in another location. You will probably need to make changes, and it will be much easier to go back to the original file to make changes than it will be to adjust the final asset.

It may not be necessary to have a source file for every final asset in the game. In fact, it can be very efficient to have multiple final assets come from one source file. If you create a button that will be re-used throughout the game but different images, icons, and effects will be used on this same button, you can put them all in one file. By turning on and off layers, you create all of the final assets.

Summary

Technical issues abound when creating an interface for a game. File size has a big effect on your game, and there are a lot of ways to reduce file size. Reducing file size has an effect on what can be loaded in the game, loading speed, how much disk space is used, and download times. You will need to make sure that all of your 2D art works under the restrictions of the game engine.

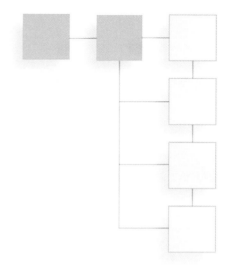

CHAPTER 10

TOOLS OF THE TRADE

As an interface designer, the only way to get your job done right is to have good tools at your disposal. I am not talking about a hammer or a wrench—I am talking about powerful software that can help you prepare artwork for a video game. Software alone won't create a great interface—solid design skills are a must—but without good software applications, you won't get far in this business.

Good software can be very expensive. Commercial software can come with a big price tag, and internally written software can cost a lot to create, but if they help speed up the process and produce a better final game, they will pay for themselves very quickly. This does not justify buying extra software for fun, but you should get the tools you need.

This chapter will cover information about software tools that can help you when you're designing interfaces. There are several commercial tools that can be quite useful, but they may not do everything you need to do. Custom-written tools can do amazing things. You may be able to have better tools created for you if you know what to ask for.

Tools for Creating Mock-Ups

The term *mock-up* refers to a piece of art that is created to look like an interface. The reason for creating a mock-up is not to have art that is ready to be used in the game, but to establish what the interface will look like. You can create a mock-up without even knowing what options will appear in the final game.

Creating mock-ups early in the design process can save time and ensure that everyone has the same vision of the final product. Mock-ups are invaluable—not only do they allow you to solidify your design, but they also give you something visual to present to anyone who needs to approve the art. You can get approval before the art is actually in the game engine. A mock-up can also help to pacify those who may be concerned about the quality of temporary art. If a producer or art director happens to see incomplete art in the game, you can assure him that it will look like the mock-up when the game is complete. Anyone can look at a mock-up and know what the final art will look like before it is ever implemented in the game engine.

Many commercial tools can be used to create a great mock-up. Use the software that you know best and that allows for quick and easy adjustments. Adobe Photoshop is one of my favorites. It is easy to keep everything is separate layers and easily make adjustments.

When most people think of a mock-up, they picture a still, 2D image. Mock-ups can go beyond the still image. Tools such as Macromedia Flash will allow you to mock up movement and interactivity. Creating a mock-up with movement that looks and even functions just the way you want it to can be particularly useful when you are in a situation where the programmer will have control over motion. In a situation wherein you do not have the software and tools to control the movement in the game interface, and you have to rely on a programmer to make the motion look good, an interactive mock-up can help. If the only thing you will give the programmer is motionless 2D art, he will have to make his best guess at what the motion should look like.

When creating an interactive mock-up, the interface designer can work out animation and button behavior. You can get everything just the way you want it. The programmer can refer to this mock-up, and there will be no question how the interface should be done. It is always a better situation when the interface designer has direct control and can change things in the game, but if this is not possible, an interactive mock-up can solve a lot of problems. Chapter 15 will describe how to use Flash to create an interactive mock-up.

Asset Management

Asset management is a large, complex topic, and the methods and theories behind asset management for video game development could easily fill an entire book. I will simply give you a brief introduction and describe some of the tools that might be used by an interface designer.

By the time a game is completed, a truckload of assets have been created along the way—including all of the files used in the final game and all of the other files used during the development process. All of these files need to be backed up and distributed to the entire team working on the game. If you're working on a team of 15, and I change 30 files in the interface, then all 14 other people on your team need to get these 30 files working in the game. Hand-adding all of the changes for each of the 14 team members could take forever. At the same time, you need to collect and keep track of all of the changes the 14 other people might make to the game every day. All of this falls under the category of asset management.

There are commercial tools, such as Alienbrain, that are made for art asset management. These tools are great and are much more stable than custom tools. The problem is that they can't do anything specific for your game engine. Custom tools not only manage your files, but they can do specific tasks that relate to your game. A custom tool could distribute your changes to everyone on the team and could rename files when they are copied to a final directory, so that they will work properly in the game engine.

The company I currently work for has a comprehensive file-management system. It is a great example of how a custom tool can be used by an interface designer. I create new files and make changes to the interface on my computer. I can then press one button and see the changes in the game. These changes only affect the game on my computer; this is good because I don't want to change something and mess up the game for everyone else. Once I have made all the changes that I want and I am satisfied with the results, I hit another button that transfers all of my changes to a central location where everyone else on the team has access to them. When I am ready, I can get all of the changes from the other team members by pressing yet another button in the tool.

This is a simple description of a complex tool. It is just important to understand the basic concept because when you make a game, it is likely that you will need to use a similar tool.

Adjusting Game Properties

Another common type of tool in game development is one that edits and changes things in the game. A level editor is a great example of this kind of tool for level designers. An example of this kind of tool for an interface designer would be a tool with which the interface designer could place buttons, create interface animations, control the flow of the menu, and adjust many other game properties. This data could then be put directly into the game and any changes would be in the game.

This is the area wherein custom tools for interfaces seem to be the weakest in the game industry. There aren't many tools that I have seen that do this very well. There may be some great tools that work directly with the game engine, but for the most part, everything is a modification or use of a commercial tool.

Using Custom Tools

Some of the best tools for working with interfaces are created specifically for the game engine. An internally developed tool can be a simple exporter that helps get information from commercial software into the game format. Many game developers hire programmers specifically to create tools for making games. These can be art tools, tools for level design, or even audio tools. Custom tools can be developed for just about anything. A tool can be a very complex piece of software that is used for creation, animation, or adding functionality, or it can be a simple script that moves files from one directory to another. This software is owned by the development company or the publisher that pays for its development. Typically, these tools are developed for internal use only, but occasionally a developer decides to sell a tool to another development company.

Unfortunately, tools for interfaces seem to be less common and a lower priority than tools for other parts of a game. Many game engines have a level editor and exporters in which a lot of game-specific properties can be set, but very few seem to have robust interface creation tools.

Many different tools could be custom-written for use when working specifically with interfaces. It is important to think about the possibilities and determine how useful a custom tool would be. You can waste time doing things by hand that could be more quickly done with a tool, but on the other hand, you also could use valuable programmer time to create a tool that does not save much time.

Using tools to do repetitive tasks can also improve your accuracy. For example, when you have to save a hundred files and name them all correctly, it is easy to make a mistake. With an exporter that saves and names these files for you, there is much less chance of a mistake. Another good use for custom tools is to perform tasks that can't be done with a commercial tool. If you want something different than is offered by a commercial software application, it may be a good idea to consider developing your own internal tools.

It is impossible to describe all of the possibilities for custom tools, and it is also impossible to tell you how to use them. Every custom tool is different, and they vary from company to company. The important thing to understand is that you can get what you want. If you need a custom tool or are already working with one that doesn't quite suit your needs, make sure you let your wishes be known. The programmer may not know what would help you the most.

Plug-Ins

One approach to creating custom tools is to create a plug-in for a commercial software program. The obvious use of a plug-in is to save the file into the proper format. This is a great place to put a lot of control. For example, a custom menu could appear that would allow you to select a property of a piece of art for the game. You could set a button to blink, and it would automatically blink in the game.

The disadvantage to adding anything more than properties that need to be exported in a plug-in is that if something changes later in the development process, you may need to re-export every file in order to change a property. If you use a separate tool to set these properties, then it is much easier to make changes later. You won't even need to open up the commercial tool to make the changes.

Stand-Alone Software

A stand-alone software tool is a software application that is not a plug-in or a part of a commercial tool and is not directly a part of the game engine. The best example of this kind of tool is, again, a level editor. A tool that could load up 2D files created in a program like Photoshop and allow the interface designer to place these files in the correct locations, add movement, and set the behavior of each button would be a great example of a stand-alone tool for interface design. The resulting file would then be saved or exported for use in the game. This tool could be very limited or very comprehensive depending on how well it was developed.

In-Game Tools

There are many tools that would be most effective if they were accessed from within the game engine. This type of tool is most effective for changes that can take immediate effect in the game. If, while playing the game, you could bring up a menu to make a change in the game it could save time. The tool described in the "Stand-Alone Software" section could be actually integrated into the game engine.

Advantages of Using Custom Tools

One of the advantages of working with highly developed, custom tools is that they usually have the exact feature set that is supported by the game. If you can do it with the tool, you

know it will work in the game. For example, you usually won't find a Drop Shadow feature that won't work in the game. The interface and program are created specifically to help you create game interfaces and the same software is not used to create Web pages. You won't run across extra features that you would find in commercial software.

If you work with the programmer who is making the tool, you can ask him to make the tool work the way you want it to and to add the features you need. Most internal tools are always changing, and features can be easily added. If you take advantage of the opportunities custom software presents, you can really speed up your workflow.

Disadvantages of Using Custom Tools

One disadvantage of custom tools is that they can be expensive to develop. It may cost less to purchase a commercial tool than it would to pay a programmer to develop a custom tool. They often have many more

bugs and problems than do commercially tested tools. Custom tools are often under constant development and features are added frequently. New features may have just been added yesterday, and so they haven't existed long enough to be fully tested. A new version of the interface tool may have a lot of cool new features, but if it crashes every time you export something, your progress in finishing a game interface will be severely impeded.

Custom tools can also be much harder to learn for a new designer, and they may come with little or no documentation. If you've been working with a custom tool from the beginning of game development, you may find it easy to use, but if you are handed a tool late in development you may have to scramble to learn how to use it effectively. With some tools, there are often important steps that must be followed in order to accomplish certain tasks, but no way to know what those steps are unless someone who knows them shows them to you.

Sometimes, experienced designers have gone through the process so many times that they forget to tell the new guy about a critical step. The game may crash because new interface art has been added and a rule has been broken. It can be as simple as not putting a colon in front of the name of every button or checking the wrong check box in an exporter.

Commercial Tools

A commercial tool is software that is available for purchase by anyone. It is not created specifically for your game engine, and when it comes to interfaces, the tools may not have been made specifically for game interface creation. There are many commercial tools that can be used for creating an interface, such as Photoshop, Flash, or Painter. Rarely does an interface designer create an interface from start to finish without using at least one commercial tool. In many cases, a commercial tool may be the only tool used by the artist to create an interface.

It may not be smart to use a custom tool to do something that a commercial tool already does well. You will find very few custom tools that are used for painting 2D images. Commercial tools are a great solution for painting pixels.

Advantages of Using Commercial Tools

Commercial tools are usually very stable. They are usually heavily tested before release, and most bugs and crashes are found and corrected.

Commercial software can be expensive, but if you compare the cost of commercial software to the cost of paying a programmer to create a tool in-house, buying commercial software actually seems quite inexpensive. Buying and using a commercial tool can often save money in the long run, even if custom exporters need to be written so the tool can be used.

Many of the big commercial tools have additional support from other companies. Other companies provide extra features that you can add on to the base software. These features usually come in the form of a plug-in that is simple to add. Plug-ins can do all kinds of cool effects that can really help you create a great interface. A product like Photoshop is a great example of a tool that is used by many game developers. You can take advantage of any publicly released plug-ins that have been created by other game developers.

In addition to the plug-ins available for purchase, there are many free plug-ins. When working with custom software, the only extras you can get will need to be created in-house.

Disadvantages of Using Commercial Tools

Commercial tools don't always include the exact functionality that you need for your game. When using commercial software, you may need to work around the existing features. You may need to find ways to get functionality from the software that it was not created to do.

I have used Photoshop to perform tasks not intended by the original software developers. I named layers in such a way that the exporter could recognize what they should be used for. A button in the normal state may be on one layer and the highlighted state on the other. An exporter was written that recognized each layer that was named correctly and saved it in the correct format. Solutions like this can be a good workaround, but a custom tool could make this process much easier. The artist wouldn't need to remember exactly how to name every layer, and a typo wouldn't cause problems. Instead, the custom tool could have a check box for each layer.

You can use many features in commercial software that may not be supported in the game engine. For example, the Renderware engine can use Flash files to create interfaces, but it does not support any of the features in the latest version, and only a very limited set of the old features will work in the game. Because the software was not written specifically for the engine, it can become confusing. You will need to be aware of the game engine limitations and make sure that all of the art created in the software will work in the game.

Middleware

Software options exist that are sort of in-between custom software and commercial software. Game engines can be purchased and used to create games. Most of these game engines come with exporters and other tools that are used during development. These products are technically commercial tools because they are sold and used by many game developers. They are similar to custom tools in that they are written specifically for making games. Often, you can also get the source code that will allow a programmer to make any changes that are needed. These game engines and tools are often called *middleware*.

The tools that come with the middleware engines can be simple exporters or very refined tools. There is a wide variety in the quality and flexibility of these tools. Some are much more like commercial software and others are exactly like something made in-house. Most of the big-name engines have really great tools. They come with exporters from most major software applications. They have tools for viewing art with the game engine but

not in the actual game. This can be helpful when, for instance, you need to figure out whether something not working correctly is a problem with the art or with the game engine.

Commonly Used Commercial Software

There are many options for commercial software you can use to create interfaces. Each has a different way of doing things and has advantages and disadvantages. There is no one best solution. The best tool is usually the one that the artist knows best. It is much easier to be efficient if you already know how to use the software.

There is one important benefit to using the most common software in the game industry, though: Files can easily be transferred to anyone else with the same software. Often a publisher will have art created by other artists from a previous version of a game or even a similar game, and it is more likely that you will be able to use these files if you have the standard software. It is also easier to find a job when you have experience in the software that is used by most studios.

The most common commercial tool used to create interfaces is Adobe Photoshop. It has been around for a long time, and it has a lot of useful features. It is overwhelmingly popular in the video game industry, and is also used heavily in many other industries like Graphic Design, Photography, and Illustration. If you make video game interfaces, you will use Photoshop at some point.

Note

I do use other tools for specific tasks, and I don't mean to rule out any other options, but I will describe techniques used in Photoshop later in this book because I know it well and I believe it will be the most useful tool for you as an interface designer. Figure 10.1 shows Adobe Photoshop.

Another very popular tool for creating interface interactivity and animations is Macromedia Flash. Like Photoshop, Flash is a commonly used software and I know it well. There are some middleware tools, like Renderware, that have tools to convert Flash files into game format and get the animation and interactive information from the Flash file into the game. Figure 10.2 shows Macromedia Flash.

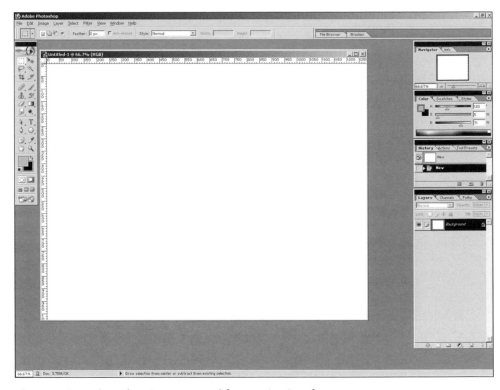

Figure 10.1 Photoshop is a great tool for creating interface art.

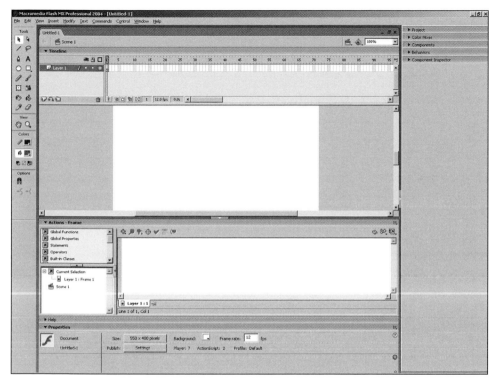

Figure 10.2 Flash is a great tool for creating animation and interactivity for interfaces.

Features of Good Tools

The mark of a good tool is that a new artist can use it to get art working in the game engine without help from anyone else. A good tool should have a user-friendly interface—the easier the tool is to learn, the greater the chance it will be fully utilized. A feature that is hard to use may simply be avoided. It should be simple to make changes and get things just right in the game. You should be able to make all the changes you want and instantly see how it works in the game. This will speed up production and encourage fine-tuning that will improve the game.

The shorter the time from art creation until the art is actually in the game the better. In the ultimate situation, the artist could hit one button and instantly see the art in the game. Once it has been set up properly, the artist would not even have to choose a destination or name of a file—it would all happen automatically. It should also be easy to get art into the final game. No other team member should have to stop what he is doing to put new art in the game.

Good tools do save you time. Efficiency is the purpose of tools. The extra speed that tools provide should not only apply to the first time a piece of art is created and put into the game, but the tool should allow for easy adjustment. A tool that is capable of this type of efficiency often includes features such as easy to use batch file processing. If the same adjustment needs to be made to hundreds of individual pieces of art, batch processing can be a lifesaver.

The Ideal Situation versus Reality

As it is with many other parts of game development, few interface artists have access to the perfect tools and ideal processes for creating game interface art. The ideal situation would be to have bug-free, easy-to-use custom software that has a complete set of relevant features—all the advantages of commercial software. Such an ideal situation only occurs at companies that have enough resources and money to create this ideal tool. Even though the tools you will use often have shortcomings, they can be very useful.

As an interface designer, you'll rarely get to use perfect tools—there may be no such thing. This shouldn't discourage you, though. Even if you can't work under perfect circumstances, it helps to know what could be possible and try to improve the tools and process anytime you can.

Software or the Artist?

I have heard so many artists say that they could create perfect art if they just had one more piece of expensive software. They are convinced that one specific plug-in will solve all of their problems and improve their art. I have also seen many of these artists get the new piece of software and still have all of the old problems—expensive and cool software can't turn a bad artist into a good one. On the other hand, I have seen good artists create some amazing art with really bad software. Software does not create art, artists do.

I don't mean to imply that software can't help in the development process. Software is essential and very important, and if there is some software that

would really speed up the process or help produce a better final result, you should not hesitate to buy it. It is simply important to understand that great software does not create art by itself any more than a great paintbrush paints a picture by itself. In the end, the skill of the artist is what matters most.

You could spend all of your time trying out every new plug-in and all the newly released software. It is good to know what is available and to keep current, but it is important to spend your time on the relevant software and, most importantly, to develop good design skills. Many artists waste their time learning new software and trying out new techniques and never really produce any great art. I am much more impressed with a portfolio full of art than I am with a list of programs that you have used. Anyone can learn to use software in a short period of time. It is much more difficult to learn good art and design skills.

It is also important to keep software from driving the creative process. A new plug-in that creates a cool neon glow effect may be perfect for the interface of a game that takes place in Las Vegas. This same effect may not be great for an underwater submarine game. Even if it looks cool, make sure it also works well with your game. Too often, an artist gets a new plug-in and uses it on everything.

Some people seem to think that a good piece of software does all the work for the artist. When I tell such people that I have painted a picture digitally, they act as if it is much less of an accomplishment than if I'd used paint and a paintbrush. I have to admit that there are some serious advantages to producing art digitally. For example, contrast, color and brightness can be easily adjusted after the image has been created. Mistakes are much less permanent. Even with these digital art advantages, good art requires good art skills. I am just as impressed with an artist who has learned how to use a pressure-sensitive tablet to paint a picture as I am with an artist who can use a paintbrush.

If you want to improve your interfaces, the best place to start is with your design skills. Study some of the basics of design. It also helps to look at a lot of great art and design. Games are not the only resource. I subscribe to magazines like *Communication Art* and buy design and illustration annuals. Take the time to understand why the art and design you discover is so effective—if you can define why it is so much better than mediocre art and design, you can apply these principles to your own art. Develop the ability to critique your own art. It can be very easy to find problems with the work of others, but much harder to see the faults in our own work. Remember that art and design skills are more important than software.

3D Tools

When you create a 3D interface, most likely you will use the same tools used to get the 3D models and animation into the rest of the game. Using 3D art is inherently much more complicated than creating 2D art, and you will encounter all of the obstacles that exist for the modelers and animators that are creating art for the rest of your game. In fact, it may be even harder for you to use 3D art in an interface than it is to use this art in the game. You may need a couple of features that are specific to the interface. For example, you might need to control the camera paths for the interface, and camera paths may not be used anywhere else in the game. If the programmers are going to grant you this control, they may need to upgrade the exporter to get this information out of your 3D software and into the game.

The struggle to determine the best 3D software can be brutal. Many 3D software users are very loyal to their favorite software package and they take offense at anyone else who expresses a different opinion. But the argument is pointless, as there is really no one piece of 3D software that is better than another. The current top two most popular packages are 3Dstudio Max and Maya. Each has its pros and cons. It is impossible to really know which is best for your game unless you are an expert in both.

Many artists are enticed into learning and using just one of these tools because it was used for a particular movie or because it was used on a particular game. I would suggest that you avoid professing your ignorance by claiming that the software you use is better unless you really know both well. If you want to learn 3D but you can't decide which software to learn, I would suggest learning the product used by the game development studio at which you want to work.

In order to make a fair comparison of software, you need to be an expert in the current versions of the programs you want to compare. Of course, it is hard to be an expert in both software packages because there is so much to learn. I have heard convincing argument for both 3DStudio Max and Maya. You can't compare the latest version of Maya with a version of Max that you used several years ago or vise versa. They both have undoubtedly added new features in the latest versions.

The bottom line is that there is a lot of great 3D software. As I've said, the best tool is the one you can use the best. If you know it better, it is better for you. There may be an instance when you need to do something very specific and a particular piece of software actually is more efficient in this area than the one you usually use. If so (and often it is more about not knowing how to do it in the other software), you also need to consider the learning curve—will you really save time by changing? Go with what you know.

Summary

You should always do your best to work with the most efficient tools possible. You will still need art and design skills but good tools can save you time. In most cases, you will use a combination of commercial software applications and custom software written specifically for your game. Both have advantages and disadvantages. You should make the most out of the tools at your disposal.

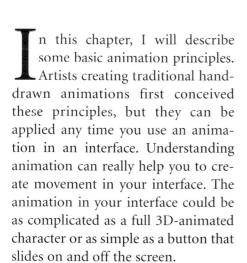

CHAPTER 11

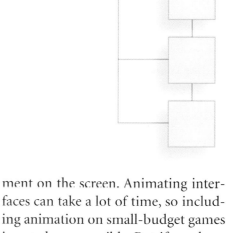

USING ANIMATION

In this chapter, I will describe some basic animation principles. Artists creating traditional hand-drawn animations first conceived these principles, but they can be applied any time you use an animation in an interface. Understanding animation can really help you to create movement in your interface. The animation in your interface could be as complicated as a full 3D-animated character or as simple as a button that slides on and off the screen.

Movement

Movement carries great visual power. If something moves, it will catch the viewer's eye. Movement will usually draw more attention than any other technique. Remember this when you are animating an interface—think about what you want the user to see, and don't create extra animations that draw the user away from actually using the interface.

When designing a game interface, you should do your best to never have a static screen. Always have some move-

ment on the screen. Animating interfaces can take a lot of time, so including animation on small-budget games is not always possible. But if you have time, make it move. Animations can bring your interface to life. Still screens are boring, and a game, of course, should be entertaining.

How Animation Works

Animation, as you probably know, is an illusion. Nothing is really moving. During animation, a bunch of still images are flashing in front of your eyes so fast that it looks as if the image is moving. This is the same way that film works: Movie cameras take a bunch of still photographs every second, and when they are played back, it looks like the objects or people in the film are moving. These images are played back so fast that the human eye can't tell that they are actually still images.

Frame Rate

Some of the terms that we use in digital animation come from the beginnings of animation and live-action film. Each of the still images in a movie is called a *frame*. During a game, images are drawn on the screen. Each one of these images is a motionless image is also called a *frame*. The speed at which these images are played back is called t he *frame rate*. The frame rate actually represents the number of these still images that are displayed every second.

Standard video is shot at 30 frames a second. A television is capable of updating up to 60 times a second (NTSC). When playing video games, it is very important that the game reacts quickly and all of the animations look very smooth. Because the user is watching every movement intensely, even slight differences in the frame rate can be seen. A game that runs at 60 frames per second appears even smoother than one running at 30 fps. Frame rates faster than 60 fps are not really detectable by the human eye.

So why doesn't every game run at 60 fps? Well, it takes computing power to draw each screen. The more calculations that must be made for each frame, the longer it takes to draw the screen. Every polygon, animation, texture, and effect in a game requires a calculation to be made by the hardware processor. The more of these elements that are used in a game, the slower the game runs. If every game ran at 60 fps, the game would have fewer polygons, textures, and animations. Many games run at 30 fps and still look great. If a game drops below 30 fps, though, the movement becomes choppy.

Interface Frame Rates

A game interface is not the most important place to have a high frame rate. Because the user does not need to react to the animations in the interface, the animations can usually run at a slower frame rate. It is still important to know at what speed the interface will run. If you are creating individual frames for an animation, then you will need to know how fast they will be played back. One thing to remember is that an animation can be played back more slowly than the game engine is actually running. For example, if one image is displayed for two frames, the animation can run at 15 fps, even though the interface is actually running at 30 fps.

The reason for playing back an animation at a slower frame rate is to save space. This is effective when you have pre-rendered frames that play back in your interface. A one-second animation at 15 frames per second can be half the size of a 30-frame animation that also only lasts one second.

Key Frames and Tweening

Back when animations were all drawn by hand, animators would choose the important frames and they would draw the character poses at these important frames. These important frames are what defined the object's movement, and so they became known as *key frames*. Creating good key frames was one of the most important aspects in creating a good animation. The experienced artists on an animation project were given the responsibility of drawing these key frames.

Less experienced artists would then draw all of the frames that appeared in between the key frames. This became known as *tweening* and the frames became know as *tweens*. Tweens made smooth transitions between the key frames. Creating tweens was time-consuming, but actually required less skill than defining the key frames. If the key frames were done well, the animation looked good.

Modern animation software works in very much the same way. The important task for the animator is to set key frames. The object's position, rotation, and scale (along with any other animated properties) are defined at each key frame. The computer does all of the tweening. The animator will also have some control of how the computer does the tweening between the key frames.

Interpolation

The term used to describe what the computer does when it calculates the frames in between the key frames (tweens) is *interpolation*. Most animation software packages' default method for calculating the tween frames is referred to as *ease in and ease out*. In real life, most motion does not start and stop abruptly. It starts slowly and then speeds up. It reaches full speed in the middle of the motion, and then there is usually a slowdown at the end, before the object in motion comes to a complete stop.

Figure 11.1 shows all of the frames that might appear in a simple animation that is easing in and out of the key frames. The frames that are closer together will appear to move slower.

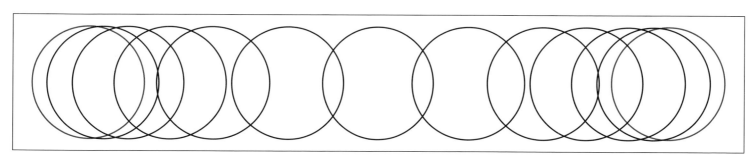

Figure 11.1 The motion changes speed during the animation.

The frames in the middle are further apart and will appear to move faster.

Most animation software applications allow the user to adjust the amount of ease in and ease out that is used to calculate the tween frames. Usually the default ease in and ease out works well, but this is not always what you want. For example, if you want an object to spin smoothly around in a circle, and you set key frames at each

of the four quarters of the circle, the default settings will not be smooth. The motion will start slow and end slow at each of these key frames. In this case, you wouldn't want any ease in and ease out. You would want the software to use what is called *linear interpolation*. In the left half of Figure 11.2, you can see what would happen if you set a key frame at the point of each of the red circles. The motion would speed up and slow down. The

right half of Figure 11.2 shows you what would happen in this same situation without ease in and ease out.

T i p

Most animation software allows you to create a path (a circle) and move an object along this path when you want an object to travel in a circular motion. This would be a much better solution than creating key frames.

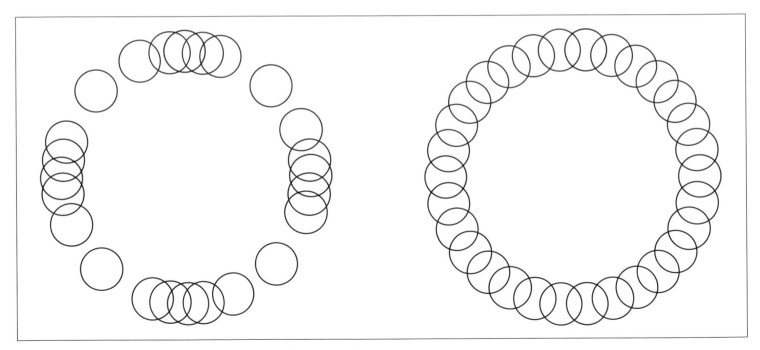

Figure 11.2 The motion on the left would seem jerky, not smooth.

Animation Principles

Back in the 1930s, Disney animators came up with a list of animation principles. These principles were meant for character animation, but many of them can be applied to game interface animation as well. In the next sections, I will cover the principles that are the most useful for interface animation.

Squash and Stretch

When some objects move, they change shape. This change in shape can be caused by the motion or because the object has come in contact with another object. This change in shape is called *squash and stretch.*

Many objects are not rigid and solid. The softer the object, the more change there is in the shape of the object. This change in shape can really add life to an animation. An object that doesn't change shape can seem as if it is made of metal or stone. If an object really changes shape a lot, it can seem as if it were filled with water.

The classic example of the squash and stretch is a bouncing ball. If the ball remains perfectly round during the entire animation, it will not look convincing—it would not seem very bouncy. In real life, when a rubber ball comes in contact with the ground, it squashes down and becomes wider and shorter. As the ball bounces off the ground and begins to move upward, it returns to the round shape. On the way back to the peak of the bounce, the ball actually stretches and becomes thinner and taller. Once it reaches the peak, it returns to the round shape.

When you're creating an interface, using squash and stretch can help give your animations a lot of personality. If your interface includes a character bouncing a ball, the application of this principle may be obvious (see Figure 11.3). But squash and stretch can be used in many other ways. Any

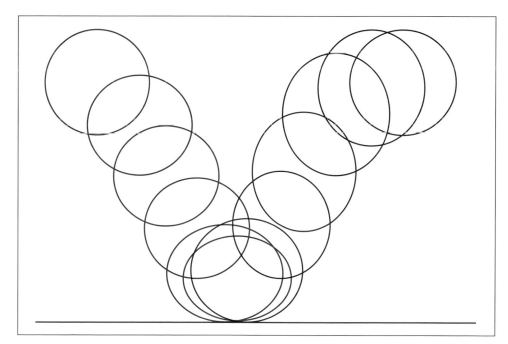

Figure 11.3 The ball changes shape during the animation.

of the animated shapes or objects could change shape as they collide or come to a stop. You could even give your buttons a different feel as they slide onto the screen. Once they reach their final destination, they could stretch a little and then return to the regular shape to give them a squishy feel. The bigger the shape change and the more times an object bounces back and forth before it returns the original shape, the squishier it feels.

This type of animation can also create a very fun and cartoon-like feeling. What kind of material do you want the user to believe the animated object is made of? Your answer will determine how much squash and stretch you will use. If your buttons are made of metal, they may not change shape at all. If they are made of a rubber filled with thick goo, they may deform a lot, but may move slower than a water balloon would.

Anticipation

Anticipation is movement in the opposite direction of the main movement, just before the main moment is made—a sort of "wind up" before making a big move. The bigger the motion, the more exaggerated the anticipation should be. Anticipation is a great way to emphasise movement.

The classic example of anticipation is the wind up before a cartoon character takes off running. The character rears back and poses briefly before shifting all his weight forward and beginning to run. This anticipation pose can almost be more important than the run.

Anticipation is typically found in human or animal animation. Applying this principle properly can really add life to an animation. Even an inanimate object can come to life with a little anticipation. Anticipation implies that the object that is moving is thinking about the next movement. It is "anticipating" this next move.

A simple application of anticipation in an interface would be to add a little bit of anticipation to the movement of a button. Once a button has been selected, you can move it backward before sliding it forward offscreen.

Just by adding a couple of frames of anticipation, you make the animation more interesting to watch. Figure 11.4 shows motion with anticipation applied to an interface button.

Ease In and Ease Out

Most motion in real life does not move at the same rate during the entire movement. It is a matter of physics. It eases in to the movement and eases out. When a movement starts, it takes a while to get up to full speed. Movements also can't stop instantly. They must slow down as the motion comes to a stop. This is the reason why many software packages have this type of movement as a default. (See the beginning of this chapter.)

If your software does not have an ease in and ease out setting, you may need to control this by hand. Even a button that flies onto the screen and stops suddenly will look strange. You can't have a button moving full speed in one frame and completely motionless in the other without the stop looking abrupt to the viewer.

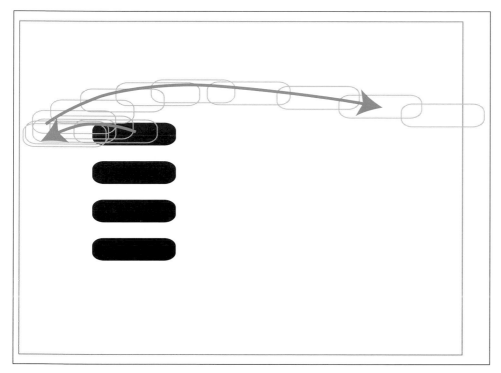

Figure 11.4 Moving the button back and then forward gives the movement more life.

and hair keep moving for a moment before swinging back into a resting position. Not only do the appendages keep moving for a while, but even the object itself moves beyond the mark and then returns back to the final position. The distance the objects move beyond the mark and the amount of time it takes to return to the final target position are based on the speed and size of the object.

Animating objects a little beyond the final mark and then having them settle into position can make motion look very realistic. When deciding how exaggerated to make the follow-through animation, you will need to consider how heavy the object should appear and how fast it will be moving.

Tip

In real life, if a heavy object stops suddenly, there is usually strong impact. If two large metal blocks collide, there would be a lot of power behind the collision even if they do stop abruptly. If you want to give the impression of a large collision, a loud sound effect and a screen shake can help. If everything on the screen bounces, it will feel like there was a big impact.

Follow Through

There is another basic law of physics: When objects or people are set in motion, they are hard to stop. Anyone who has ever been in a car when it stopped suddenly understands how this principle works in real life. When you are riding in a car, both you and the car are moving. When the car

stops suddenly, your head wants to continue moving until you can stop it with your neck muscles or it is stopped by the dashboard. Heavy objects are harder to stop than light objects, and the faster an object is moving, the harder it is to stop.

This principle is seen also when a person stops short and his or her arms

Arcs

When people move, they do not do so mechanically. Human movement does not occur in straight lines. Instead, natural motion occurs in arcs. If you were to trace the motion of parts of the human body, such as hands, hips, or even the head, you would notice that the motion creates smooth arcs and not sharp turns and angles.

Using arcs when animating an interface provides the illusion of natural motion. This may not always be the desired effect, of course. If you want an interface to appear mechanical, then it is much better to keep the animation linear and avoid arcs. If you understand the effect of both approaches, then you can better control the look of your interface.

Figure 11.5 shows three positions of a circle. If the motion between these three positions were linear, as in the top part of Figure 11.5, it would seem very stiff and mechanical. If the motion were more of a smooth arch, like at the bottom of Figure 11.5, it would seem much more smooth and lifelike.

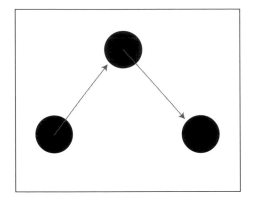

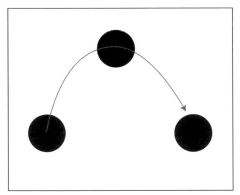

Figure 1.5 Different types of motion.

This arcing movement is often the default method for interpolation between key frames in most animation software. If it is not the default motion, you may need to add this arc by hand. Many animation software

applications also have a feature to draw a path and move another object along this path. Using this method, you could ensure that your object moves in smooth arcs.

Exaggeration

When animating, it is almost always better to make the motion a little bigger and more exaggerated than one would expect. You will always be surprised at how normal an exaggerated motion will look in the game. Choose the most important aspects of your animation and exaggerate them. In traditional animation, the extreme poses were often exaggerated. When a fist was moved back for a punch, it went *way* back. If you stick with motion that appears to be closer to realism, you may run the risk of creating drab and boring motion. You almost can't exaggerate too much.

Designing Transitions

Many interfaces pop from one screen to the next. This is the simplest way to change screens, and it can save a lot of time and money. If you really want to add the quality touch to your animations, a great transition between these screens can do the trick. Adding a transition will take more time and effort, but the results will be well worth the work.

Transitions should be quick so that the user is not left waiting. There are few things more annoying in a game than a slow-moving transition. A cool-looking but long transition may be impressive the first few times it is seen, but after that is just becomes frustrating. I would recommend keeping all transitions to less than a second.

Transitions can vary in complexity. A simple transition solution is a fade. The fade is often done by the programmers and does not take much time or effort for the artist. A fade in and fade out often looks much better and more smooth than a pop between screens. Using fades is a way to have a transition without spending too much time and money.

Some very complex solutions—that really look good—are possible. For example, all of the objects on the screen can animate in different directions or at varying speeds. You can create a custom animation for the transition between every screen. This type of animation can take a lot of time, but it can look quite impressive. The motion must be organized, though. This is not always a case of the more animation the better, but small variations can add a lot. If you decide to slide all of the buttons off-screen, it'll look really cool if they don't all start sliding at the same time. You can add a frame or two delay from button to button or stagger the start from top to bottom.

There are many cool possibilities for transitions. You could make all of the objects at the top of the screen begin to fall, and as they collide with the objects below them, the second set of objects begins to fall. In the end, everything falls off the screen. Animating all of the falling and colliding in a way that everything appeared to have weight and impact

---

Don't Make Them Wait

One of the big mistakes that new interface animators make is to create animations that take too long. The user should never feel as if he is waiting around for an animation. Slow animations can be particularly painful to endure with transitions, as I've said. Get them there fast. It doesn't matter how cool an animation looks—if it takes too long, don't use it.

If you are new at animation, it is important to learn and understand just how fast *fast* is. One second is a really long time to wait for an animation during a game. Count "one, one thousand" and think about how much could happen in that second. If your transition takes longer than one second, it is probably taking too long. You can make it much shorter and still have a very interesting animation.

It is amazing how much the human eye can perceive in a single second. If you watch a commercial or video clip that rapidly flashes images, you will notice that your eye can pick up dozens of images every second. Gamers have been exposed to this type of rapid stimulation and have even come to expect it. Give them this fast-paced action. Don't be afraid to make things happen quickly.

would be very complicated, but it could be really fun to watch.

Be creative when creating transitions. The best thing to do is to look at the still screen that you are starting from and the screen where you want to end up and think about how to get from one to the other. There is no limit to the things you can come up with.

Consider Experienced Users

You want a user to play your game over and over, right? After a user has played a game a lot, he knows what he wants to do right away. He knows which options he wants, and he wants to get into the game quickly. Such experienced users should not be slowed down because you wanted to show a really cool animation that takes forever to play out. Experienced players often memorize the pattern of button presses that will get them into the game. They can press the buttons as fast as your interface design will let them. Consider these experienced gamers when designing the interface.

Short transitions and quick reactions to button presses are a must. If you

feel you must include that cool, long transition, you could maybe skip the animation when the user presses a button during the transition. Just jump to the next screen. No matter what you do, you want to make the interface quick to navigate. As you are designing, time yourself and see how fast you can get the settings you want and start a game when you are very familiar with the interface.

Properties That Can Be Animated

Many properties of an object can be animated or changed over time in an interface. Some of the most common properties are translation, rotation, scale, and color. Learn which of these properties your game engine will support and take advantage of these features.

Translation, Rotation, and Scale

There are three basic properties that can be animated: translation, rotation, and scale. It will help you become a better animator if you

understand these three types of motion. The animation data that is typically stored in the files used in the game falls into these three categories. These animation types can be used separately or animated at the same time. Space-efficient file formats leave out unnecessary information. If you never animate the scale of an object, the scale animations data is not put into the final file. The absence of data means that the scale does not change.

Translation is what most people think of when they think of animation. It is one of the very basic animation properties. Translation refers to the position of an object. Translation is even called *position* in some software. When you move things around on the screen, you are animating translation.

Rotation is just what it sounds like. If you spin an object or turn it upside down, you are animating the rotation. When animating rotation, it is important to establish the pivot point. This will be the center of the rotation. It does not have to be in the center of the object. In fact, it can be far away from the object. The location of the pivot point can greatly affect how the object behaves as it is rotated. Figure 11.6 illustrates how different an animation can be if the pivot point is moved to a different location.

When you animate the *scale* of an object, you are changing the size of the object. Most software and game engines will let you distort an object by scaling more in one direction than the other. The important thing to remember when changing the scale of

a 2D graphic is that if you scale it too large, it will become blurry. If you want a big image at one point in your animation, make the image big and scale it down during the rest of the animation.

Transparency and Color

Transparency and color are two other common properties that can be animated in addition to translation, rota-

tion, and scale. *Transparency* refers to how see-through an object is. An object can be totally opaque or it can be just barely visible and mostly see-through. This property can usually be animated and changed over time. A simple way to create a fadeout is to place a solid black box over an object and animate the transparency from 100 percent transparent to 100 percent opaque. Another common use of animated transparency is to place a highlighted version of an object directly on top of an un-highlighted version. The transparency of the highlighted version could be animated to make the button appear to pulsate.

Many game engines offer the ability to animate the color of a 2D image. This can be a little trickier than animating other properties of an object. Typically, you will need to save an image in the right format for a game engine in order to change the color. As you can imagine, if you change the color of an already colored image, it could look really strange. The best way to use color animation is to produce a grayscale image, with no color, and let the game engine do the

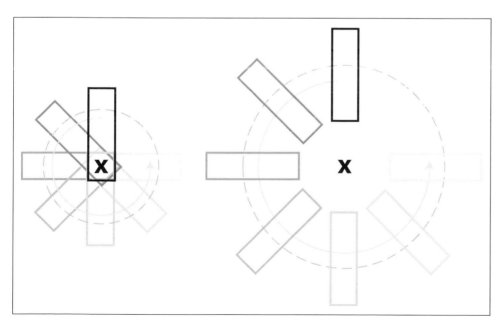

Figure 11.6 The location of the pivot point can really change the effect of a rotating animation.

coloring. This technique will not allow you to use multiple colors in an image at once because the entire grayscale image will be colored using only one color, but it will be easy to animate a color change.

Transparency and color are both aspects of an interface that a programmer can often control. If the programmer animates these properties using the game engine—instead of giving him multiple 2D frames that he plays back—it can save file space.

As I mentioned in the chapter on tools, good software can allow the artist to control the animation of transparency and color in the same way the programmer would change it in the code. The tool would simply provide a user interface to make these changes and provide a way to save them in a format the game could read.

Using Effects

In addition to the basic animation, there are countless animated effects that you can use when creating an interface. These effects can be either simple or elaborate, and they can be impressive to behold. There are many different techniques and methods to create these effects; I will cover some of these techniques in the sections to follow. It is best to decide what kind of effect you want and then decide on the best way to pull it off.

Overlaid Animations

A common and simple effect technique is to play a sequence of semi-transparent frames over the interface. For example, when a button becomes highlighted, a little sparkle could appear. These frames can be a pre-rendered animation created in a 3D program, or they could be hand-animated in 2D software. In either case, there are a number of files that will be played back by the game engine. The concept is simple, but the possibilities are endless. There are so many ways to create this type of animation that I can't begin to list them here. Any software or method that will generate a series of numbered files (in the right format for your game engine) for each frame of your animation will work.

Note

As I mentioned previously, in order to save space, these animation may need to be kept small, and they might even be played back at a low frame rate. Animations that require playback of pre-rendered frames can take up a lot of space.

A huge variety of animated effects can be created by playing one of these sequences. Objects onscreen could melt, shatter, squirt water, or do anything else you can think of. Use your imagination and come up with animations that look cool and fit well with your interface. Some of the best effects are those that fit well with the theme of the game. If you are making a game that takes place underwater, bubbles could come out of your buttons when they are selected. If you are making a gangster game, machine gun bullet holes could cover the screen when a user leaves it. You will only be limited by time and file-size constraints.

Particle Systems

Many game engines support particle systems. Particle systems use 2D images created by the artist and the game engine then animates these textures based on the settings for that particular effect. Many small versions of these 2D images move around, scale, change transparency, change color, and blend with other particles in a way that produces the overall effect. There are a number of parameters that are supported by the particle system. These vary greatly from particle system to particle system. Changing these parameters changes the way that the particles (2D textures created by the artist) behave. There is really no limit to the number of effects that can be created with a particle system, but some of the common effects you'll see are smoke, fireflies, explosions, and moving water. Figure 11.7 shows a spaceship with a trail of smoke and flame. This trail was created with a particle system.

These particle systems have a variety of properties that affect the animation. Some of the common parameters not already discussed in this chapter are life (how long they last onscreen), decay (how long they take to disappear), and the way they blend with the other particles onscreen. These parameters can often be randomized to produce a natural effect. Particle systems can be very complicated, but they can produce great effects.

Because every game engine has a different particle system, I can't tell you how the system works in your game engine. If this technology exists in your game, you might be able to use it in the interface. The technology and features will vary greatly from game engine to game engine. If you want to take advantage of these effects in your interface, then you will need to learn how the particle system in your game works. If you take the time to learn how to use this feature, it can become a powerful tool.

Other In-Game Effects

Many other in-game effects can be used in your interface—you are not limited to particle effects. If you know all of the effects that are planned for the game, you should also ask the programmers if these same effects could be easily used in the interface. If the work is already done to support these

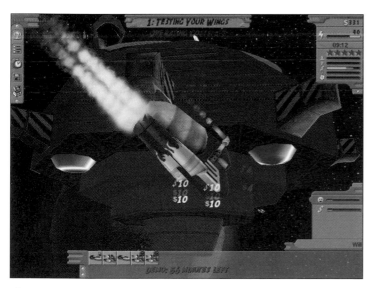

Figure 11.7 These flames are created with an in-game particle system.

effects, you might as well take advantage of them. A great example of this would be a screen shake. If the screen shakes in the game when there is a large explosion, this effect can also be used in the interface. Again, these features are very game-dependent. You will need to see what your game engine can do. If you see something you would like to use, don't hesitate to ask if you can use it. Most likely, it won't be hard to do it in the interface if it can be done in the game.

Summary

The best interfaces use great animation. Learn the basic principles of animation and apply them to your interface. Think big and create interfaces with amazing movement. Use the power of movement to attract the user and help guide him through the interface.

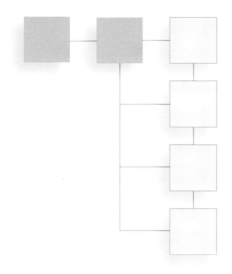

CHAPTER 12

ICONS, ICONS, ICONS

Icons are an important method of communication in an interface. Displaying information graphically is always more interesting than displaying a lot of text. If you must show an amount of money, consider using gold coins instead of a number amount. If you must display the amount of energy your character has left, consider using a fill bar. You can use icons for almost everything in your interface. They usually take a lot more time to create than would a paragraph of straight text, but they make your game a whole lot more fun.

Use Text Sparingly

Text should always be used sparingly in a game interface. (I jokingly say that I promote illiteracy in my games.) If you can leave text out of an interface, then by all means leave it out. I believe an interface is only finished when there is nothing else that can be taken out. If you must use text in your interface, do everything you can to reduce its length. Short sentences and phrases are much more likely to be read than a large paragraph of text.

Gamers don't like to read too much while playing a game. I have seen countless gamers glance at a page of text and immediately hit the button to skip the screen. It doesn't matter how important the information is, they will skip it—or try to, anyway.

It does not matter how cool your story is—if there are too many words, your interface will suffer. It is always better to impart important story elements using music, voiceover, and images. If you went to see a movie and found you had to read the story while only a few images drifted by onscreen, you'd probably feel cheated—if you'd wanted to read a book you would have stayed at home! You expect a movie to be a visual experience, and players expect the same from a video game. Many great video games have gorgeous cinematic sequences—sort of mini-movies—that use sound effects, music, voiceover, and animation to tell a compelling story.

There is nothing wrong with including text in your interface to support the visuals. Doing so can help gamers who prefer to play without sound. Just make sure that players aren't *required* to read text in order understand what is going on in the game.

Budget Constraints

Once again, budget and time constraints will affect your ability to deliver the perfect product. An interface with a lot of text is often a sign of a small budget because, of course, it is easier and cheaper to use text instead of creating custom art and icons. There will be times when you must take shortcuts in order to meet a budget or hit a deadline, but resist giving up and filling the screen with text.

I recently designed an interface for a game with a small budget. The development team did not have time to make movies or even enough money to record voice actors, but we had a great story that was important to communicate to the user. In this case, I had no choice but to use text to tell the story, but we went to great lengths to leave out extraneous detail and only use text to tell the most important pieces of the story. We broke the story up into little online pieces and presented these lines throughout the level, and we spent a lot of time re-writing to make sentences and phrases shorter—sometimes by just a couple of words. In this way, we spared the player from as much unnecessary reading as possible.

Note

A truly great interface can be navigated by a user who doesn't speak the language in which the text is written. Imagining that your players don't read English is a great way to make sure you're communicating the necessary information without relying on text. What would the user assume each button does?

Using Icons Instead of Text

You may be wondering, "How can I create an interface that doesn't require the user to read?" The user needs to understand how to navigate and control the interface and the game, and he must understand what every button does. Using icons that indicate the functionality of a button or control is often a good solution.

Great icons can accommodate the game to the user without text. Text can be used to reinforce an icon, but the better the icons are, the less this text will be needed. It is not easy to create great icons, but it can be done.

Image Choice

The key to creating great icons is choosing the right image to represent the functionality. What image will communicate the concept to the player without any reading? Choosing the right image is not as easy as it may seem—it can be quite difficult to find an image for an abstract concept. For instance, for a button that allows the player to build things, a hammer icon may be a great solution, but what about a button that is used to display a character attribute, such as bravery?

Standard Icons

Many standard icons, or icons that always mean the same thing, are used in video games. Players already know what these icons mean and can get up to speed more quickly if these standard icons appear in your game. For example, many game have a Save feature, and a common icon for the Save feature is a floppy disk. (This is sort of funny, as no one really saves games on a floppy disk anymore.) A character/player's health in the game is sometimes represented by a box with a red cross, which symbolizes a first-aid kit. Hearts also often represent health of a character. A shield often can be used as an icon for a defensive action and a sword for attack.

Take advantage of players' past experience by using images that they are probably already familiar with. Even if you use an object that is commonly used in other games, you can customize it to fit the look of your game.

You will also need to consider your target audience when you design icons. You should consider what games your players have probably played before. You can expect a completely different type of user with different experiences depending on the type of game you are making. You may not be able to assume previous game experience if you are making an educational game that is aimed at young gamers. If you are working on a space combat game, it is likely that the user will have played many video games.

Non-Game Standard Icons

A red octagon means *stop*. Green means *go*. It is not hard to figure out which bathroom to use, even if there is no text on the door. Symbols are all around us, and we learn early in life what these symbols mean. Many icons and images that have nothing to do with software and games are great references for creating icons for games. Think of all the buttons in your car, on your DVD player, and on your kitchen appliances—most people can figure out what these buttons are for even if they aren't labeled.

When creating icons for games, you can draw on these same universally understood symbols. Why reinvent something that already works well? Use red for a button that stops an action and green for a button that starts an action. Use a plus sign to add a knight to your army or a minus sign to drop a flask from your inventory.

Software—other than games—is a great source from which to draw standard icons. It is safe to assume that anyone playing video games has used a computer for other tasks, and there are many standard icons used by operating systems and software that can be used in your game. For example, a magnifying glass with a plus or a minus is often used to zoom in and out. A lowercase "i" often means *information*. Figures 12.1 and 12.2 both show a number of buttons from commonly used software.

Many of these icons would be a little bland for a game if they looked exactly like the icons in a common software application, but the concept might still be good—you can take the idea and improve on it. Figure 12.3 shows how a standard icon of a magnifying

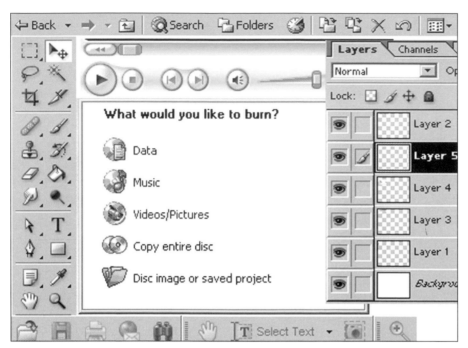

Figure 12.1 These are icons and symbols found in Microsoft Windows 2000, Windows Media Player, Adobe Photoshop, Adobe Acrobat Reader, and Nero Express. Just by looking at these icons you might be able to guess what each button does.

Figure 12.2 The symbols for playing audio and video are well known. These are the buttons found in the Apple Quick Time Player. These symbols have been used on radios and VCRs for many years.

Figure 12.3 This is an icon you have seen many times, but this version looks more like it belongs in a game.

glass with a plus sign can be improved to look more like it belongs in a game.

Be consistent. If you use a red octagon for a Stop button in one location, make sure you don't change to a black square (the audio symbol for Stop) in another location. The user will learn what the symbols mean in your game. If the player can perform the same action from two different places in your menu, make sure the icon is the same in both locations.

Use color wisely. Defining groups of similar icons and keeping color consistent within the groups to help the user learn and use your interface. For instance, make all of the icons that result in player action green and all of the preference icons (like sound, effects, and game resolution) blue. Be careful not to make it confusing by changing icons and icon colors randomly.

> Never actually use copyrighted artwork that is used in other games for your icons—it is illegal. Besides, using someone else's art is never as rewarding as creating your own. This does not mean you should not look at other games and use their solutions to help yours, though. Build on the strengths of the art done for other games. Many artists have spent a lot of time determining what symbols to use for each icon.

If you aren't sure if an icon you created works well, show someone the icon and ask what he or she thinks it represents. This person doesn't need to be another artist—after all, you aren't looking for information on how pretty it is. You're just trying to determine whether the symbol communicates what you want it to.

Every Pixel Counts

Their small size is one of the things that make icons such great tools in a game—they don't take up a lot of screen space. When you're working at TV resolution, you must keep icons small. It can be quite difficult to make a recognizable image when you only have a 24×24 pixel (or smaller) area to work with. The smaller the icon, the less space it takes up. Keeping your icons small is particularly important for in-game icons. The more screen space left open—not covered by interface buttons and controls—the better. The player needs to be able to see the action in the game.

After you have decided what symbol to use for your button or control, the next big challenge is to create an image that fits into a limited number of pixels. Many novice icon designers simply take a large image and reduce it down to make a button icon. This might work in some cases, but often most of the image detail will be lost and images will become blurry. If the small details are important, these details may need to be exaggerated so that they can still be seen when the image is reduced.

Figure 12.4 shows how a large image can become blurry when it is reduced. It also demonstrates how a little hand editing of the reduced image can sharpen up the lines.

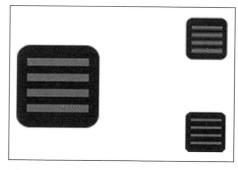

Figure 12.4 When it is reduced, the image in the upper-right corner becomes blurry. This can be easily cleaned up once the image is reduced, as has been done to the image in the lower right.

Your pixel limitation may affect the subject matter of your icon. The image will need to be small enough to be an icon, but still be recognizable. I have had a publisher sit and describe to me an icon that was to depict a complex scene that needed to be recognizable in 32 pixels. It is impossible to show a Ferrari driven by a smiling man with one missing tooth all in a small icon. The driver's head may only be a couple of pixels big, even if you do crop out most of the Ferrari. Think big, simple shapes when designing icons. If the driver's missing tooth is the key concept, then you might just use a smile with a missing tooth, not even the driver's whole face.

When editing icons, you will need to make adjustments at the pixel level. Zoom way in on the icon and make changes. It can be hard to see what these changes look like at actual size when you are zoomed in, so it is a good idea to constantly zoom in and out while working on your icons. Slight changes to a pixel can make a big difference.

Photo Reference

Very rarely will you be able to use a photo for an icon without changing it drastically, but photos can give you ideas for good silhouettes. Finding a good silhouette is the key when using photos. You will almost always need to repaint all of the details before it will make a good icon. Photos can still help you know what the object really looks like.

Summary

Great icons can make for a great interface. Keep away from text by using symbols and icons to let the user know how to use your interface. Hone your icon-creating skills. The ability to create a great icon is a very valuable skill when creating game interfaces. You might be surprised how much more fun the interface seems to be when you use icons in place of text.

CHAPTER 13

DESIGNING THE HUD

The acronym HUD stands for *Heads-Up Display*. *HUD* refers to the interface and display information that is onscreen while the game is in progress. This in-game interface is very important because it affects game-play. If the HUD is hard to understand and use, then the game will also be hard to understand and play.

HUD design is a very complex subject—an entire book could be written on it. This chapter will give you only an introduction to designing HUD.

Many of the same principles that apply to the front-end menu also work for HUD. In this chapter, I will cover the aspects that are specific to the in-game interface.

Screen Space

One of the basic rules to follow when creating HUD is to take up as little screen space as possible. With PC games, screen space is always limited; space is even more limited in a console game that is played on a television.

Players want to see what is going on in the game. If you cover the screen with a distracting interface, it can be like looking out of a car windshield that is covered with stickers. Designing HUD for multiplayer games that use split screens is even more difficult than designing for console games because, of course, the screen space is cut in half.

When it comes to HUD, less is more. The trick is to display a lot of information in a very little space. Try not to fill up the screen with unnecessary information—it is all too easy to end up filling up a lot of space with HUD and getting in the way of game-play with cool-looking but unimportant details. If the player does not need the information to play the game, you should consider taking it out of the HUD.

There are many ways to organize the HUD on the screen. Think about the shape of the screen that is not covered by the HUD. If you want a wide screen, you may want to place the HUD at the top or bottom of the screen. If you prefer a screen that is closer to a square shape, you can put the HUD on the left or right of the screen. You can also spread the HUD into every corner. Figure 13.1 shows several different types of layouts that you can use. The black areas represent possible locations for the HUD.

When you're working with HUD, it is good to keep the extra stuff small. Part of your HUD will be decorative—the beveled edges on buttons and rivets in the rusty metal are there just for looks—you want your HUD to look cool, but you don't want this extraneous detail to be too large.

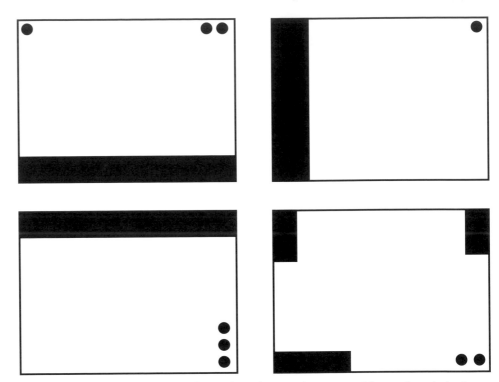

Figure 13.1 Here are several different basic layouts that you could use when designing the HUD.

There is no need to use a lot of pixels; it is amazing what you can do with a two- or three-pixel border. (See Figure 13.2.)

 Figure 13.2 A lot of detail can be added with only a few pixels.

Again, if it is not absolutely necessary to display the information onscreen during play, then put it in another location. For instance, one small button in the HUD could open a page of information or options that are rarely needed while playing the game. This approach still provides the player access to this information when he does want it.

In-Game Information

A great way to reduce the amount of information that is displayed in the interface is to put more information into the actual game and take it out of the interface. For example, if a character in a game is becoming fatigued, you might indicate this to the player by changing the character's animations rather than by displaying a fatigue bar in the interface. This technique works best when the player does not need the specific details. If the player needs to know only that he is not at full strength and not his exact numerical fatigue amount, then having three sets of animations—one each for energetic, tired, and super tired—may be enough information.

Many games use icons in the actual game environment. Rather than put a 2D piece of art in the HUD to display the mood of a character, you could place a 3D icon that floats over the character's head when he is mad, and

another icon (or the same one in a different color) when he is sad. Instead of displaying in the HUD the number of bullets that your character has left, you could change the 3D model in the game so that the player can see the ammunition on the character's belt.

It is much easier to display information in the HUD than it is to develop more game content to display information; that is why you see so many games with cluttered or boring HUDs. Putting an icon in the HUD to show that the player is carrying a jewel is much easier than actually putting a jewel in the character's hand, but it doesn't look as good. If it is a big jewel, you might have to change the run animation so that the character uses two hands to carry the jewel. Several animations would need to be created, and it may be expensive and time-consuming to do so—but it would be much more fun for the player to see the character carrying a huge jewel than it would be to stare at a 2D image of a jewel in the corner of the screen. It is always easier to throw up another icon when the player is using

his super strength, but an in-game effect such as the muscles on the character beginning to bulge or shrink would be much more impressive. You will need to work within the budget of your game, of course, and find ways to put as much information into actual game-play as you can.

You can also allow the player to select in-game objects instead of automatically putting an interface element onscreen. Once the player selects the objects he wants, the important information can be displayed. The in-game objects basically become the buttons that might normally appear in the HUD. If the player needs information about the prices of objects in a magic shop, for example, you could allow the player to select the objects by walking around in the game world. Once the object is selected, you could display the price and item description.

An even better but more difficult way to reduce the amount of information displayed in the HUD would be to allow the player to get all of the information he needs just by looking at the character. A character's facial expression can reveal his mood, the animations can give information about his energy level, and when the character is selected, a voice can tell the player what the character wants.

All of these options take much more time to create, and so they cost the publisher more money, but they are more interesting than a set of boring bars on the screen.

Pop-Up Menus

Pop-up menus are just what the name implies. When the player presses a button in the HUD, an in-game object is selected, and a menu can pop up with new information. The game can pause or continue in the background. Using pop-up menus is a great way to keep the screen clear—if the player needs to know about the status of a character, he can press the small character status button and up pops a whole page of information.

A great place to use a pop-up menu is in a tutorial. When a player is first learning how to play a game, you can

have information pop up to help him. It can be really effective when the game can tell when to pop the menus up. For example, if the player seems to be confused and is not progressing through the game at a certain rate, the game could pop up a menu offering hints. Figure 13.3 shows a pop-up menu that appears early in the game to teach the new player how to play.

Figure 13.3 A pop-up menu provides extra information.

Dynamic Content

The basic idea behind dynamic content is that the HUD changes depending on the game situation. Only the information that is important at the moment is displayed. When the situation changes, the HUD changes to match. For example, the player's shield strength may only appear onscreen when meteors are hitting him. Once the meteor shower has

subsided and the player's shields have returned to full power, the shield-strength information could disappear.

Obviously, the amount of oxygen a player has left should only be displayed when the character is underwater, and the amount of ammunition a player has left should only be displayed onscreen when the player has his weapon out. The player may not know how much oxygen is left in his tank when he is on dry ground, and he may not know how many bullets he has when his gun is put away, but this information is not important at these times.

You might think that it is important for the player to know how much health he has at all times. I have played several games that brilliantly take another approach: The health meter only appears when the character loses some health. This meter

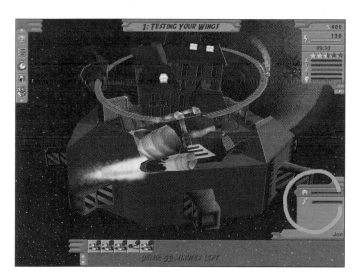

Figure 13.4 An interface with a dynamic HUD that only appears when the player needs it.

remains on the screen for a short time and then fades away. This saves screen space and really improves the game experience.

A very simple example of dynamic HUD can be seen in Figure 13.4. The HUD in the bottom-right corner of the screen only shows up when a ship is selected. It contains information about the currently selected ship. When no ships are selected, nothing appears in this spot.

Evaluate your interface and decide whether you really need all of the information onscreen all the time. If you think that there may be times when some information is needed and other times when it is not needed, change your interface to fit the situation.

Combining Information

You can combine information in order to have fewer objects on the screen. When playing your game, the player may need information, but he may not need all of the details. In a game where the player controls a theme park and tries to make visitors happy, it is important to know how a visitor is feeling, but it may not be important to know all of the details that make up the happiness. The game may keep track of a lot of information in the background, but not all of it needs to be displayed. If the player just ate a hamburger and it made him happy, but then he couldn't find a drink, rather than displaying all of this information, you could just display the a bar that says his hunger is half filled.

The choices you make of what to display not only affect the HUD, but they also have a lot to do with basic gameplay. In the theme park example, for instance, do you want to spell everything out for the player or let him discover how to please this visitor on his own? If possible, reduce the amount of information on the screen by making logical combinations.

Legibility

All HUD elements should be as small as possible, but it is also very important that they are clear and legible. If a player can't tell what it is, then there is no use putting it on the screen. In order to achieve the right balance of smallness and legibility, you must often test and re-test your design, and you may have to adjust the art after you see it in the game.

I have already discussed the fact that gamers don't like to read text. If the HUD is fuzzy and hard to read, they will be even less likely to read it. While this same concept applies to a front-end interface, it is even more important in the game. Usually, the game does not pause so that the player can read the information and the player can only pay half attention to the HUD because he is busy playing the game. Don't make the player break his

concentration because it is hard to see something in the HUD.

You can get a pretty good idea of the clarity of your image during the creation process, but the best place to test it is in the game on the target platform. See how your art looks in the game engine. It can often look very different in the game engine than it does in Photoshop.

If you are working on a console game, you must also check your art on a television. There is often a huge difference between what you see on a computer monitor and what you see on a television. Some colors are harder to see on a television. Because there are a limited number of pixels on a television screen, even small images may appear much larger than you expect. This can reveal flaws that may not have been seen on a computer monitor. Just because everything is clear and legible on your computer does not mean it will be clear and legible in the game.

Eye Movement

As I've said, the information displayed in the HUD should be vital to the player; if it's not, it should be displayed elsewhere. Important information should be clearly visible, and the player should be able to read it quickly. The player does not have time, in the heat of battle, to search the screen for information on how much health he has left—he needs to know this immediately. The HUD design should communicate such information quickly and clearly.

When designing the HUD, consider the player's eye movement. Where will he be looking and how easy or hard will it be for him to see the information? Placing information into groups with similar information can help the player find the information he needs quickly, as he will only have to look in one place. Looking back and forth across the entire screen over and over can take valuable seconds and be quite frustrating.

In an RTS game, the player might need to build units and buildings. It is helpful for the player to find all of the building actions in one location. Other interface buttons, such as buttons used to control the action of a selected unit or units, could be placed near each other in another location. Attack, Patrol, and Guard are actions that might go well together. It would be awkward for a player to have to push a button in the upper-left corner to attack and another button in the bottom-right to guard an area.

Ease of Use

A well-designed HUD should be easy to understand and use. The player should know how to navigate the interface without thinking. When designing for a PC game, think about how far the player will need to move the mouse. How many clicks will it take to perform a common action? Is it obvious to a new player what to do?

Use as many visual clues as you can to help the player understand the interface. Small interface animations can help the player understand the effect of pressing the buttons. If the player is spending money, it can be helpful to see animated dollar signs pop up after every purchase. If the player is changing a weapon, it is helpful to show an image of the current weapon after the change.

Use all of the same techniques that are used in the front-end menu to get the player's attention. Color, size, and movement can all help the player see what is important. (These concepts are discussed in Chapter 7.) Your goal is to help the player understand how the HUD works and understand all of the information. You are communicating with the player through the interface. Don't distract the player from game-play, but if you are going to display something important on screen, make sure the player notices.

Organize the interface. For example, placing all of the information about the player's character in the right-hand corner and all of the information about the enemy in the left corner of the screen will lessen any confusion about whose health meter the player is looking at. It is also helpful if all the information onscreen is organized according to color—the player's character data can appear in blue and the enemy's can appear in red, for instance.

Making HUD Look Cool

With all this talk of functionality, don't forget to make your HUD look cool. A good-looking interface can really add to the game. Make sure the HUD fits the look and feel of the entire game.

If the front-end interface has successfully captured the feel of the game, then this is a great place to start when designing the HUD. If you can pull off a good theme, it can really add to the feel of the game. If the game is in space, for example, make sure that your HUD feels like space—dark, star-filled backgrounds with lots of glowing lights may be appropriate for such a game. If you are working on a fishing game, you might go with a backwoods, rustic look, with a lot of wood grain and "hand-painted" text.

Game-Play Adjustments

The design of your HUD will be greatly affected by any changes made to the game-play during the development process. Unfortunately, it is hard to make all of the decisions about game-play before a game is made and not make changes during development.

As the game gets to a point where it is playable for the first time, testing begins and so do the changes. The game designers may decide that the player may need a lasso in addition to a gun, and you may need to fit in an interface that is used to throw a lasso into the HUD you have already designed. If the game designer finds that the game needs to display the number of enemies in the game, new interface elements may be required. If the decision is made to allow the character to pick up and carry game items, you will need to add this functionality to your HUD. These items in the player's possession may need to be displayed in the HUD.

When the game is finally playable, you will have a chance to test out your interface. You will often find that new players are confused by elements that you thought were going to be painfully obvious. If no one who plays your game can figure out how to turn the

ship's shields in a space combat game, for example, you may need to make some adjustments to the HUD so that it is easy to understand how to turn on the shields. A good icon might really help.

While you should do your best to avoid having to make changes to the HUD, knowing before testing that changes are probably inevitable will help you resign yourself to making improvements when the time comes. Willingness to make a change is particularly important when there is consensus on your team or among test players that a problem exists. No matter how much you love your HUD, if the testers are all having trouble with it, it's got to go.

Graphic Information Display

Display as much information as you can graphically. It is much more interesting to see information displayed in a fill bar than as a number amount. There are many ways to take information and turn it into an icon, chart, or graph.

Use visuals that will help the player better understand the information in the HUD. Instead of labeling a health meter with text that says *High* and *Low*, for example, you can change the color of the bar from green when the player's health is high to red when it is low.

In Figure 13.5 you can see how a lot of information can be displayed in a graph. The icons on the left side of this piece of the HUD represent each of the desires that visiting spaceships have. The green section of the fill bar represents how much of that desire your space station is capable of meeting; the red section of the fill bar represents the amount of the desire that you cannot fill. Using this graph, it is simple for the player to see how well he is doing. Even when the scene is filled with ships, a glance at this menu will give him a lot of information. The more green sections displayed, the better he is doing—this is much easier to understand than it would be if numbers were used to show the same information.

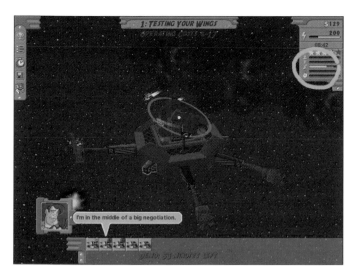

Figure 13.5 You can display a lot of information in a simple way if your HUD is designed well.

Standard Elements versus Non-Standard Elements

There are many standards for in-game interfaces. Familiarize yourself with your competition, as players may be familiar with and like the way interfaces in other similar games work. Play the other games in the same genre and pay attention to how their designers have designed their HUD. Using this information can help you create an interface that is easy to use. Learn about all of the standards for your game genre and stick with them in most instances.

When you vary from a standard interface, it can result in much more work. It can be risky, as well. When making a golf game one time, I and the other game designers decided that it would be cool to change how the basic swing mechanic worked. Most golf games at that time used a gauge at the bottom of the screen, and the player would simply click as the meter reached the correct point in the animation. This worked well, but we decided that a new way to swing could make our game even more fun.

We wanted the player to pull back and push forward on the joystick so that it felt more like swinging a club. It ulti- mately worked, but it was not easy to design. We tried many different inter- face elements to tell the player how to swing. Before we settled on the final mechanic and HUD, we tried all kinds of three-dimensional meters that sat in the club's path. In the end, these meters did not work well for game- play.

We ultimately took away a great deal of the interface and created a particle blur behind the club. The color of the motion blur changed as the player neared the sweet spot; we even added a little ding sound so the player would know when he should swing forward. A small club head also displayed a number that represented the percent- age of the full-power swing. This number animated as the player took his back swing so he would know when to swing forward. It would have been a lot easier to use the same type of meter that had been used in other golf games.

You can make cool innovations to your HUD, but you must understand how much longer it takes to come up with a new solution compared with something you know will work because you have seen it done in a thousand other games. When you decide to innovate, don't throw out the baby with the bath water—only change the one item, don't change the whole menu's functionality. If you present the player with too many new tasks and unfamiliar functionality, he may get confused.

Summary

Many of the basic design principles and techniques used for the rest of the interface can also be applied to the HUD. The HUD is the part of the interface that is tied closely to gameplay. Make the HUD easy to use and understand and don't forget to make it look cool.

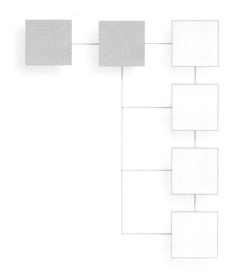

CHAPTER 14

DESIGNING AN INTERFACE

U p to this point, I have been discussing interface design principles. This chapter will provide a real-life example of how these principles can be applied, by taking you through the steps of designing an interface. This "tutorial" will, I hope, help you understand how complex and difficult it can be to create a good interface. Good design is not easy to create—it is just easy to use. The best interfaces require planning and careful thought. You can't just whip them out in a couple of hours.

As I go through the design process, I will explain how I created an interface using Adobe Photoshop. I will not try to teach you how to use Photoshop. Instead, I will demonstrate basic techniques that I use and show you the design process.

In this chapter, I assume that you have a basic understanding of Photoshop. But even if you don't know the software, you'll still be able to understand the design concepts—and I will focus more on the concepts than on the specifics of Photoshop. I can't cover all of the details of Photoshop in this book. If you need a Photoshop tutorial, pick up another book on the program.

Nomad Design Goals

In this chapter will show you the process I recently went through as I designed an interface. Because the game is not complete at the time of this writing, I'll refer to the game with a code name—*Nomad*. This game is a space trading game at the core. The player can fly from space station to space station, trading goods for profit, accepting secret missions, purchasing weapons, and upgrading his ship.

This game may sound familiar to you—many space trading games out there fit a similar description. *Nomad* does have several new and innovative features that aren't found in competing games, but what really sets this game apart is that it is accessible and easy to learn. It is deep enough for hard-core gamers, but it will not scare off a casual gamer. Most of the existing trading games are aimed specifically at hard-core gamers. They can be very technical and often require a lot of time to learn. *Nomad* is much more simple to understand. This was a primary design goal for *Nomad*—make the game easy to play. This is always a difficult goal to meet, but if you can meet it, you will have a successful game.

Nomad is based on an existing intellectual property (IP) that was used in a previous game. The characters and ships were originally created for another game, *Outpost Kaloki*. Because it is based on this IP, the basic art style for *Nomad* is already set. The game must not break completely from the previously created *Kaloki* universe, but this does not mean we can't improve on what was done for that game. *Nomad* shouldn't have the exact same look as *Outpost Kaloki* but will retain the feel.

Play *Outpost Kaloki* if you want to familiarize yourself with its look and feel. A demo version can be found on the CD that is included with this book. You will be able to see how the interface design for *Nomad* fits into the *Kaloki* universe.

The Rough Sketches

I started my work on *Nomad* by sitting down with the game designer, and together we began to work out the HUD design. We determined that we should first design the most important part of the interface. We could then use this to guide us in the design of the rest of the interface.

We needed to identify the piece of the interface that would be seen the most and could potentially cause the most confusion. One of the core game-play elements of our game was trading goods. The player would spend a great deal of time using the Trading menu. It was very important that this interface be easy to understand for an inexperienced player; simplicity was the major goal here. This interface also needed to be flexible enough that it could handle the most difficult scenario the game would present. If we did not get this part of the interface right, the whole game could suffer.

We first looked at many similar games to see how their trading interfaces were implemented. We found that this part of the interface was one of the biggest problems in many competing games; the trading interface was often a screen full of text and data that was difficult to understand. Consequently, these games often had a high learning curve—they were very difficult to understand at first, and a new player had to be willing to spend a significant amount of time learning how to play. Many players would probably look at these screens and decide, based only on the visual complexity, that the game itself is too hard to bother with.

Nevertheless, the game designer and I began by sketching some very rough layouts that were similar to the interfaces in other trading games. We then asked ourselves the question, "How can we make this interface easy to understand and use?" What was really important and what could be left out? How could we remove as much text as possible?

We started with the basic layout that seemed to be the most common in competing games. We were not completely satisfied with this approach, but we needed to use it as a starting point. Figure 14.1 shows some of the sketches we came up with.

These sketches are probably illegible to anyone who was not present when they were jotted down on paper. The purpose was to quickly see potential layouts. We explained to one another what each scribble represented, but we did not waste time trying to make a pretty sketch.

We then began the stage I call the "what if" stage. We would continue to scribble on paper and ask each other things like, "What if we left this out and moved this over here? Would it be easier to understand?" We moved elements around on the paper. We scribbled on a whiteboard.

All of this moving and scribbling helped us determine that there was some basic information that was important for the player to understand:

- Amount of money he has
- Number of holds he has in which to store items
- Quantity and type of items he is carrying
- Items that he can buy
- Cost to purchase items
- Price at which to sell items
- How these current prices compare to a standard

This last item is interesting. Many of the games we looked at required the player to remember if a price was high or low before deciding whether it was a good idea to sell or buy. Tracking this price information in your head did not seem fun—it seemed like too much work. We decided that it would be much more fun to get this information quickly and spend the extra time determining trading strategies.

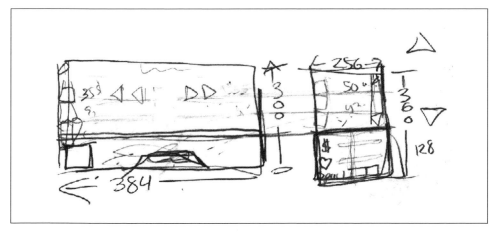

Figure 14.1 These are very rough sketches.

We also decided that the game would be much easier to play if the player could easily understand whether each purchase was a good deal or if he could make money by selling off items. Competing games displayed enough information that the player could calculate how good of a deal each price was—if he could remember the details—but this information was not always displayed in the current trade dialog box and often required a lot of calculation. There wasn't a good reason why we shouldn't make this information simple to find.

We also decided that it was important to display this information graphically rather than using text. We needed an icon or another way of indicating whether the price was high or low.

After the player processed all of the information displayed in the HUD, he needed to do one of three things: buy, sell, or leave. The player should clearly understand how to buy, sell, or close the dialog box and move on. The buttons for these actions needed to be big enough to see easily and needed to

be colored in a way that the player would instinctively know what to do.

We then moved on to sketches of a different approach. We were still not at a point where we needed to have pretty sketches. If we could look at a sketch and understand the layout, then it was good enough. Figure 14.2 shows a rough sketch of a vertical layout.

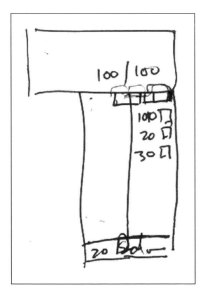

Figure 14.2 This vertical menu approach seemed to take up less screen space and it could naturally grow out of the ship information that would already be on the screen.

The buttons for purchasing items did not need to be displayed all of the time. We decided that it would be a good idea to have these buttons pop up on the side of the menu when an item was selected that could be bought or sold. This would also help the player better understand what the Purchase and Sell buttons did. The highlight would move down to the row where the item was located. The Purchase button would not just visually signify *purchase*, but *purchase this*.

Figure 14.3 is a very rough sketch of the buttons appearing to the side of the highlighted object.

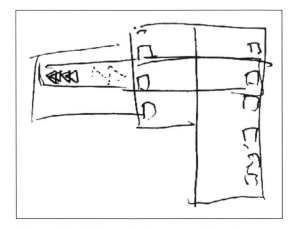

Figure 14.3 These sketches are still very loose. The purpose was to quickly see potential layouts.

Temporary Art

Before spending much time on final art, the game designer and I began creating some temporary art. The interface programmer was then able to take this temporary art and put it in the game. He could start displaying information and making buttons work. The game began to be playable at this point—the player could buy and sell things and make money.

Of course, this was a long way from a fun, finished game, but it afforded us the opportunity to do some early evaluation. We handed the game to new players and tested whether they could quickly understand the interface. We also could begin to see whether this approach made it fun to trade items. If trading was tedious, we had to change how it was done because trading was what the player would be engaged in throughout the game. The only way to know if a game is fun is to try it. An experienced game designer can make some good assumptions about the relative enjoyableness of a game, but there is no substitution for an actual trial involving new players. Because it was so early in the process, we knew we'd have to make many changes.

Spending time on polished artwork is a big temptation—it is really rewarding to look at pretty art in the game. I have worked with many producers and publishers who want something cool to show off—they want to show a version of the game to the press or to their boss, so they ask for polished art early. While creating finished art early on is sometimes a necessity, you should realize that doing so will create extra work when things need to be redone. It also can take the focus off the game's functionality and put it on the quality of the art. In these early stages, it is better to get the functionality correct. You can then follow up with pretty art.

On *Nomad*, we used some pieces of art from a previous game and created some new art. Luckily, we were working with experienced game developers who understood what they were looking at. Some of the art we used was purposely bad—the program-mer even made some of the art himself. Making bad temporary art is sometimes a good idea—if you make temporary art really ugly, then there is no doubt that it is temporary. If we were dealing with less experienced directors, we might not have taken this approach—they may have believed that the art was final if it looked too good. The goal here was just to test out the game's functionality.

Figure 14.4 shows some temporary art used to test the functionality of the interface.

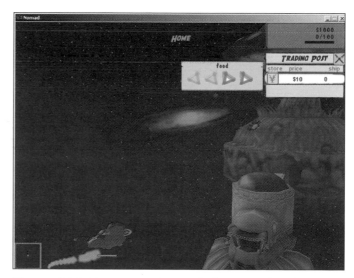

Figure 14.4 You can see the poorly drawn Purchase buttons and the general poor quality of the art here.

Re-Do's

There is one area in which we did waste a little time—re-do's. We tried hard to avoid spend time on re-do's, but it is almost impossible to avoid completely.

The programmer set up the temporary art and made it work in the game. As we reviewed it, we came up with a better solution than we had implemented at first. This new solution meant that the artwork must be done differently, and the programmer would have to make the changes. If we had guessed correctly the first time, the temporary art would have only needed to be replaced with final art, and it would have taken little or no programmer time. The programmer spent time setting the art up the way that seemed best at the moment—he just had to take his best guess. This is one of the reasons for using temporary art; at least I did not waste time creating final art and then have to change it.

I try hard to get an interface completely right the first time, but I don't think I have ever actually done so. This is because I am always open to improvement. Once I see an interface in action and see how other players play the game, it seems I always find ways to improve it. If there is time and budget to make it better, then I want to do so. I have seen too many game and interface designers get an idea and cling to it tightly. This can be damaging to the final game.

The early stages of a game are the best places to make changes. When I am told that the direction of a design is set and it cannot change—simply because it is the way the designer wants it and not because of time or budget constraints—I assume the game will not end up as good as it could be. If you fear change, you might miss out on opportunities to make a better game.

Don't come away from this book thinking you should demand radical interface changes late in the game process or when there is not enough time or budget to make the changes. Be open to new ideas but wise about your schedule. In real life, an unfinished game is worse than an imperfect game. An unfinished game can't be sold. (Although I have seen a couple of games that have made me question that statement!)

Nomad Colors

The game designer and I tried several color combinations for the trade interface in *Nomad*. This color decision would also affect the entire game, as all of the HUD and front-end interface would follow this same color scheme. These colors might also have been used on the box cover. What we were really deciding was what the color of the game should be.

The colors used in *Outpost Kaloki* were fairly saturated colors. We needed the color scheme for *Nomad* to match the already-established look of the in-game art. The spaceships in the game were bright and had sort of a cartoonish look. This bright, cheerful look was not an accident; it was carefully chosen. We believed that this look would help *Nomad* appeal to a broad market.

Neither of the two common styles for space games—rusted metal with dirt and grime or clean, glowing, and high-tech—was perfect for our target audience. These two art styles might appeal to the serious gamer, but they might also scare off the casual gamer. Our goal for *Nomad* was, you'll recall,

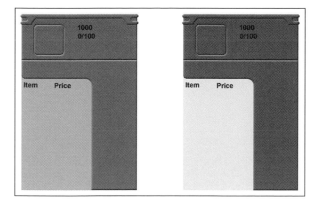

Figure 14.5 These are some color schemes that we looked at for the game.

Figure 14.6 The final colors are a little more edgy than in *Kaloki*, but they still fit well within the look and feel of the *Kaloki* world.

to reach this casual gamer while still appealing to the hard-core gamer. The interface colors played an important part in reaching this goal.

Two possible color schemes for *Nomad* are shown in Figure 14.5.

In *Nomad*, we added combat elements that did not exist in *Outpost Kaloki*. *Nomad* was going to be slightly edgier than *Outpost Kaloki*, and the look could therefore be a little more geared for the serious gamer. We came up with a predominantly gray and purple interface with bright orange accents. This was a very non-traditional color choice for an interface. It would really

stand out, but it also fit well in the *Kaloki* universe. We hoped that these colors would become recognizable as the colors of *Nomad*. The final color choice can be seen in Figure 14.6.

Using Color as a Tool

The game designer and I made a decision to use color as a tool to help the player. Our simple sketches didn't have color, but we began discussing ways we could use color to make the interface easy to understand while making these crude sketches. Talking

about color in this early stage also helped us to visualize the final product.

We decided that it was important for the player to understand what items he had in his ship and what items were in the store. As items were purchased and sold, they would change from one side of the Trading menu to the other. As always, we did not want to rely on text to solve this problem. The standard solution is simply to label the top of the columns of items Ship or Store, but we wanted to leave such labels off the screen. If our label-less approach turned out to be unclear, we could always add text later. We wanted the player to know what was in his ship without having to read a single label, so we used color to provide visual clues.

Some information, such as the amount of money the player had and how much space was left to carry items, needed to be displayed all of the time. We decided it would be a good idea to have a small portrait of the ship next to this information. This would make it clear that this was information about the player's ship.

This small piece of HUD with the portrait of the ship was mostly purple. We therefore decided that all of the icons and information about the ship should appear on a purple background. Any of the items in the virtual store would appear on a gray background. We also decided to make a visual connection between the pieces of HUD that were displayed all of the time and the store interface that appeared only when the player parked at a space station. We wanted this art to appear to be one big piece—the player may never have consciously noticed that the ship information always appeared on purple, but we hoped that it would give him intuitive clues.

Figure 14.7 shows how all of the information about the ship had a purple background.

We listed all of the important items that we thought would appear in the game. We then assigned each item a color. If we kept these colors consistent, the player would eventually learn what the colors meant. If warp gates were always blue, then the player

Figure 14.7 You can see how the basic ship information seems to connect to the list of items carried in the ship.

would learn to instantly recognize that a blue gate was a place to exit the area and warp to another. Figure 14.8 shows the chart we made for the use of color in the game.

A great place to use this color-coding was in the mini-map. The mini-map displayed a bunch of moving dots that represented a number of objects in the world. The player would need to look at the mini-map and instantly understand what all of the dots on the map represented. Labels could have

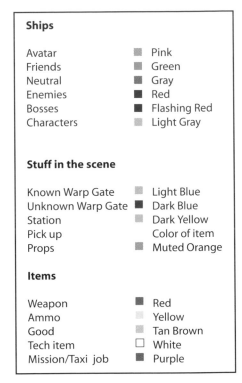

Figure 14.8 This chart was made not only for the interface, but also as a guide for the entire game.

been a solution here too, but they would have made the mini-map much harder to understand than it would be if we colored-coded the dots.

A good use of color in the mini-map went a long way. If all of the enemies appeared as red dots in the mini-map but the space station was also red, then the player would have a hard time telling the space station from the enemies in the mini-map. But if the enemies appeared as red dots and nothing else onscreen was red, then the player would have no trouble spotting them.

Creating the Art

Once the initial pencil sketches were done and the temporary art had been tested, it was time to create some good-looking art. This was our first shot at art that might be final. While we understood that the art would probably change again later, we attempted to create art that could be final if it worked well. You never know—you might get certain parts perfect. That was the goal, anyway.

Breaking Up the Art

It may have been faster to simply create the entire piece of art needed for the trade interface and give this to the programmer. While this technique might appear to save time at first, it is usually a poor solution, and in the long run it will take longer. Although breaking up the files into smaller pieces will require more effort for the artist and more programmer time at first, it will actually save time.

Once this initial work has been done, this one piece of art can be used in many different locations at various sizes. If a solid piece were used instead of a file that could be scaled, file sizes would end up being much larger than needed because a new file would be needed for each different-size menu. A piece of HUD that can be scaled also allows a lot more flexibility.

We examined the *Nomad* design and decided how to break the art up into the smallest and most flexible pieces possible. It wasn't easy to arrive at the best solution. Finding the most efficient way to break up the menu also required some very slight changes to the design. These changes were small, and making them allowed us to use fewer pieces of art.

At the time, it seemed like we were doing more talking than creating art, but all that discussion was necessary in order to avoid having to re-do the art several times. Taking out a little variation in the middle of the menu and squaring off a rounded corner reduced the number of pieces that was needed to create a dynamically scaling menu.

The art needed to be flexible. The Trade dialog box needed to be dynamic and change for each situation. Each store where this dialog box would appear included different items to sell, and every store could sell a different number of items. The player also had a varying number of items aboard his ship. The size and shape of the dialog box needed to change for each of these situations. The two sides of the dialog box, the ship inventory side and the store inventory side, needed to change independently. The side on the left, which included the store items, needed to change to accommodate the number of items in the store. The side on the right needed to change to accommodate the number of items carried in the ship.

The same art we created for the Trade dialog box would also be used in the dialog box for accepting missions.

This Mission dialog box would have the same basic layout and be based on the same concepts as the Trade dialog box, but the amount of information would be different. More information needed to be displayed in the right side of the dialog box, as this was where the information about the missions the player had already accepted would be displayed.

Figure 14.9 shows two different sizes of the Trade dialog box that can be created with the same art.

It is always best to design an interface with breaking up the art in mind. Even when doing the rough pencil sketches, I was thinking about how it would be best to break up the art, and so I designed it accordingly. This meant that I needed to think about pixel sizes of each element in the design in powers of two, as most game engines require that pixel dimensions of each piece of art be a power of two (see Figure 14.10). There are ways to work around this by leaving extra space in the file, but it is much more efficient to have art that works well with this limitation.

If I designed it correctly, the interface would be easy to break up into powers of two. For example, the horizontal rows in my mock-up are all 32 pixels tall. As I sketched them, I made the assumption that I would have 32 pixels of space. If I needed more, I knew I would need to jump to a 64-pixel tall row. If I'd had a 34-pixel tall row, those extra two pixels would have actually added another 32 pixels to the height.

After a lot of thought, the game designer and I came up with what we felt was the most efficient way to create the art for this interface. This plan required six pieces of art. If you look at Figure 14.11, you can see our crude sketch that we scribbled on the whiteboard—I added the green stuff digitally to help identify the different pieces. All of the pieces of art are labeled with an R to indicate that they need to be

Figure 14.9 Different situations required different sizes for the Trade interface. It was designed to be flexible.

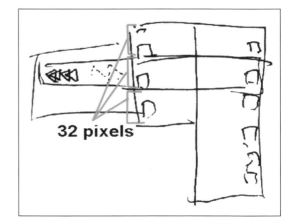

Figure 14.10 Each section had to be created in a size that was a power of two.

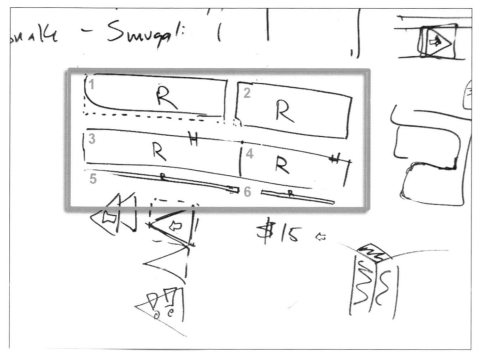

Both pieces 1 and 2 were made to look as though they connected to the purple ship information box that appeared at the top of the dialog box. Both of these pieces of art were 32 pixels tall and 128 pixels wide. The left 32×32 pixel square served as the end piece. The second 32×32 block was the tiling center. The third 32×32 section was the right end piece and the last 32×32 section was blank. You can see more about how this scaleable art works in Chapter 9. You can see what this art looks like in Figure 14.12.

Figure 14.12 These two pieces of art are the final ones used for the top row on the Trade dialog box.

Figure 14.11 This is the final sketch on our whiteboard; it shows how the interface would be pieced together.

dynamically re-scaled. (The size of the dialog can change based on how many pieces of art are tiled together.) The pieces marked with an H need to have a highlighted state.

The piece of art labeled 1 will be mostly purple but will also include the transition to the gray store sec-

tion; this is the section where the title will appear. The piece of art labeled 2 will be at the top of the list of items in the ship. It will be all purple except for a small corner piece that will round off the transition from the purple to gray.

The pieces labeled 3 and 4 in Figure 14.11 are also 32 pixels tall and they are scaleable because they can be tiled and made any size, just like the two pieces of art above them. This is where the store items and the ship items will be located. If there are five items in the ship, piece number 4 will be duplicated five times.

In order to make the interface clear, I put a line to separate each row. These lines were placed at the top of each section, and they appeared as though they connected across both pieces of art. You can see what the final art looks like in Figure 14.13.

Figure 14.14 These two pieces of art work like the others, but they are much smaller. They form the cap on the end of the vertical columns.

Figure 14.13 These two pieces of art are the final pieces used for the middle rows on the Trade dialog box.

The pieces labeled 5 and 6 in Figure 14.11 are only eight pixels tall and 32 pixels wide. They are scaleable bars, just like pieces 3 and 4, but they are broken up into 8×8 sections. These pieces of art are purely decorative. They create the bottom caps on the Trade dialog box. Pieces number 5 and 6 also included a bar at the top. The line on this bottom piece of art separated this piece of art from the horizontal row above it. You can see the final art for the bottom piece in Figure 14.14 and everything put together in Figure 14.15.

Figure 14.15 This is what it looks like when all of the pieces are put together.

I have worked with several programmers who always want the art in one big piece. Often, this is a sign of inexperience. There may be a rare case when submitting the art in one piece is actually the best solution, but most of the time it is worth the effort to break files up into pieces, as it saves space. In our game, we were very concerned about file size because we planned on creating a downloadable demo. The entire download needed to be as small as possible. In the end, we didn't have many files and they were all small. The file size of the total game was also small.

As you can probably tell by this description, creating the initial art for the Trade interface was not a quick process, but doing it this way actually saved time in the end. I created six pieces of art and with these six pieces of art we were able to create a dialog box that scaled to every situation. Breaking the art up into small pieces not only saved space, it also allowed for a lot more flexibility.

Many different dialog box boxes were needed for the game. We could not have anticipated all the different sizes that would be needed in the game, and even if we could have, creating all the various size dialog boxes would have required a lot more art. Scaleable art allowed the programmer to adjust the size of the dialog box to fit the amount of information that needed to be displayed.

Selected Rows

The pieces of art that are labeled 3 and 4 in Figure 14.11 are items the player can select in the game. These two pieces of art were placed next to each other to form horizontal rows. The entire horizontal row could be selected by the player at once. Because this entire row could be selected, a highlighted state was needed for both of these pieces of art, just as is needed for a button.

More art was created for this dialog box. When each row was selected more information was displayed to the left of the row. The Purchase buttons appeared and information about the item that could be purchased was displayed. All of this art had to work well together.

It was important that the player understand what the Purchase buttons could be used for and that it be easy for the player to connect the information to the item that was available for purchase. He needed to

know what he was buying when he pressed the Purchase button. In order to make this clear to the player, we needed to make the buttons look as though they could be pressed; the buttons also needed to communicate what would happen when they were pressed.

As I mentioned previously, the background of these additional pieces of art was gray so it was similar to all of the art used for the items in the store. The information was about the items for purchase, and the gray color was used to make this fact clear. We used buttons with an arrowhead shape to indicate which way the selected item would move if the button were pressed. It would either move from the store into the ship or from the ship into the store.

Figure 14.6 shows the highlighted bar, the Purchase buttons, and an area where information could be displayed.

Figure 14.16 When each row is selected, it highlights and more information is displayed in the additional dialog box.

Photoshop Techniques

I created all of the art for this section of the HUD using Adobe Photoshop. This is my favorite program for creating interface art with this look. Other software has a lot of the same features, but Photoshop is by far the most commonly used software in the industry, and I know it best. Photoshop includes many features that I am familiar with that make tasks easy and fast. I will show you how I used Photoshop.

When it comes to creating interface art, my favorite features in Photoshop are the layer effects that can be created using the Add Layer Style button. These features should not limit your vision, though—that is, you should not rely on the layer effects so much that you don't create anything that doesn't use one of them. If a layer effect gives you the look you want, then go for it.

The green circle in Figure 14.17 indicates the button in Photoshop used to access the layer effects.

A big advantage to using the layer effects is that it is easy to maintain a consistent look throughout your entire interface. Once you have created a layer effect and adjusted it just the way you want it, you can easily use this same effect through your entire interface. After you save the layer

style, it will appear in the Styles menu. It can be applied by simply clicking on it when the correct layer is selected.

You can see where to add a new style in Figure 14.18.

I used the Bevel and Emboss effect on the *Nomad* interface. You can see this effect on the purple areas of the interface. I first created this effect on the Ship Information panel. Once it was

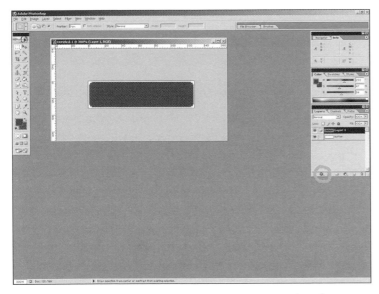

Figure 14.17 This little button gives you access to a lot of different effects that can be very helpful when creating art for an interface.

Figure 14.18 Once you have an effect adjusted just the way you want it, you can save it and use it in other places in your interface.

created, I saved it and used it on all of the purple pieces in the Ship section of the Trade interface. I also used the same effect, saved in the Styles menu, for a great deal of the HUD and even in the front-end interface. This allowed me to be very accurate—I could add the same two-pixel bevel with the lighting coming from a consistent angle to any piece of art with a single click. This would have been much more difficult if I had created the bevel effect by hand.

Using the effects in Photoshop not only allows me to keep the same look across the entire interface, but it also offers precision and consistency across a single piece of art. This is very important when you're creating art that is tiled and pieced together in the game. If there is any variation in a drop shadow, for example, it can look bad when tiled, so you will still need to be careful.

For example, a curve that gets too close to a middle section can cause problems—a slight difference in the color of a pixel becomes much more noticeable when it is repeated. Figure 14.19 shows how this can happen. You can see how a curved area comes very close to the right edge of the first 32×32 section of the art. Because the drop shadow is affected by this curve, the first pixel in the next 32×32 is slightly lighter than the rest of the drop shadow. You can see in the lower part of Figure 14.19 how this shows up when it is tiled.

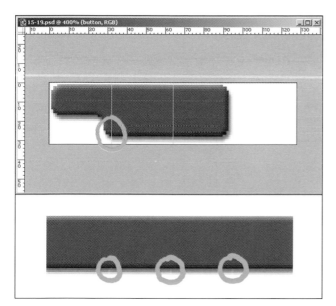

Figure 14.19 A very slight difference, even in only one pixel, can be visible when this section is repeated several times in a game.

Step-by-Step Art Creation

In this next section, I will take you thorough the step-by-step process I used to create the art for the Trade interface. I hope that reading about this process will reveal more information that you can use in your interface design.

The Ship Information Panel

As I previously mentioned, I began by creating the art for the Ship Information panel. I created the shape of the top orange bar. As I made this top bar, I knew that this entire section would be created out of a scaleable box (see Chapter 9 for more information). Because it was a scalable box, all four corners had to fit within a 32×32 box, and the top edge had to be repeatable. I filled it with the orange color and applied a layer effect to give it the beveled edge. You can see this decorative bar in Figure 14.2

Figure 14.20 This decorative bar at the top of this piece of the HUD is created in such a way that it can work with a scaleable box.

I then created a new layer below the orange bar. I created a square selection that was not quite as wide as the top bar. I inset this box several pixels from the edge of the top bar so that the top bar would extend past the edge of the box slightly. When I saved the final file, I made sure that the file format supported transparency so that the player could see through these pixels to the game. I placed the same bevel effect on this layer that I placed on the bar above. Figure 14.21 shows the box behind the top bar.

I then used the Ellipse tool to create a small circle. The advantage to using a vector shape is that it could be easily scaled, yet you can apply effects just

like with a raster level. (You can always right-click on the layer in the Layer window and convert it using the Rasterise option.) I applied a bevel that made it appear like a little bump or rivet. I made copies of this layer and positioned one in each of the bottom corners. You can see these rivets in Figure 14.22.

Figure 14.21 The purple box is on a separate layer and has the same bevel effect applied to it as the bar above.

Figure 14.22 I added small circles that appeared to be some sort of rivets.

Note

Photoshop is a raster-based program. This means that most features and the final file are based on the use of pixels. There are a few vector features. This means that the shapes created using these features are not pixel-dependent. They can be scaled and moved easily. Only when the file is saved in a format other than a PSD or when the layer is "rasterized" by right-clicking on the layer and choosing this option are these shapes converted to pixels.

I saved this file in a Photoshop format. This format retains all of the layer and layer effect information so that I could always open this file and easily make edits. Another benefit is that you can use the separate layers in other areas. If I need a rivet in another file, I can open the Photoshop file and drag this layer onto the new file. Whenever I need a bar similar to the top bar in this file, I can drag this layer and place it into a new file. The layer effect will also be transferred.

I then merged all of the visible layers. This makes it possible to select and copy pieces from all of the layers. After all of the layers have been merged, when I select and copy the only layer the layer effects are included. Before the layer is flattened, the Copy and Paste functions ignore the layer effects. If you don't merge layers, you will only copy the base art.

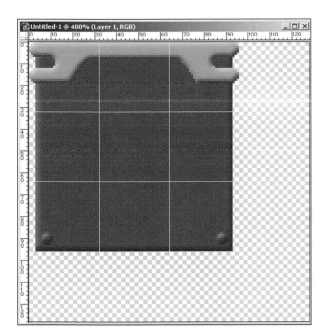

Figure 14.23 This is the final art used for the Ship Information panel.

I then coped 32×32 sections of this merged art and pasted them into a new 128×128 file. I copied the four corners, the sides, the top, the bottom, and the middle. I then placed these nine sections into the correct spots in the new file in order to create a scaleable box. The tricky part about this art was that the sides and bottom corners had to be inset so they would line up correctly. Figure 14.23 shows the final art.

Next, I needed to create the box with the ship logo in it. I created the background box and gave it to the programmer so that he could place it where it belonged. The image of the ship was a separate image—I created a new ship image for every ship possibility in the game. These ship images were small renders of the actual 3D model. We did it this way so that the ship image would change as the players ship changed during the game.

The ship needed to be larger than a 32×32 so that I would have plenty of room. A 32×32 image was not enough to see the ship clearly so I had to jump to the next size, 64×64. I only needed a few more pixels so the ship image did not fill this entire file, so—I left extra transparent space. The programmer placed this box based on the upper-right corner of the file, so the extra space ended up at the left and bottom of the file.

First I created the render of the 3D model and used it to determine the right size for the ship image. The player needed to recognize the ship. I tried several sizes until I found the smallest size where the details of the ship were reasonably recognizable. There was no need to take up space with a ship image that was too large. I then knew how big this file was and I used this information to determine how big the box in the background should have been. I created a square selection that was the size of this outer box. I used the Smooth Selection option in the Select/Modify menu to round off the corners of my selection. Once I had the proper selection shape, I filled it with a dark purple color. I added a Pillow Emboss effect to this layer.

Next, I duplicated this layer, locked the transparency, and filled it with the menu's orange color. I left-clicked on this layer in the Layer window while holding down the Ctrl button; this gave me a selection around the edge of the layer.

I again used the Select/Modify menu, but this time I chose the Contract option. I entered 2 in the Contract Selection dialog box and then hit the Delete key. This created a two-pixel border around the background. I added a two-pixel bevel to this layer to give the border a little depth.

You can see where to lock the transparency of the selected layer in Figure 14.24. You can see the final result in Figure 14.25; Figure 14.26 shows the final piece of art for the background of the ship icon. Notice the extra space.

I placed the ship icons in a 64×64 file to match the background. These icons were transparent around the ship. The ship was placed in the right location in this file so that if it the ship icon file were laid over the background file, it would be positioned correctly. This made it easy for the programmer to position the image of the ship over the background. He simply put these two pieces of art in the same location and the ship was in the right spot. You can see this in Figure 14.27.

Figure 14.25 The background and border are each on a separate layer with different layer effects applied to each layer.

Figure 14.24 If you lock the transparency and then press the Alt + Delete, the opaque portions of the layer will fill with your foreground color.

Figure 14.26 This is the final art for the ship image background.

Figure 14.27 The ship icon appears to be in a weird spot in the file, but this will allow it to be positioned correctly over the background.

The Trade Dialog Box

The next step was to complete the Trade dialog box that would be located under the Ship Information bar I just created. I began to create the Trade dialog box by starting with the Photoshop file that I had just completed. It contained the art used in the Ship Information bar. I started with this file so that I could see both the completed Ship Information box and at the same time see the Trade dialog box I was working on. This way, I could make sure that both pieces worked well together.

I started by creating a new layer below all of the existing layers. I made a rectangular selection the same width as the Ship Information bar that was already in this file. I then rounded the corners of this selection by using the Select/Modify/Smooth option, with a radius of 6. I filled this selection with the gray color. I did not worry about the three corners that did not need to be rounded because they would all be covered up. The only corner that really needed to be rounded was the lower-left corner.

The next step was to create the title bar area for my design. I created a new empty layer on top of the gray layer I had just created. I changed the grid in the options to have two subdivisions in every 32-pixels and used this grid to see how tall each section would need to be. I wanted to create a purple section in this layer that did not completely fill the 32-pixel tall section. In this new layer, I made a rectangular selection just below the Ship Information bar. This selection was the same width as the entire gray section of the background. The selection was 24 pixels tall, so it was short enough that a small portion of gray would fit into the 32-pixel height. The gray area needed to be big enough to have the curved area circled in green in Figure 14.28.

I needed enough gray at the bottom of this 32-pixel tall section to create this curve, but I also needed enough room on the purple area for a title. Once I had the right selection, I filled it with the purple color. I then rounded the selection with the Smooth option and then inverted the selection. I used the Eraser tool to round of the bottom-left corner of this purple selection (see Figure 14.29).

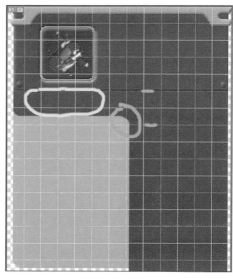

Figure 14.28 The gray area needed to be big enough to fit this curve.

Figure 14.29 This is the first block of purple I added to the lower section.

This curve needed to fit within the 32-pixel height, which is marked in green, but I also needed room to place a title in the area marked with yellow.

Next, I made a large rectangular selection that started at the left edge of the gray area and then I selected beyond the area where I wanted the lower half to be (see Figure 14.30). I then made another selection with the left side right where I wanted the edge of the lower section to be. I smoothed this selection and deleted part of the purple area, leaving a rounded edge (see Figure 14.31).

I added the same bevel effect as on the Ship Information bar. I also added the same rivet-looking circle as the Ship Information bar. I was able to duplicate the layers that contained the other rivets and move them down into position. (See Figure 14.32.)

The next step was to add lines to separate each row. I created a new layer above the purple layer. I made a two-pixel tall selection the entire width of both the purple and gray area and then filled it with the gray color. I selected the part of the line that was over purple background area, locked the opacity, and filled this part of the line with purple. At this point, the line

was not visible because it was the same color as the image behind it. I then added a one-pixel bevel to this line and duplicated it several times. I moved each copy down 32 pixels. Each line would be placed at the top of the 32-pixel row. Placing these lines at the top of each row rather than the bottom meant that a line would need to be placed at the top of the bottom caps.

I had already created the bottom cap with the rounded corner when I created the gray background area. The bottom of the purple side of the menu was still needed. I went back to the

Figure 14.30 This addition is a little wider than the final goal. I will use the selection to delete the rounded corner.

Figure 14.31 Smoothing the selection and deleting the extra purple leaves a rounded inside corner.

Figure 14.32 I added the bevel and rivets.

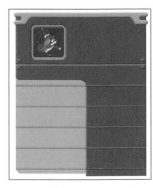

Figure 14.33 These lines have a bevel effect and have been spaced 32 pixels apart.

purple layer and made a rectangular selection that was the width of the purple area and was eight pixels tall. I rounded the selection using the Smooth option.

The problem with this selection was that I only wanted the bottom corners rounded, so I added these corners back to the selection by holding down the Shift button while using the Selection Marquee tool. Once I had the selection shape I wanted, I filled this selection with purple. I then used the Select/Modify/Contract option with a setting of 2 and deleted the area in this selection.

Without changing the selection shape I just used, I selected the gray layer and filled the selection with gray. This entire bottom piece was only created to make the dialog box look better—it is a way to add a smooth corner. This is why it was only eight pixels tall. You can see the final effect of the bottom-right section of the dialog box in Figure 14.34.

I saved this file so that I could make changes to it later. The final art used in the game would not have the layers and layer effects that could be easily changed. A Photoshop file stores this

information that is not in the final format. Once I had saved this file, I needed to break it up into pieces. The easiest way to do this was to merge all of the visible layers, select each section, and then paste them into the correct size files. I also put the art in the correct layout so that it could be used as scaleable bars. You can see all the final pieces in Figure 14.35.

Figure 14.34
Smoothing the selection and deleting the extra purple leaves a rounded inside corner.

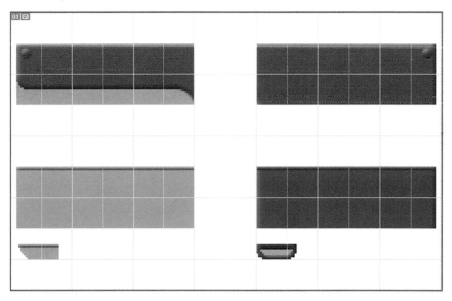

Figure 14.35 This is what each of the final pieces of art looked like. This is the art actually used by the game engine.

Showing Selection

The next step was to create a highlight for the entire row that actually extended out past the row. I also needed an area in which extra information about the item for sale could be placed. The horizontal row was made up of two halves, a gray half and a purple half. I needed to make a highlight for each of these pieces of art that fit together to look like one long row.

I used the Inner Glow effect to make the bar look as though it were highlighted. This effect also enabled me to use the same-size art as on the unhighlighted row because the glow did not extend beyond the row. The Inner Glow effect also did not cover any information on the rows above and below. If I wanted to use an Outer Glow effect, it wouldn't have fit into the 32-pixel tall selection.

I needed to pull a couple of tricks to make the inner glow work. If I had just put the inner glow in the existing art, it would cover up the lines used to separate the rows. Just placing a glow on each piece of art would also cause the effect to separate the two halves because the row was actually composed of the purple half and the gray half, each on separate levels. What I wanted was for the glow effect to appear to affect the entire row, not the two halves. I got around the problem by putting the glow effect on a new layer that extended past the center area, where the two halves met. I then added a blank layer above this piece of art, linked the two layers, and then merged them. I merged the layers because this merge embedded the glow effect in the layer. The layer effect looked the same, but it was no longer really a layer effect. This allowed me to select and delete the extra glow effect that I had created past the center where the two halves met. If I left the inner glow effect and the image in the layer would have been the correct size, the glow effect would have split the two halves.

I then pasted a copy of the line on top of this art so that it was not covered by the Inner Glow effect. If you look at Figure 14.36, you will see that the two highlighted halves look as though they could be combined.

Figure 14.36 These two pieces of art were used in the game.

When a row was selected in the Trade interface, the bar extended further to the left. I created the piece of art for this extension of the row. I used the same technique that I used for the other two pieces, but I added a piece of art that served as an end cap on the left. Just like the other pieces I just created, I had to create the glow effect on a larger piece of art and then cut it down to size. The entire piece of art that was place to the left of the row was also created as a scaleable bar so that the size could easily be adjusted.

Figure 14.37 shows the highlighted effect before the art was cropped. You can see the final art in Figure 14.38.

Figure 14.37 This is the side piece before it was cut down to size. It includes the unwanted glow effect on the right edge.

Figure 14.38 I removed the left edge in the final art so that it would visually connect to the rest of the row.

The last piece of art I needed was a background for more information about the item for sale. Just as for the area I created for the ship information, I created a scalable box so the size of this background also could be adjusted. This way, it was easy for the size of this box to dynamically change depending on the amount of information that was displayed for each item.

Figure 14.39 This is the final art for the scalable information box.

Figure 14.40 This is what all of the art looked like when it was put together.

Notice in Figure 14.39 that this piece of art had a gray background because it contained information about the items in the store. You can see how it is all put together in Figure 14.40.

The Big Change

After all of this work, the game designer and I decided not to use this art for the Trade dialog box. We ended up using this art in other areas, like for the Accept Mission dialog box. Why didn't we use the art for the Trade dialog box? Well, we put the art in the game and tested it out, and despite all of our careful planning, it was still difficult for new players to figure out, and we still had to do a lot of explaining. We realized that *Nomad* still would have required a complicated tutorial. This new interface was better than any of the other trading games we had played, but we had not gone far enough. It was very important to make this game easy to understand and fun to play.

After watching a new player struggle to understand *Nomad*, the game designer came up with a great idea: Get rid of the Trade dialog box altogether. If it isn't working, then why use it? Skip the interface and put the ability to pick up and sell stuff right into the 3D game world. This new idea limited the amount of information we could easily display in the 3D game world, but it also really simplified trading. It was more fun. There was no longer a break from the game world into a dialog box.

I chose to share this example because I feel that this is an important part of game design. Many of the big, blockbuster titles are done this way. Some of these developers have an almost finished game halfway through development and basically redo the game to make it better. If you have a huge budget, you can get a great game with this method. It is always difficult to leave something behind after you've spend a lot of time on it, but hanging on to a flawed solution can limit your game. We worked out the new method for "trading." This new solution made *Nomad* easier to understand and more fun to play. The basic trading action was simplified, and the boring part, in which the player compared numbers in the old style of menu trading, was gone.

Willingness to make improvements is the only way to develop better games. You need to make changes to the important areas. It is important to make sure that the basic game-play is fun—adding more stuff to a game won't fix a problem with basic game-play. It is important to identify this core game-play early so that the extras don't distract you. As in this case, the menu and HUD had a big effect on the game-play and getting this right was very important.

Summary

I hope that reading about some of the challenges I had in creating this small piece of an entire interface helped you to have a better understanding of how complex the interface design process can be. Don't let technical limitation dictate the final look of your interface. Design it first and then find a way to create it.

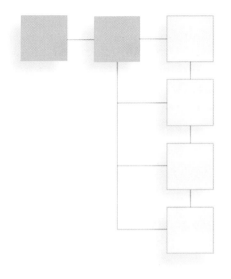

CHAPTER 15

CREATING AN INTERACTIVE MOCK-UP

In this chapter, I will show you how to create a simple yet effective interactive mock-up. Creating something more than just a still mock-up can be incredibly helpful—you can see your design in action before it is put into the game.

Creating interactive mock-ups can help you in many ways and is well worth the effort to learn. Not only can you work on the details of the interface yourself, but also others can see your interface in action and give you input in the early stages of the design,

when you need it most. Once you know how to create such a mock-up, you will want to do so every time you design an interface, I guarantee.

There is so much software out there that can be incredibly useful to you when you're designing interfaces. Many applications are so deep that it is almost impossible to master every aspect of them. In this chapter, I will use Macromedia Flash. This chapter is not meant to teach you how to use Flash, though—Flash is a complex application, and it would require an entire book to teach even the basics.

Instead, I will do my best to give you a brief introduction to ways in which Flash can be used for game interfaces.

I will keep things simple in this chapter, and will give you only a brief explanation of how Flash works. The purpose of this explanation is to help you understand how Flash, or a similar program, can aid you in interface design.

This chapter may not contain enough information to begin using Flash if you have never used similar software. However, when you combine this information with other material—such as a Flash primer book or maybe your existing knowledge of a similar application—you'll be on your way to using Flash to create super cool video game interfaces in no time.

The Ideal Situation

In the ideal situation, you would be able to control all of the movement and interactivity of the interface in the final game. You would be able to create the art and get it completely ready for the final game—you'd control animation, button behavior, and everything else.

You could control all of the features of your game using a software tool, and then you'd simply press a button and export a file, run the game, and see the changes. The programmer wouldn't even know how the buttons move and highlight until he saw them working in the game. Be grateful if you are in such an ideal situation—most of us will have to count on the programmer to animate our interfaces and make the buttons function correctly.

Realizing Your Vision

It is very satisfying to have control of the animation in your game and be able to make the buttons actually go to the right screen yourself, without the help of a programmer. If the programmer controls the animation and interactivity of an interface, you will rarely get exactly what you want. The programmer may not understand what you mean when you say something like, "Have the buttons scale up and down and look bouncy." He may envision something totally different than what you see in your head.

Sometimes the programmer just doesn't care about your vision—he might do what you ask him to, but he really doesn't think how a button bounces is really all that important. To him, the simple animation you're asking for does not show off any new and cool technology, and it isn't nearly as fun and rewarding to create.

It would be great to have complete control, but as I've said, you rarely will. Handing the programmer an interactive mock-up can help you show him exactly what you want, and

give you the influence over the look of screen items you might lack without the mock-up. The programmer doesn't have to pick your brain—he can just check the mock-up to see how you want things to function and move. There is little room for confusion when he can see it.

Experimentation

If you can control motion and interactivity, you can experiment with your design. You can easily try things out and see how they look. It is much harder to experiment when it takes a long time to go from concept to the point where you can click through a menu in the game engine. Creating the art in Photoshop and then going through all of the steps—including opening the file up in another program, converting it to a different format, saving it with a different file name, and so on—to prepare it for the game can take a lot of valuable time (and it's tedious, to boot). This is especially true when the process involves another person; if you need to wait for a programmer to put the art in the game, you might have to wait a long time before you can see it in action.

When it is hard or takes too long to try out new ideas, most designers will be inclined to do what they already know works. Creativity is discouraged by complex processes. It might be difficult to explain to a programmer that, after all the effort that you and he put into a ripple effect, you think it looks dumb and you want to try something else.

The ability to create an interactive mock-up can provide you the opportunity to be more creative because it can be much easier to experiment.

Commercial Tools

Many game engines use commercial tools. For example, the RenderWare engine has the ability to export Macromedia Flash files and use them in the game. Many interface designers who are using RenderWare don't even know that they can use Flash. When you use Flash, you can animate and design the menu flow. My guess is

that, in the future, more and more engines will allow interface designers to use commercial tools effectively.

It's not easy to use a program like Flash to create interfaces for a game. It usually requires a lot of technical understanding and a lot of time. This may be why some designers choose not to use programs like Flash to create final assets. It can be tricky to learn how to give information to the game engine. If the player chooses Expert mode, the game engine will need this information. If there are three saved games, the interface will need to display these saved games, and it will need to know how many games are saved and maybe even the name of the saved game. In these cases, you will need to give the programmer (or game engine) the ability to affect the interface. The interface will need to change, based on direction the game engine gives the interface. This can be the toughest part of this approach, but it can be done. It just requires good planning and communication with the programmer who is working on the interface.

Using a program like Flash is great, but rarely can you use all the features in Flash in the game. There are often many limitations in the engine that are not in the software. This is the case with RenderWare. Make sure you understand what you can and can't do, as you will need to work within these limitations.

Even with the possible difficulties of communicating with the game engine and determining which features will work in the game, it is worth it to spend the time to use some commercial tools. Doing so can result in a much better interface than if you left it up to someone else.

Why Flash?

I will use Macromedia Flash to create my mock-up. I chose Flash because of the flexibility and control it gives me. It is one of the most popular and fully featured tools on the market today for creating all kinds of interactivity. Flash is powerful enough that you can make an entire game start to finish using it. You don't need to know how to use all of these features in Flash, though, to create a simple interactive mock-up.

When you use Flash, it is easy to let others check out your results. Flash has the ability to export an EXE file that will run on just about any Windows PC. You can export into Mac format or even into HTML that can be used in any Web browser (with the appropriate plug-ins). The professional versions of Flash allow you to export into PDA and cell phone formats.

Compatibility is seldom an issue when you're using Flash. You can send your interface to a computer-illiterate producer, and he can review it without installing anything.

Introduction to Flash

The most difficult part of learning new software is simply figuring out the basic logic of the program. Even if you don't know all the features or understand what every button does, if you understand the program's approach, then you can begin to use

it. If you don't have this basic knowledge, then learning a program's new features is pointless.

Using Frames

The terms used by Flash will be familiar to anyone who has used animation software, as it uses the same terminology and logic found in the animation industry. As you probably know, animation is really a bunch of still pictures, called *frames*, that are played back rapidly so that they appear to move. Flash's use of this approach makes it logical. One thing that might be a bit confusing is that the term *frame* is used in Flash even if objects in the scene do not move—for example, if you jump from one screen or page to another, you are *changing frames* in Flash. A frame is a basic unit of time if the file is moving forward. You can stop on a single frame. Images, text, and objects all exist within a frame.

However, a frame in Flash is a little different from those in an animation. In an animated movie, frames are played back at a constant rate.

Because Flash is interactive, you can stop on a single frame, move backward, and jump around. The concept of time even gets a little more complicated than that. You can have several frames of a movie clip or a button within a single frame of the basic timeline. This allows you to have an animated button that has a five-frame animation appear in one frame (or screen) of the overall timeline. Understanding this concept is key to understanding Flash.

Note

It may be helpful to follow along in Flash as I walk you through the process. It will be much easier to understand how this mock-up was created if you try it yourself in Flash. You will find a trial version of Flash on the CD that comes with this book.

When you first open Flash, you will have one empty frame. If you look at the timeline across the top of the screen, you will see a red rectangle with a thin, red line extending down. This is how you move through the frames in your scene. As you start, you only have one frame, so you can't drag this slider. Once you add more frames to your scene, you can use this slider to move around. (See Figure 15.1.)

If you insert a single frame by selecting Insert/Timeline/Frame from the menu across the very top of the screen (or by pressing F5), you will see the white block under the red indicator get twice as big. You now can click and drag on the red time slider and move between these two frames, but noth-

ing changes because nothing is in either frame.

You now can put something in both of these frames. There are tools for creating vector objects within Flash, but when working on interfaces for games, most often you will use images created in other programs (like Photoshop) and import them into Flash. You can do this using the File/Import/Import to Library option from the top menu. This will place the image into a library associated with this file.

In order to save space, Flash will import one image into the library. You then can use this image as many times and in as many places as you want throughout your file. Re-using images in this

way saves file space because it does not need to be saved multiple times. After you have imported your images, you can open a Library window and see all of the objects in your library. You can then drag these images and drop them onto your page.

Once you have placed an image into the scene, the two frames in the top of your screen turn gray (see Figure 15.2). They were white when there was nothing in the scene, but they turn gray to indicate that there is something in that frame.

There is still no difference between the two frames in your scene because the image is in both frames. If you want to see a difference between frames, you will need to place a second image in the second frame but not in the first frame. The best way to do this is to create a new layer.

Using Layers

In Flash, layers function much like they do in other programs, such as Photoshop. Any object on a higher layer will cover an object on a lower layer. You can put many objects into

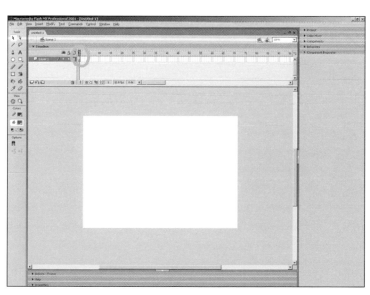

Figure 15.1 This file contains only one blank frame. You will need to add more frames before you can move from frame to frame.

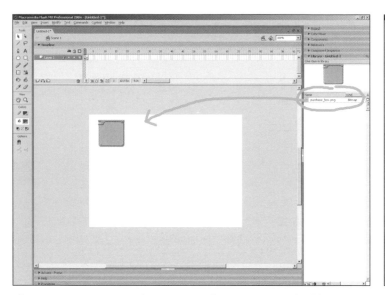

Figure 15.2 Once you have imported an image into the library, you can drag it into your scene. Once you have done this, the frames turn gray in the timeline.

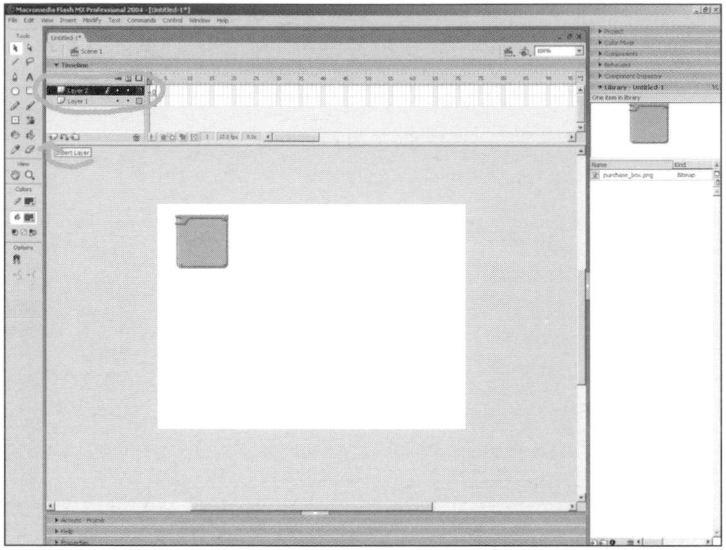

Figure 15.3 This button will create a new layer.

one layer, but it is easier to keep track of all of the images and to animate them if you keep them all on separate layers.

You can create a new layer by pressing the Add Layer button, the icon that looks like a page with a corner turned up. It has a plus sign next to it and is located in the upper-left section of the screen. Once your new layer appears, you can add a new image to it. Figure 15.3 shows you where the button is to add a new layer.

Now you will need to put an object in the second layer. You can import another image into your library and drag it into the scene. This time, when you drag the image into the scene, make sure that the correct layer is selected.

You can select the layer by either clicking on the bar with the layer's name (by default, Layer 2) or by clicking onto the frame in the time line. This will put the object into the proper layer.

Figure 15.4 shows the correct layer selected.

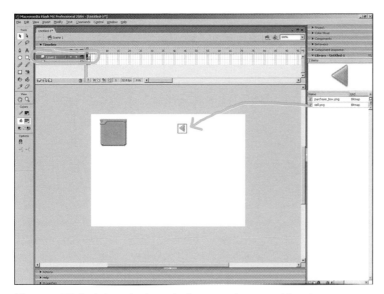

Figure 15.4 Select the layer before you drag an object into your scene. The object will be placed on the selected layer.

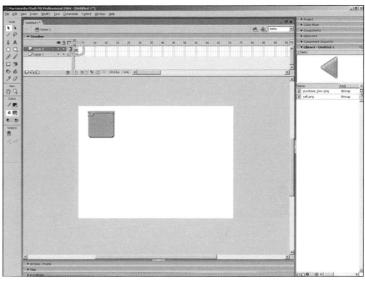

Figure 15.5 Layer 2 is empty in frame 1 and includes an image in frame 2.

The frames in this layer will turn gray once they contain an image. Like before, the frames are still the same—there is no difference between frames 1 and 2. Both placed images are in both frames.

You can remove the image on the second layer from the first frame by clicking once on the black circle in the first frame, on Layer 2. Once this frame has been selected, you can click again and drag this circle into the second frame. You can use this click-and-drag method to extend or shorten the life of the images in a layer.

Layer 1 is empty in frame 1 and includes the image in frame 2. You can see which frame is empty in Figure 15.5.

Finally, the two frames are different. You can drag the red bar back and forth to see the differences between the two frames.

Working with Flash can, of course, become much more complicated, but this is the basic idea—create a bunch of frames (screens) and move from frame to frame, based on input from the user.

Animation in Flash

Working with animation in Flash can be very complex. I will keep this discussion simple and describe only some of the basics—the principles that you will often use when working with game interfaces. I covered some of this material in Chapter 11, you might recall, but I think it bears repeating here.

A common term in animation is *key frame*. This term has its roots in traditional hand-drawn animation. A key frame was an important frame drawn by the animator. Usually, the more experienced animators would draw these frames.

These experienced animators would also specify the amount of frames in between these key frames, and less experienced artists would then draw the frames that blended between the key frames. This process became known as *tweening*.

Flash uses these same terms. Like in traditional animation, you can create key frames in Flash. In these key frames, you set an image's position, rotation, scale, and any other attributes that can be animated (such as transparency). After you set the next key frame, you can tell Flash to create the frames in between the key frames. Flash refers to this as *motion tweening*.

Before you can create an animation in Flash, you will need to extend the layer so it lasts the entire length of the animation. There are several ways to do this. The simplest way is to select the black dot in the timeline that represents the image in your scene. When you select the image in the timeline, notice that the image is also selected in the scene below. You can add one frame at a time by pressing the F5 button. Just keep pressing F5 to make the layer as long as you need for your interface. In my example, I made the animation last 20 frames.

Figure 15.6 shows what the timeline looks like when it is extended for 20 frames.

Once you have enough frames to work with, you can tell Flash that you want the object to animate by right-clicking on the section in the timeline and choosing Create Motion Tween. You can select any of the area between the black dot on the left and the

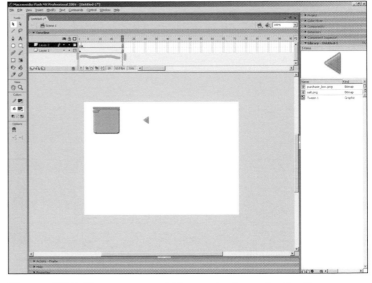

Figure 15.6 There are now 20 frames in the entire timeline.

empty box on the right. When a tween has been added to an image, the background turns blue and a dotted line appears.

You can see the change in the timeline in Figure 15.7.

Even though a tween has been added, nothing moves yet. A key frame must be added at the end of the animation, and changes must be made to the image at the point of this key frame. Simply select the frame where you want to add a key frame. Select the last frame in the blue area with a dotted line. (The shortcut to add a key frame is F6.) You can then make adjustments to the image on this frame.

If you simply move the image to a new position in your scene, you will create an animation. Once you have done this, you can drag the red slider back and forth and watch your image move (see Figure 15.8).

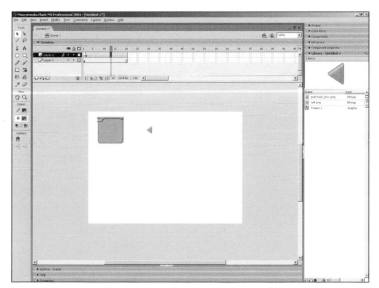

Figure 15.7 A dotted line appears when a motion tween has been applied to an image.

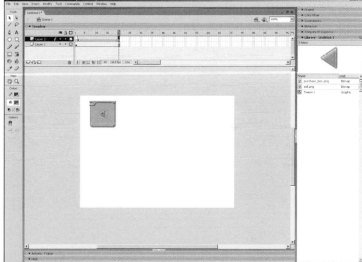

Figure 15.8 Once a key frame has been added and the positioned changed on this frame, you can see movement.

Playback Speed

The *frame rate* of an animation is just what it sounds like. It is a number that refers to the number of frames that are played every second. Most game interfaces run at 30 frames per second (30fps). By default, Flash is set to 12fps. This is easy to adjust. The current frame rate is displayed just below the timeline. If you left-click the box with the frame rate displayed, you will find a variety of parameters that can be adjusted. Frame rate is one of these parameters. Figure 15.9 shows you where this box is located.

Changing the frame rate will have a big effect on the speed of your animations. You should adjust this frame rate before creating any animations. If you change it from 12fps to 30fps after you have created animations, then everything will move more than twice as fast as the default 12fps. Everything will look smoother at 30fps.

Using Scripting

You control the interactivity of anything in Flash through scripting. Scripting allows you to give directions on what to do when buttons are pressed or when the file arrives at a particular frame. These directions, or *scripts*, can be located on a frame or on an object like a button. If the script is on a frame, the file will do whatever the script directs when the file reaches that frame. If the script is on a button, it will execute the orders when the button is pressed. Again, scripting can be very complex and powerful, and I will present only the basics here.

With a few simple commands—such as stop, Play, and Go to Frame—you can create some basic interactivity for the images in your scene. These commands are pretty straightforward, and do what you'd expect. Flash has many other capabilities, but I would suggest concentrating on the Stop, Play, and Go to Frame actions first.

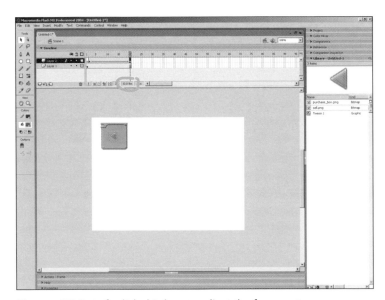

Figure 15.9 Left-click this box to adjust the frame rate.

If you want to add a script to a frame, the best method is to create a new layer that will contain all of the actions placed on a frame. You can put these actions in layers that also contain other images, but it is much easier if you keep things organized and use a separate layer for all actions placed on any frame in the file. Once this layer has been added, you will need to select the frame where you want to put the action and add a key frame. This is a case where the key

frame term and concept are still used, even though this key frame will not have anything to do with animation.

For this example, you can add a keyframe on frame number 2, as shown in Figure 15.10.

I wanted to add a Stop action to the second frame. When you have the key frame in the correct spot in your action layer, you can add an action to this frame. Select the key frame in the second frame in the Actions-Frame

window, located at the bottom section of the screen, then hit the plus icon (+). Choose the Global Functions/Timeline Control/Stop option. This will add the Stop action to this frame. When the scene arrives at this frame, it will play until it comes to a Stop action.

You can see how to get to the Stop action in Figure 15.11.

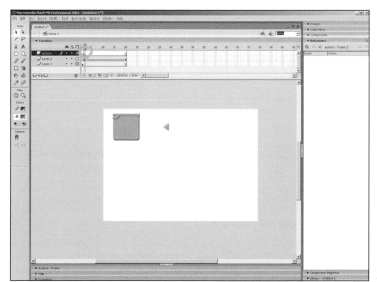

Figure 15.10 You will need to add a key frame before you can add an action.

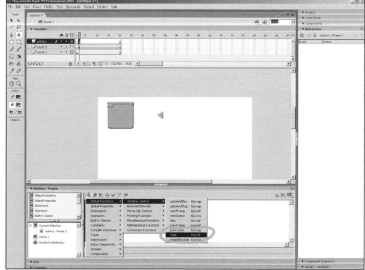

Figure 15.11 This selection will add a Stop action to the selected frame.

When an action script is added to a frame, a small letter A will appear in the timeline. These small letters can be hard to see; this is one of the reasons to create a new layer for your action scripts. It is even more difficult when other images are on the same layer. It is also a good technique to space still frames a fair distance apart, even if the frames in the middle are not being used. If you have a little more room between two frames, it is much easier to see what is going on. Keep your files organized.

Creating Buttons in Flash

Like everything in Flash, the basic button concept is fairly straightforward, but because of the depth of the program, working with buttons can become complicated. The easiest way to create a button is to select an image that you want to use as a button, right-click that image, and choose the Convert to Symbol option that appears in the menu that appears when you right-click the image. Several options appear in this menu; choose the Button option. You can also name your button in the same dialog box where you choose the button option.

You can see where to select the Convert to Symbol option in Figure 15.12.

Once you have converted an image to a symbol, the image becomes a button. This means it has certain functionality that it did not have before. If you look in your library, you will see both a new button and the old image. The image can still be used in your scene in its non-button form, but at the same time, that same image is also used inside your new button and the button appears as a second object in your library. This image is currently contained within the button.

Now this is where it may get a little confusing. If you double-click on the button in your scene, you will open up the button. In essence, you will be *inside* the button. The confusing part is that everything still looks very similar to the scene you were just in. The only visual difference is that the items that are not contained within the but-ton are slightly dimmed. This way, you can tell what is actually part of the button. If you look at the title bar at the very top of the screen, just above the timeline section, you will notice a change—you will see the name of the entire scene followed by the name of your button. You are always working inside the last item on this list. In this case, you are inside the button. You can return to the main scene by selecting the text in this title bar. In Figure 15.13 you can see the extra name in the title bar.

When creating simple interfaces you will not need to go deeper than what I've presented here; but it can get even more confusing—you can put a movie or another button inside of a button. Although the multiple levels can be hard to navigate, the ability Flash offers to put an animation or button inside of a button can be a powerful feature. For example, you can place a looping animation in a button in the mouseover state. This movie will play when a button is high-lighted.

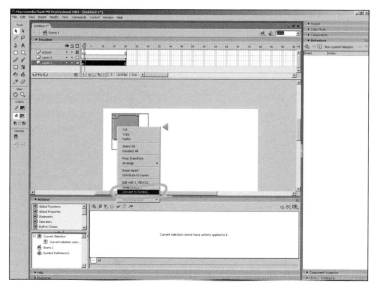

Figure 15.12 This option will convert an image into a button.

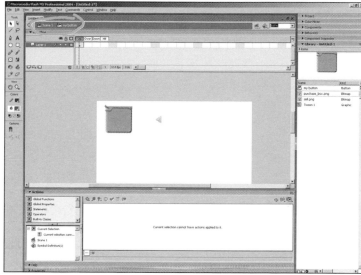

Figure 15.13 These icons and text let you know that you are working inside of a button.

Because this animation exists inside the button, the whole button—including the animation—can be placed in one frame of the overall timeline, even when there are many frames in the animation. Just remember to look at the text at the top of the screen if you get lost. Click on the text to get back to the level where you want to be. For now, you can stay inside the button.

You might have noticed another change when you opened the button: the timeline changed. You can no longer see the timeline of the entire file; instead, you see the components of the button. A button is a specific type of object in Flash and it has some unique properties. Each button has three button states (Up, Over, and Down) and a hit area that can be all adjusted in the timeline. Just like with the overall timeline, you can scrub

back and forth to see these different states. Check out Figure 15.13 again—it shows a button open so that you can see how the timeline changed. Layers can also be added within a button, just like in the timeline for the entire file.

As I said, even though there may not be any animation inside a button, the concept of key frames is used when working with buttons. If an image changes from frame to frame, you must add a key frame to make a change. For example, if you want the button to look different in the Over state (when the mouse moves over the button), you will need to set a key frame in the frame below the word *over* and then make your change to the image in that frame. I usually just replace the normal button image used in the Up frame with another image, created in Photoshop, in the Over frame. It is always easiest to use images that are the same size for every state. This way, they all go in the same place and they work together perfectly. Make all of the images as large as the largest image—you may need to account for the size of the outer glow or drop shadow in the highlighted state.

A simple approach is to place the image for the Up state in the spot where you want it. Then select each of the other frames and press F6 to create a key frame for every state. Drag the time slider around and make changes to each of these frames. If you have created the art in another program, you can just replace the old image with a highlighted version for the Over frame and a pushed-in-looking version for the Down frame.

The Hit Area

The hit area is the location that will trigger the button. When the user moves the mouse over a hit area, the button will change to the Over frame. If the user clicks on the hit area, the button will be triggered. The simple solution for a hit area is to use the same art you used in the Up frame. This is what you will do most of the time. However, the ability that Flash gives the user to designate a hit area that is different from the image in the Up frame allows you to do many different things.

There are times when using the same image for both the Up and the Hit frames can be problematic. For example, using text in both the Up and the hit area can create problems because the spaces in between the letters do not count a hit area and so the highlighted state can flicker on and off as the user moves the mouse across the button. The simple solution to this problem is to create a box in the hit frame that encompasses the entire button.

You can also use the ability to have a different image in the hit frame, even more creatively. For example, you could have an image that looks like a button and use this same art in both the Hit and Up frames. You could then have an image in the Over frame that was in a completely different location and did not seem to be a part of the button. When the player moved his mouse over the button, it could highlight a totally different location on the screen.

Putting Scripts on Buttons

Once you have created a button, you can place an action script on the button rather than on a frame. The action will then be triggered when the button is released. This is the default action, but there are several other options when placing an action on a button. For example, you can trigger an action when the mouse moves over a button or even when it moves off of a button. You may not use these other events as often as the button release event, but it is good to know that they are available.

To put an action on a button, start by single-clicking to select the button in your scene. (Double-clicking on the button will open it.) With the button selected, open the Behaviors panel on the right side of the Flash interface. Click on the blue plus sign in the upper-left corner of this panel. Choose the Movieclip/Go to and Play

option. A dialog box will appear; leave everything at the defaults in this dialog box and just enter the number of the frame to which you want to go.

Once you have placed an action on a button, you can see it in the Behaviors window every time you select the button. It also can be modified here. You can see where to do this in Figure 15.14.

The option right below the Go to and Play option is Go to and Stop. Use the Stop option if you don't want the scene to play when it jumps to the frame number you entered. Use the Go to and Play option if you want the frames to advance after arriving at the specified frame. This action will be executed first, and then any action on the frame will be executed. If there is no Stop action at the end of the scene, the file will start over at the beginning. The file will loop continuously if you do not stop it.

Seeing Your Button Work

When you're working in Flash in the Standard mode, you will not be able to see how your button works. When you move your mouse over the button, it does not highlight and you can't press it. The reason for this is that you will probably need to select and modify this button, and these behaviors would get in the way. The button will work just fine when it has been published and saved in the final format, but it won't work when you're editing the Flash file. Flash has a way

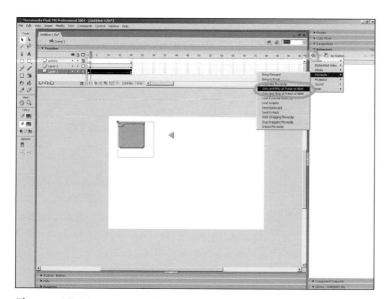

Figure 15.14 You can add a Go To action to your button.

around this: You can turn on the simple functions of a button to test them out by choosing Control/Enable Simple Buttons from the menu across the top of the screen; the buttons will then function like buttons should. Once you are done testing the button, you can switch back by de-selecting the same option.

Publishing Files

Once you have completed your interface, you will need to save it in a format that other people can use. When you save your file using the File/Save option in the main menu, you save a FLA file that can be opened by anyone who has Flash. Saving a file in another, final, format is called *publishing*. These files can't be opened and edited in Flash the way a FLA file can, but they don't require Flash to be opened.

The Publish option is found under File/Publish in the main menu. You can adjust the setting that will take effect every time you publish your file. These settings can be found in the File/Publish Settings option in the main menu; there you will see a number of file formats that you can choose. Every time you check one of these boxes, a new tab that contains all of the settings specific to that file format appears. You can specify the name of the files that will be saved when you publish, and if you click on the folder icon, you can choose the location of these files.

Once you have made all of these adjustments, all you need to do is choose the Publish option and all the files you specified will be saved. You can see the Publish Settings dialog box in Figure 15.15.

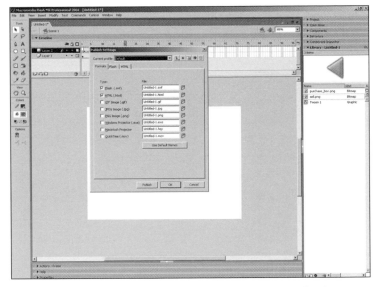

Figure 15.15 There are a variety of options for a final file format.

Flash Summary

You can create simple interactive interfaces by creating all of your screens on different frames. You can move back and forth in these frames using the Go to and Stop action placed on a button. When you are ready to see the file in the final format, you can publish it and get results in many different file formats.

I left out a lot of the details of Flash and have described concepts and actions that I wish someone would have described to me when I was starting out with Flash. As I began learning how to use Flash, it took a lot of reading for me to figure out these basic concepts. I hope that, with this brief introduction and the help of other information and tutorials available about Flash, you will be able to learn the program much faster than I did. Consider this chapter a jump-start to learning Flash.

The Sample Flash File

Now that you have a glimpse of how Flash works, it may be helpful to take a look at a file created in Flash. I used this file for some early tests on the Trade interface for *Nomad*, described in Chapter 14. I will give you a quick explanation of how this file works, and will assume that you have read the "Introduction to Flash" section of this chapter and have a little understanding of how Flash works.

This file is created in a very simple way. There are more efficient ways to use Flash to create this exact interface than those I'll explain in this book, but they would require quite a bit of knowledge about Flash. The method used for this file is good for an introduction to Flash—it was intentionally created using only the principles discussed earlier in this chapter. This example will give you a hint of how much you can do with only a few simple techniques.

The mock-up I created is not a complete interface mock-up. The way the menu functions in the mock-up is not exactly the way the menu worked in the final *Nomad* game. There are several features that do not even work in the mock-up I created.

The menu in this mock-up was created to test the validity of the approach that the game designer and I came up with. We did not want to painstakingly create a perfectly functioning menu only to have to reproduce it in the game. We just wanted to know if pressing the Buy and Sell buttons seemed like the logical way to buy and sell things in the game. On this particular project, there were a couple of key aspects that we wanted to test and perfect; these aspects were important enough that we spent a little time to make this mock-up.

Mock-ups are great for testing. It is always a good idea to test with a functional menu; a user can get a lot more information when he can see movement and buttons that highlight. It is much harder to show someone a menu in a flat, concept image and know if he is really going to understand how to use the menu. No matter how well you can envision something in your head, it is always a little different when you actually see it working.

The CD that comes with this book includes several files named Trade Mock-Up. You can open any of these files. There is a self-contained file for both Windows (EXE) and Macintosh (HQX). You can also open the HTML file with any browser that has the correct files. (This HTML file refers to the SWF file, and it must be in the same directory.) I have also included the original Flash file. If you have Flash installed, you can open this file up and see how it was made.

Actions on Frames

Most of the actions in Figure 15.16 have been placed on the actions layer. The lowercase "a" designates a location that contains a script. If you select these lowercase a's, you can examine the script. When you've selected one of these frames, open the Actions-Frame window. As the name implies, this is where the actions are created and edited for a frame. You can see how the file should behave when it reaches this frame. This file is located on the CD if you want to open it up and look at it. You can see the actions in Figure 15.16.

Frames 1, 15, and 23 all have a Stop action. These three different frames are the three different possible looks for the interface. All of the frames in between these frames are part of the transitions.

Frames 31 and 46 have an action that moves the file to another frame and then stops. These Stop actions are located at the end of transitions.

Actions on Buttons

There are four buttons that control the interface in this file (located on the CD). The main Ship tab that appears on frame 1 is a button. There is a Purchase and Sell button and a Close Dialog button. It is pretty simple, yet there is still a lot of stuff going on. If you have too many buttons and animations, as I've said before, your interface can become very confusing. Organization is the key.

If you scrub the timeline to frame 1 and select the Ship Information box, you will see that it has been converted into a button. You can see the script applied to this button in the Behaviors window on the right. There is a stop on frame 1. The file will stay

on this frame until the button is pressed. Then the Go to and Play action on this button will send the file to the next frame and begin playing. The file will play until it reaches the Stop action located on frame 15. The frames between frame 1 and frame 15 contain the transition of the trade interface opening up.

In the game, this menu and animation will be triggered when your ship docks at a trading post. This button was created just as a way to trigger this transition. You can see the action on the button, created out of the ship information bar, in Figure 15.17.

There is a key frame on the layer that contains the ship box, at frame 15. Key frames are added, as I've said, so changes can be made. Visually, there is no change in this layer from frame 1 to frame 15; the difference is in the button. The same button is in frames 1 and 15, but the action has been removed from the button on frame 15. In the first frame, the script on the button goes to frame 2 and opens the dialog box. Once it is open, you don't want this button to do anything, so I removed the script at this point.

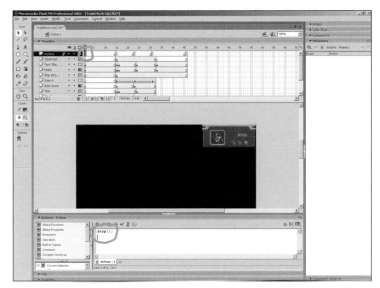

Figure 15.16 If you select a frame that contains an action, you can see the script in the Actions-Frame window.

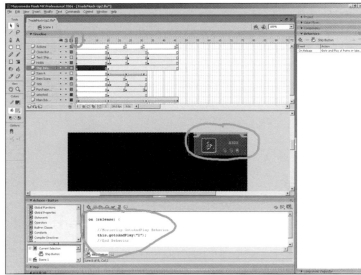

Figure 15.17 Select the button in the scene and you can see the action on the button in the Behaviors window.

Once the dialog is open and the file has stopped on frame 15, the two buttons become available. A Close Dialog button appears in the upper-right corner of the Trade dialog. If this button is pressed, the file goes to frame 32 and plays to frame 46. This is the close animation where the menu slides up. You can see this script by selecting the Close button on any frame where the button appears and looking in the

Behaviors window. This button should do the same thing on every frame where it appears.

At the end of this transition, on frame 46, there is an action. This action directs the file back to frame 1. This happens as soon as the animation arrives at frame 46. Because this frame looks exactly like frame 1, the user will never notice anything amiss.

The Purchase button looks like an orange arrow. On frame 15, it contains an action that directs the file to go to the next frame and plays the animation. The file will stop on frame 23. On frame 23, the Purchase button is very transparent and does not contain any actions. Once the item has been purchased, it can't be purchased again.

Just as with the Purchase button, the Sell button is not always available. Because you don't have any of the selected items in your ship on frame 15, you can't sell anything. Once the Purchase button has been pressed and the item has been purchased, the file moves to frame 23. On this frame in the layer with the Purchase button, there is a key frame. The button contains a script that sends the file to the next frame and plays. On frame 31, the file reaches the end of this animation and is redirected to frame 15.

You will notice that if a purchase is made, the dialog is closed and then re-opened, then the item does not show up in the ship. There are ways in Flash to retain this information even when the dialog has been closed, but these methods all require more complicated scripting. Making this work like it should have worked in the final game was not important for the test that we needed to do.

Poke around in this file and see how everything was done. You can see the movement by scrubbing the red box in the timeline. You can also see the final result by opening any of the files that have been published.

This file may be simple, but it is easy to see how useful it is. You can try and test all kinds of things using Flash. Creating iterative files is a great way to build a strong portfolio with functional art. You can also make an incredibly strong presentation of a new concept—no programmers needed!

Summary

You now have the basic skills that will allow you to design a game interface. Review the principles in this book often and continue to learn more. There is always more to learn. Get as much real-life experience by designing interfaces for games as you can—the best teacher is experience.

I hope that you have been inspired to improve your skills and in turn improve your interface designs. I have seen some amazing interfaces, but that does not mean that you can't create an interface that is even better. Aim high!

INDEX

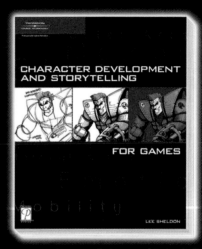

License Agreement/Notice of Limited Warranty

By opening the sealed disc container in this book, you agree to the following terms and conditions. If, upon reading the following license agreement and notice of limited warranty, you cannot agree to the terms and conditions set forth, return the unused book with unopened disc to the place where you purchased it for a refund.

License:
The enclosed software is copyrighted by the copyright holder(s) indicated on the software disc. You are licensed to copy the software onto a single computer for use by a single user and to a backup disc. You may not reproduce, make copies, or distribute copies or rent or lease the software in whole or in part, except with written permission of the copyright holder(s). You may transfer the enclosed disc only together with this license, and only if you destroy all other copies of the software and the transferee agrees to the terms of the license. You may not decompile, reverse assemble, or reverse engineer the software.

Notice of Limited Warranty:
The enclosed disc is warranted by Thomson Course Technology PTR to be free of physical defects in materials and workmanship for a period of sixty (60) days from end user's purchase of the book/disc combination. During the sixty-day term of the limited warranty, Thomson Course Technology PTR will provide a replacement disc upon the return of a defective disc.

Limited Liability:
THE SOLE REMEDY FOR BREACH OF THIS LIMITED WARRANTY SHALL CONSIST ENTIRELY OF REPLACEMENT OF THE DEFECTIVE DISC. IN NO EVENT SHALL THOMSON COURSE TECHNOLOGY PTR OR THE AUTHOR BE LIABLE FOR ANY OTHER DAMAGES, INCLUDING LOSS OR CORRUPTION OF DATA, CHANGES IN THE FUNCTIONAL CHARACTERISTICS OF THE HARDWARE OR OPERATING SYSTEM, DELETERIOUS INTERACTION WITH OTHER SOFTWARE, OR ANY OTHER SPECIAL, INCIDENTAL, OR CONSEQUENTIAL DAMAGES THAT MAY ARISE, EVEN IF THOMSON COURSE TECHNOLOGY PTR AND/OR THE AUTHOR HAS PREVIOUSLY BEEN NOTIFIED THAT THE POSSIBILITY OF SUCH DAMAGES EXISTS.

Disclaimer of Warranties:
THOMSON COURSE TECHNOLOGY PTR AND THE AUTHOR SPECIFICALLY DISCLAIM ANY AND ALL OTHER WARRANTIES, EITHER EXPRESS OR IMPLIED, INCLUDING WARRANTIES OF MERCHANTABILITY, SUITABILITY TO A PARTICULAR TASK OR PURPOSE, OR FREEDOM FROM ERRORS. SOME STATES DO NOT ALLOW FOR EXCLUSION OF IMPLIED WARRANTIES OR LIMITATION OF INCIDENTAL OR CONSEQUENTIAL DAMAGES, SO THESE LIMITATIONS MIGHT NOT APPLY TO YOU.

Other:
This Agreement is governed by the laws of the State of Massachusetts without regard to choice of law principles. The United Convention of Contracts for the International Sale of Goods is specifically disclaimed. This Agreement constitutes the entire agreement between you and Thomson Course Technology PTR regarding use of the software.